# BENEATH the Vines

MIKE MASS

# BENEATH the Vines

TATE PUBLISHING
AND ENTERPRISES, LLC

Published by Tate Publishing & Enterprises, LLC
127 E. Trade Center Terrace | Mustang, Oklahoma 73064 USA
1.888.361.9473 | www.tatepublishing.com

Tate Publishing is committed to excellence in the publishing industry. The company reflects the philosophy established by the founders, based on Psalm 68:11,
*"The Lord gave the word and great was the company of those who published it."*


*Cover design by Lirey Blanco*
*Interior design by Richell Balansag*

Published in the United States of America

ISBN: 978-1-68352-219-5
1. Biography & Autobiography / Political
2. Biography & Autobiography / Personal Memoirs
16.06.30

To my mom and dad, Lois Payne Mass and Fred Mass, Jr.

Mom was a nurse, cook, field-hand and spiritual leader for a family of ten. In 1961, with a flat tire on a dark country road, older brother and I witnessed as she stood her ground against an armed assailant....an escapee from a nearby work-farm; and that.... without the aid of a concealed carry permit.

Dad fought a war, raised eight children and set by example the values of hard work and integrity. His generosity and kindness to the poor and underprivileged were a hallmark of his life.

# Acknowledgments

Foremost to my daughter, Elena, who for two years never missed a day sending a letter, while I was in the federal penitentiary. Her collaboration, along with my return mail, were the ingredients that made *Beneath the Vines* possible.

Many thanks to my entire family and a host of friends. Without your help, the manuscript would have never made it to Tate Publishing. I love all of you.

On the twenty-sixth day of June 2009, I got out of bed a little before daylight, put on a pot of coffee, and hit the shower. After getting dressed, I poured my coffee, grabbed a cigar, and headed to my garden. As the sun peeked over the Southeast Oklahoma hills, I walked through the rows of sweet corn, purple hull peas, and tomatoes, carefully examining each plant. Just a few more days and there would be an abundance of fresh, ripened garden vegetables. I was hoping to find a ripe tomato today, but no such luck.

I wouldn't be working the garden that day or any other day for the next two years. Within the hour, I would be on my way to the Federal Transfer Center, a holdover facility for federal prison inmates in Oklahoma City.

A mockingbird was raising hell atop one of the peach trees in the corner of the garden when my two sons drove up the driveway to pick me up. The two of them, along with my wife, would be my escorts to my new temporary home. On the way, we would stop by my sister's house, where I would share a farewell breakfast with Mama and my siblings. The day before, I had said my farewells and hugged on my grandbabies, as well as my two daughters. There were lots of tears but few from me, at least in their presence.

By 8:00 a.m., we had left my sister's and headed west. It would take nearly three hours to reach the transfer center, and my reporting time had been set for 11:00 a.m. sharp. On the way, we made mostly small talk. What do you say when you're taking your dad to prison? The closer we got to the city, the quieter we all got. We'd never so much as had an encounter with jail, much less a federal penitentiary.

We reached the facility with fifteen minutes to spare. The massive seven-story octagon-shaped building surrounded by razor wire was intimidating. As we pulled through the guard shack, the officer on duty promptly pointed out where we were to park and the entrance I should use to enter. All trying to outbrave the other, we hugged and said our brief good-byes. With my cigar clenched between my teeth, I strolled across the hot pavement toward the entrance as if I were in full control. In my peripheral vision, I could see my boys and wife reluctantly driving away.

The cigar had become somewhat of a trademark, and the habit came about in sort of a practical way. Diagnosed with a mild heart attack in the mid-90s, I gave up smoking three to four packs of cigarettes per day. I weaned myself from the habit of smoking but never kicked the nicotine craving. Subsequently, I found myself chewing cigars but never lighting up. If I was awake, I had a cigar in my mouth.

The Federal Transfer Center was a last-minute notion of the feds. The judge had originally ordered me to a minimum-security pen in Texarkana. My oldest daughter had checked that facility out online and found that it had outside facilities that included a softball field, visitation area, and walking track. It also had dormitory-style sleeping quarters and supposedly a rather nice library. My lawyer had also told me that it was geared more toward white-collar crime and that I would blend right in. The way my daughter and lawyer were describing Texarkana was almost making me look forward to the trip! Having only been notified three days before the switch, we knew absolutely nothing about the FTC. From the outside, the place looked like Fort Knox.

I entered the large, heavy glass doors into a rather nice-looking waiting area. Portraits of past wardens encircled the walls. The tile floor was like a mirror. To my right was a dark, tinted glass encased with a microphone. I could make out the silhouette of what appeared to be a woman sitting on the other side. A voice came through the microphone. "Have a seat. We'll be with you in a minute." Although I'd been through my share of hell over the past few years, it takes a lot to slap the vanity from a politician, especially one who was called Mr. Chairman. Somewhere in the recesses of my mind was a vague notion that a petite young receptionist would soon appear and say, "Follow me, Mr. Mass, and I'll show you to your room."

The minute gradually turned into an hour, and being thin blooded, I was beginning to shiver a little, both from the intense cool air inside the waiting area and the anticipation. Suddenly, a large male figure burst in through an obviously heavily locked door, and he came directly toward me. His hair was pulled back in a ponytail, and cuffs hung on either side of his waist. He wore combat boots, and on his hands was a pair of bright blue tight-fitting latex gloves. Before I could get out of my chair, he reached and pulled the cigar out of my mouth, ordered me to place my hands behind my head, and gave me a thorough frisking. The greeting was somewhat of a shock, and the latex gloves were sending a clear message: I was no longer fit to be touched by naked hands.

He led me through the heavy metal door into a maze of concrete walls and floors. At frequent intervals, we would reach another locked metal door where we would wait to hear a buzz before it would open. We would step inside an enclosed sally port where we would wait for another buzz before passing to the other side. We entered a long corridor with heavy metal holding cells on either side. All were filled to the brim with inmates. As we approached the end of the corridor, I could see a long line of inmates, all bound in waist chains. All were wearing T-shirts and khaki pants. The smell of chemicals, the sights, and the sounds were surreal. I was in the bowels of a so-called minimum security federal penitentiary. I would hate to see a maximum.

We entered another hallway off to the right of the main corridor and approached a long, waist-high counter. My escort handed me a cardboard box and ordered me to undress. He pitched my belongings into the box. I was then ushered into a partition-filled room where another guard would take over. I was given a thorough cavity search. The guard then tossed me a stained yellow T-shirt, a pair of elastic waist khaki pants, and one pair of canvas shoes.

We hurriedly moved down another hallway bordered by cells of solitary confinement, with unfamiliar faces of inmates peeking through the narrow glass windows. We passed by a large glass-front cell where an inmate wearing only a smock was being held on suicide watch. Even though this place was only a three-hour drive from home, I never felt so far away.

We approached another counter where I was handed a form on which to notify next of kin should I die while incarcerated. From there, I was placed in a line of inmates, all waiting to be processed. We'd have our blood drawn for various tests such as TB, with an adequate amount left for DNA purposes, then fingerprinted. The final station was a room where I was examined for any special markings such as tattoos or distinguishing moles. After that, I was stood against a tape and photographed for my inmate account card. Within minutes, the Polaroid picture was laminated. Underneath the picture read, "Mass, Michael. 04581-063." I was told to keep the card on my person at all times, handed a small plastic-covered pillow, a sheet, and a laundry bag, and then escorted to a large elevator.

When the elevator doors opened, it was packed with inmates, their eyes as piercing as the pain I felt as I listened to the judge hand down my sentence. One guard inside was operating the controls. As I squeezed in to take my place, a young, slender black inmate with braided hair was quick to tell me, "Get out my face, mothafucka." There was no place to go. The guard operating the elevator didn't flinch or act alarmed. I'm sure he was accustomed to the rhetoric. I wasn't. The elevator doors opened again. I was now on the seventh floor. The clock above the door read 3:30 p.m. This was cadre unit, another word for *work unit*. There were three cell pods in the unit labeled D, E, and F. Each unit housed approximately sixty inmates, two per bunk in a nine-by-ten-foot cell. The E pod would be my home for the next two years.

I often reflect on the time I spent there at the FTC, as I'm sure most former inmates do—how I came to be there, the guys I met there, and those initial days of shock and disorientation. I still carry that laminated inmate card in my wallet as a reminder, as if I needed a reminder. Just a few months back, I was totally embarrassed when I went to the bank drive-through to cash a check and mistakenly placed the inmate ID in the plastic container, along with the check I wanted to cash. I thought I had grabbed my driver's license.

The month of April means three things to most folk in Southeast Oklahoma: tax time, garden time, and time to catch the crappie spawn in our abundant area lakes and streams, but not necessarily in that order.

Foremost on my agenda is tending my larger-than-needed garden. It's the time of year when we're a smidgen past the average frost date, but the nights are still cool enough to be threatening. I'm outdoors during daylight hours, tilling the soil, planting, and occasionally sneaking off to Lake Eufaula with my sons, a good cane pole, and a few dozen minnows.

I rarely spend time in front of the television, and my cell phone is obsolete, so I rely on my wife to watch the local eight-day forecasts. When I catch a week's forecast with the lows above forty degrees, it will be safe to put my several dozen tomatoes and pepper plants in the ground.

The other night, I came in at my usual dark thirty, kicked my boots off by the kitchen door, poured a glass of ice tea, and asked my wife what the low temperatures were forecasted for the coming week. She had just finished watching the news and the complete weather forecast but drew a blank when trying to remember the morning lows. Trying to soothe my obvious disdain, she said her brain had like this little merry-go-round that carried her thoughts with it. If one of her thoughts got past before she snatched it off, she'd have to wait until it came back around, which sometimes took longer than others, depending on how many thoughts were riding it. It gave a whole new meaning to "the wheels are turning!"

At our age, that made perfect sense to me, so how could I get mad about that! Besides, being forewarned is forearmed, and it did make me realize that I'd better share my story while my own merry-go-round is still functional.

Except for a brief period in the early 1970s, I've lived most of my life in Southeast Oklahoma. I was born and raised here and, in all likelihood, will die here. But soon after high school graduation, in the spring of 1969, I left home, mostly to get away from my father, who I thought at that time was the meanest SOB who ever lived. With ten bucks left of some hay-hauling money, I purchased a Greyhound bus ticket that got me just across the Red River into Denison, Texas. With high school diploma in hand, I proudly set out in search of a career and found one real quick too! I landed a job with Brookside Division of Safeway Foods, a plant that packaged, bottled, and shipped everything from peanut butter to dish detergent. That's where I got the first pair of britches and shirt that ever matched—gray khakis and a gray khaki shirt, along with a green hard hat. They guaranteed a whopping two forty per hour, handed me a Weedwacker (the kind with a wood handle and no motor), and told me when I finished cutting the seven-foot tall Johnson grass around the perimeter of the plant, they'd try and find me some inside work.

I was seventeen going on eighteen then, and it seemed as though everyone I knew or came in contact with was considerably older. They all had advice too! That's what we old folks do best. We lurk in the shadows of our own miserable failures, waiting to impose our great advice and wisdom upon some unsuspecting youngster, whether they want it or not!

Although it's been well over forty years, I'll never forget a tidbit of advice I got from an older white-haired lead man at that plant. "Two things you should never discuss," he said, "politics and religion." He went on to say, "Those two subjects will only turn off your friends and turn on your enemies!"

Little did I know at the time, I would go on to become chairman of the most powerful committee in the Oklahoma House of Representatives, chairman of one of the state's largest political parties, an ordained minister, and later a pathological gambler and convicted felon.

In Oklahoma, politics and religion go hand in hand, two peas in a pod; they just match, kind of like the shirt and britches to that gray khaki uniform. Best of all, neither require a formal education to make one eligible to participate. Only in Oklahoma could you fail eighth grade math and still qualify to preside over the entire state budget. Also, where else could you be deemed unfit to be a politician yet retain your license to preach?

Although I held the rank of advice taker instead of advice giver, those days back at the old Brookside division were the best days of my life. The job was steady and allowed me to buy my very first new, used car. It was a candy apple red 1963 Ford Galaxy with bucket seats, a souped-up 390 engine, and an eight-track stereo tape deck. It was then that I married my high school sweetheart, Suzanne. She was a member of Hartshorne Highs honor society, runner-up football queen, drum majorette, and baton twirler. I was the envy of all my buddies. I had not only the prettiest girl in the old hometown but also the sweetest. It was during those days that we bought our first house and started our family. First, we had two beautiful little girls, then two adorable boys.

God, what I wouldn't give to turn back the hands of time and sail down Highway 69 in that little red Ford, gazing at the legs of the majorette who had worn those short skirts so well, to fit once again into that gray khaki uniform and, yes, not only hear the advice from some of my peers but to take it!

My first days of officially representing the good people of House District number 17 in Southeast Oklahoma were like an episode of the *Twilight Zone*. I rode in a Lincoln Continental with a severely weathered vinyl roof. I was thirty-nine years old, and so was the Lincoln—in car years, that is. The Lincoln belonged to a great man whom I will refer to as John. He was one of the few remaining old guard politicians still serving the House, and he and that old Lincoln were a perfect reflection of one another. New parts wouldn't fit the car, and new ideas didn't fit John.

Being beaten out of office the previous term, he had regained his seat in the House and was so considered the ranking and literally the oldest freshman in our class. John was from Muskogee. His personal anthem was Merle Haggard's hit song "Okie from Muskogee," and rightly so!

I was introduced to John by a mutual friend and supporter in my hometown. The supporter, who was the longtime mayor of Hartshorne and in his own right a member of the old guard, recommended that I hook up with John. He had also asked him to "take me under his wing," so naturally, I made friends with John, and we shared a room at the old Central Plaza Hotel located just a few blocks from the state capitol building.

Two years earlier, John had lost his seat to a young and upcoming attorney in Muskogee, who had run his campaign based on "out with the old and in with the new." But after only one term, he underestimated John's ability to mount a comeback. John pulled every political trick in the book, most of them dirty, even compared to current standards.

Running from well behind most of the race, John hired a couple of unsavory young women he'd met in a bar in Oklahoma City. He then instructed them to attend his opponent's campaign rally, where they would join the young lawyer's campaign team and come away with T-shirts and other campaign paraphernalia proudly proclaiming both the colors and name of John's opponent.

Just a few days before the election, the women cut the T-shirts off just below their breasts, wore the matching caps, and, on a beautiful Sunday morning, held their own campaign rally just one block from one of the largest Baptist churches in Muskogee. As church let out, the cars would slowly stream past the women who would raise the young lawyer's posters well above their heads, exposing their breasts with every wave of the signs. There simply wasn't enough time for John's rival to undo the damage. Thus, old guard John was "back in with the new!" He was also my roommate and political mentor for my first session in the Oklahoma House of Representatives.

I blended in well with John and the dated Lincoln. His old friends were all gone, and I hadn't made any yet. After the campaign that year, I had lost most of my hair, eyebrows and mustache included. The doctor said it was stress and nerves. I was broke and exhausted. The first day of session, I wore a secondhand suit that was about an inch short in the legs and a thirty-dollar wig and had my eyebrows and mustache colored in with mascara. Adding insult to injury, I had missed all the presession freshman orientation, caucuses, training sessions, and the standard welcoming gigs put on by lobbyists, where you mingled with all the state officials and the who's who in Oklahoma politics.

I was too embarrassed by my own looks to be seen. So my first day of official duty, I literally didn't know where the bathrooms were. That entire first session went on much the same. While the other legislators in my class were off to a half dozen receptions every evening for cocktails and hors d'oeuvres, I loaded up in the old Lincoln with John. We'd go straight to the hotel, change clothes, and eat dinner at the same Waffle House that was across the street from our room. In keeping with John's old ways, this routine never changed.

The downside of that first session was like missing the first semester of school and having to catch up fast while maintaining the second semester. My freshman colleagues were already learning all the technical aspects of stewarding their bills from committee to the House floor: how to file amendments, how to work with their senate counterparts, and what a committee report was. They were becoming familiar with the whole process and how it worked. They were also getting familiar with all the state agency executives and which lobbyist they could depend on for lunch or dinner or, in some cases, a good round of golf. More importantly, they were already forming coalitions and finding out who they could depend on for an affirmative vote.

There was, however, an upside for me. Old John was a living history book in politics. He delighted in telling me story after story of the characters and past events of his long legislative career—where all the bodies were buried, where all the land mines were, years' worth of campaign strategies you can't learn in school. The stories poured out whether in our shared hotel room, at the Waffle House, in the hotel lounge over a glass of Crown and Coke, stories of how he'd short-circuited the leadership or managed to get a bill killed or passed and, yes, even the story of his latest campaign.

In Oklahoma, the legislature convenes every year in February. The legislative session ends by the last day of May. Two legislative sessions equal one legislature and are numbered accordingly, so every two years at the end of each legislature, new elections are held, and all 101 House seats are up for grabs. The senate elections are held every four years.

The end of that first legislative session was a big relief for me. There were no midterm elections, and I had eight months to recuperate. By then, I had a steady paycheck coming in from the state of Oklahoma, something I hadn't had for the previous two years. My garden, which is nearly an acre in size, would keep me preoccupied for the next six weeks.

I've always made a garden. Even back in the Denison, Texas, days, I dug up a small corner of our backyard and managed to grow a couple tomato plants, a small row of onions, and enough cucumbers to make a salad. Now the rows are one hundred feet long. Several rows of sweet corn, tomatoes, potatoes, green beans, peas, okra, onions, lettuce, squash, and an assortment of flowers. During that first term in office, my boys were preteens but plenty old enough to help keep it weeded and tilled while I was at the capitol. When the corn was ready to gather, I'd take them to town and let them sell it. They always made enough money to buy new jeans, cowboy boots, and a new straw hat for the upcoming Fourth of July hometown rodeo. The rodeo was always their big summer delight. For me, though, the garden was always more than just a means to buy clothes or enjoy the fresh vegetables. It was and still is my sanctuary. It's a place to process my thoughts, a place of familiarity that brings me back to my own childhood. I spent many an hour there that summer, pondering the stories John had shared and reliving over and over in my mind the sights and sounds of that busy capitol building.

By the time the second session of that first legislative term rolled around, I was fully recovered. The garden had come and gone. I had spent the fall mostly in the woods with my boys and enjoyed our traditional deer camp. My hair had grown back and was maybe even a shade darker, with a little more wave. I had my confidence back, some new slacks, shirts, and blazers that fit. And at least I knew where my office and the bathrooms were in that big capitol complex. No more cheap wigs! No britches tugging at my crotch with every step and even a few bucks in my pocket.

I hit the ground running that session. I didn't miss a reception, a caucus, a party, or a dinner. Guess you could say I didn't miss a trick! I was catching up on lost time and doing it with a vengeance. And it was like being the new kid on the block. It seemed like everyone wanted my company and got a big kick out of my homespun stories. I enjoyed being the life of the party. The only one at the capital who wasn't enjoying the new me was old John. He'd already been down the fast lane and didn't have the inclination or the energy to do it again. I could tell it aggravated him a bit that I had not stuck to our old routine, and this session left him pretty much alone at the old Waffle House. I was having way too much fun to worry about old John, though, and although I still didn't know "come here" from "sic 'em," as far as the whole process, I was gaining ground fast! After all, in John's own words, "You can have all the friends at home you want, but without a lot of them up here, you won't get anything done for your district."

I was beginning to learn that you really didn't need to know much. The House staff was made up of brilliant young attorneys, analysts, wordsmiths, and number crunchers. They were well capable of drafting your bills, analyzing its fiscal impact, and even filing it for you. Heck, they could and would write your speeches and press releases that made even a country bumpkin like me look smart. Of course, I'd have to ask them what some of their words meant, just in case someone asked. Most people wouldn't question them anyway. Some of those words and terms they used were intimidating to Joe Six-Pack and Aunt Minnie, so most folk would just marvel at my newfound brilliance. I had even learned some coined phrases to use on the college presidents, all of whom spent more time at the state capitol than they did on campus.

The big surprise, and one I thoroughly enjoyed, was the nightly dinners sponsored by the lobbyists, and there certainly wasn't a shortage of them. The oilies, optometrists, ophthalmologists, pharmacists, electric co-ops, and a myriad of other utility reps—I can't name them all, and one can only imagine. The dinners weren't at the Waffle House either. Only the finest dining spots in Oklahoma City would do. I'll never forget the first time I went to Michael's and Junior's. Both are some of the more elaborate restaurants, and I could order anything I wanted on the menu and some stuff that wasn't. Cocktails always preceded dinner. My first few trips, I'd drink the cocktails as fast as I could order them for fear they'd surely run out with so many legislators all participating! I enjoyed it so much, I was eating some stuff I couldn't even pronounce! The lobbyists seemed to never run out of dinner money! One of my buddies who had been around a couple terms longer than me used to lean over and whisper, "Wonder what the poor folks at home are eating?"

Meanwhile, back at the capitol, I was beginning to learn how important I was. Those guys in the green coats would nearly break their necks trying to open a door for me. They were the House "sargeants" and some of the finest salt-of-the-earth people I'd ever been around. Then there was the ever-present House photographer with the *National Geographic*–looking vest on, snapping pictures of us politicians every thirty seconds. Little baskets of fruit or cute new coffee mugs would appear on my office desk every morning from some organization. My new name, Representative Mass, even impressed me! I can't speak for others I served with—or for politicians anywhere else, for that matter—but for me, the seeds of narcissism were slowly being planted.

One of my freshmen friends summed it up pretty well. He was a well-dressed, well-groomed, and well-liked representative from Tahlequah. He had met the incoming governor during a campaign stop in Tahlequah, and the governor elect asked my friend why he didn't run for the House seat in that area.

My buddy said, "Oh, shoot, I like to goof off too much, and besides, I curse a lot."

The governor elect said, "That won't hurt you."

"Well," my friend said, "I'm also bad to drink whiskey and carouse a lot."

The governor elect said, "Nobody cares about that!"

To which my friend grinned and said, "Why, hell," sounds like just the job for me!"

The federal transfer center wasn't more than ten miles, as the crow flies, from my old office at the state capitol building. The facility was designed to house federal prison inmates waiting to be assigned to a permanent prison. A cadre unit of low security inmates are assigned there to perform food and maintenance duties for the nearly 1,500 inmates in holdover. I was one of them.

Since the facility houses inmates with varying security levels, protocol for operating procedures are based more on a maximum security level. That meant I'd be locked in a nine-by-ten cell, on average, no less than ten to twelve hours a day—from 3:00 p.m. to 5:00 p.m. for the daily count and from 9:00 p.m. to 6:00 a.m., when the cell was unlocked for the daily work routine. Except for a small landscape detail, all inmates are confined inside. There were very limited medical and no mental health services available, and any recreation would be limited to a small rec deck that sported a basketball hoop. Although the deck had twenty-foot concrete walls and was covered with steel mesh and razor wire, you could see the sky from there.

I was still in shock by the time I'd been processed and escorted to my new and unfamiliar home on the seventh floor. There were no classes in the public school I came from back in Hartshorne that taught you how to prepare for prison. Neither the judge nor my lawyer had given me a manual on how to be an inmate. So there I stood in my BOP issues, holding my laundry bag, plastic pillow and sheet, with dozens of inmates all staring down the latest arrival.

The guard in a small office where I got off the elevator had handed me a piece of paper with my cell number scribbled across it. I was literally forcing one foot in front of the other as I made my way around the wall of adjoining cells, glancing above each metal door for the number E-6. I figured I was the only "wimp" there, as all the other inmates seemed to be going about their business like they'd been there forever. Some were standing in line waiting to board the large elevator, some were staring at a small TV hanging from a metal pole in the center of the pod, others were playing cards and slapping dominoes on the fiberglass tables scattered about, and a handful seemed content just staring a hole through me while I circled the pod looking for my new bunk.

When I found the cell, it was obvious that the bottom bunk was occupied, so I took the sheet from my laundry bag and began making my bed on top. All I wanted to do was crawl up there and suck my thumb. The bunk itself was made of solid metal sheeting, and the mattress was just short of a plastic bag stuffed with a handful of fiberglass shredding. As I would find out later, new arrivals are always given the worst accommodations, including their cellmate. It was not anything designed by prison officials, just a natural order of seniority protocol among inmates.

While I was in the process of trying to tie the torn sheet to the flimsy mattress, I was approached by an inmate who introduced himself as Powell. He occupied the bottom bunk, and he was quick to inform me that E-6 was his cell and more or less insinuated I was welcome as long as I adhered to his cell rules.

Powell was a couple of years my senior, medium build, and had the disposition of a cranky German shepherd dog. He was fine so long as he was being petted but quick to snap on occasions. He was a former truck driver from Talladega, Alabama, who was stopped while hauling a couple of marijuana bales for a little extra cash. He was on his final eighteen months of a sixty-month sentence. He explained the basic ground rules of prison life, and when lockdown for count occurred twice a day, then he ambled back off to his plastic chair facing the TV pole. I climbed atop the bunk, curled up facing the concrete wall, and tried my best to go to sleep. I was hoping to wake up later realizing it was all just a nightmare. I couldn't sleep to save my life. The deafening echoes of dominoes slapping against the hard-surfaced tables and sixty inmates all trying to talk louder than the other outside the cell was maddening. Within the next few minutes, old man Powell was back in the cell, and a guard was locking the heavy metal door for the 4:00 p.m. count.

After count, the guard made his rounds, unlocking all the cell doors, and inmates scrambled to line up for the evening chow. Although eating was the farthest thing from my mind, I took my place in line, forcing myself to learn the prison routine. There were lines formed from each of the three pods. As we neared the elevator, I could see that the guard was taking about a dozen men at a time into the large elevator. From there, we went to the basement floor and formed another line. I felt odd being the only one in line with the T-shirt and elastic-waisted khakis. Everyone else had on green khakis with button-up shirts and work boots. I stuck out like a sore thumb. It would be a couple days before I received my work unit issues.

The smell coming from the cafeteria was a far cry from the smell that had come from the nice restaurants near the state capitol. The closer in line I got to the entrance, the worse it smelled. Of course, nothing about the place I'd been for the past five hours smelled good. I was still in shock and very disoriented. I didn't eat much that evening. The tea I had poured from a tin canister even reeked. All the other inmates appeared to be enjoying the meal, the way they were gulping it down. I soon learned they were inhaling the stuff on account of the time we all had to do it in. This definitely wasn't a cafeteria where you took your time and kicked back for a relaxing dinner. The line never stopped moving. You had to eat quickly if you wanted to eat. On the way back to the seventh-floor unit, I asked one of the guys if the food down there was always that bad. He said, "Hell," man, this place feeds better than any of the other federal pens. You ought to try eating the slop they feed down at Big Springs." I would later learn that the chefs in the cafeteria were none other than my fellow cadre inmates, and they weren't just cooking for the work unit upstairs, but the inmates in holdover as well. You sure can't expect much from a bunch of inmate cooks who are serving up three squares a day to 1,500 people, especially when they're using frozen meats that are ten years beyond their expiration date. I couldn't help but recall my first wining and dining experience as a legislator, when a senior colleague leaned over and whispered, "Wonder what the folks back home are eating?"

It took until 9:00 p.m. that night for reality to set in. That's when the guards ushered us into our cells and twisted the metal lock on the cell door. It would remain locked until the 6:00 a.m. chow call. I was sick at my stomach but wasn't quite ready to sit on an open toilet two feet from a guy on the bottom bunk I didn't know. What it felt like to be locked in that eight-by-ten concrete cell with a total stranger is beyond my capacity to describe. Trauma, panic, despair—take your pick. Up until then, I thought I was a pretty tough customer, but I had serious doubts about handling another six hundred days like this one.

By 4:00 a.m., I was dressed and standing at the cell door, staring through the narrow glass window at the empty pod. I guess it's a natural instinct, wanting out of a locked cage, especially the first time you're in one. I stood there until 6:00 a.m. when the guard finally unlocked it for the 6:00 a.m. breakfast call.

I didn't get in the breakfast line that morning. I instead went out on the small rec deck and paced circles around it until well after daylight. It made me feel like I was going somewhere. I was soon joined by a young black kid pacing the same circle I was. He was a truck driver from Little Rock, Arkansas. He was thirty-five years old and had seven kids at home. He'd dropped out of high school and learned to drive a truck to help support his mother and siblings. Originally being from Mississippi, that was the nickname he would be called by at FTC.

I asked him what he was in for, and he was quick to tell me. "Looky here, man, I was hauling eight Mexicans across the border in the back of my truck for a little extra cash. They done caught my black ass and throwed me in this place." He said his lawyer argued that "they ain't never throwed anyone in prison for the first offense," but the judge said, "This nigga needs to go to prison and get his GED anyway." He finished with, "So here my black ass is. Now I don't know how my wife gonna take care of those babies."

His story made my own plight seem somewhat less severe, and I couldn't help but feel some compassion. That kid didn't have any business being in prison. He needed to be back in Little Rock taking care of his family. They'd have to fend for themselves, however, at least for the next eighteen months.

The rest of that day, I pretty much just roamed around in the pod and out on the rec deck. No one had as yet given me any instructions other than my cell number. I noticed on a bulletin board next to the officers' station that prison orientation would take place, but that was two weeks away. At that point, I was just following the herd.

That evening, I was approached by a young man from McCurtain County. That was one of the areas I represented back in the early nineties. He introduced himself as Rick and said he'd heard me speak on several occasions back when I had joined forces with the local cattleman association in an effort to keep the Choctaws from selling Sardis Lake water to the Texans. Rick was on his last five-month leg of an eight-year sentence for a firearm offense. Back in his youthful years of sewing his wild oats, he got caught growing some pot in buckets on the back porch of his mother's house. She didn't know what it was, and Rick couldn't help but chuckle while telling about it. Anyway, when the local authorities busted his marijuana operation, it went on his record as a felony even though he did no jail time. Of course, being a felon means you're no longer welcome to own or be in close proximity of a firearm. Twenty years later, Rick found himself very involved with the cattleman association in a dispute with the US Forestry Service over a land swap between the Forest Service and Weyerhaeuser. The dispute turned personal, as often occurs in local matters. Someone in the Forest Service was aware of Rick's prior felony and managed to get a valid warrant to search his home. Of course, Rick had some hunting rifles, as do most ranchers in the hills of Southeast Oklahoma. By the time the feds added the ammunition to the handful of guns, Rick got the mandatory federal sentence. Rick didn't have a violent bone in his body.

Anyway, it was a big relief meeting someone there from the same general area as I had come from. Rick gave me all the lowdown on prison fundamentals and made me much more at ease. He had also already put in a good word for me to get a job in laundry where I'd work side by side with him.

By the end of the first couple of weeks, I was well on my way to becoming a more confident federal convict. I was issued the green khakis and boots, which made me much more comfortable. I got a job in the laundry room right alongside Rick. I found out that the young black man who cursed me on the elevator that first day was really harmless, and I was making friends fast.

My ability to make a lot of friends there came about by sheer coincidence. A young Hispanic named Oso worked in commissary, which was only separated by chain-link wire from the laundry. Oso was finishing the last two years of a five-year sentence for gang-related activity in south Oklahoma City. Oso had the demeanor and the distinct tattoos that went along with gangster life. At work in laundry one morning, he put his hands through the chain-link cage and gave it a good rattle while calling out my name. I was both afraid to approach him and afraid not to. The guy had not so much as looked my way back in the E pod. I didn't know what to expect. As I approached the cage wire that separated us, he began to grin—wide enough that I could see his gold-capped teeth. I was glad to see he was grinning. He asked me if I knew a guy named Richie who he'd met in the holdover unit while delivering some commissary items. Richie, having seen the news accounts, knew I was in the facility somewhere and had asked Oso if he knew of an inmate named Mike Mass. He went on to tell Oso that I had gotten him out of a scrape or two while I was in office. It thoroughly impressed Oso that I was that kind of politician, and we became friends on the spot. Before finishing our brief conversation, Oso said, "Look here, man, we gonna call you da Governor from now on." Within days, every inmate in cadre referred to me as the Gov, and there wasn't one of them I didn't get along with.

I was really relieved at going to work in laundry. Most newcomers are assigned to kitchen detail, where their entire work shift is done on greasy floors amid hot water flying in every direction. Besides, the odor of that place didn't set well with me. I was in the portion of laundry called laundry fold. The washing and drying was done by a crew in a separate space, between our work station and the mess hall. We were responsible for rolling up socks, T-shirts, and boxers inside a pair of brown khaki pants, taping them in a roll, and stacking them in a four-by-four laundry cart. We would then deliver them to the holdover units on a daily basis. A stockpile for new clothing was also kept there but put in use only when the clothing in use was beyond repair or cleaning. We worked in pretty cramped quarters, and it was all done on our feet for six to eight hours a day. The pay was less than twenty cents per hour and either went to our commissary fund or to pay off pending court costs or fines. Of course, even encaged, we were closely monitored by surveillance cameras.

Time in prison goes by at a snail's pace. It went especially slow that first couple of weeks before I got in a routine of work in laundry fold. Locked in that cell with Powell was an experience of its own. Turns out the old fella had mental problems. One night in the wee hours of the morning, I woke up gagging and choking. Through the dim light filtering in through the narrow window of the cell door, I could see Powell puffing a cloud of medicated powder. We had a tense confrontation, but neither of us threw a punch. The next day he wanted to "talk about it." I guess that was his way of apologizing. Old Powell never missed a prison-sponsored devotional, and ironically, the old guy even had a certificate he'd earned in the prison's anger management class. Nevertheless, at least every other night, he'd throw a tantrum of some sort. The following day, like clockwork, he'd apologize and invite me to the next devotional. I told him I was beyond saving—I just needed a good night's sleep. After a couple of weeks, I gave in and went with him, along with a dozen or so other cadre inmates. The prison chaplain met us all at the elevator one evening and escorted us all to the chapel. Old Powell was pleased as punch that I'd went with him. I thought if a trip to the chapel would get me a good night's sleep, it was well worth it. The chaplain droned on for nearly an hour about forgiveness and how that even he was a lowly sinner and had to depend on the blood of Christ for salvation. I thought it a little funny, him talking about forgiveness while standing in a prison with 1,500 kids locked in a cell. Why in God's name didn't someone forgive them! After the service, the kind chaplain led us through two metal detectors, handed us off to a guard for a thorough strip search, and delivered us back to our cells. I never went back. I'd rather listen to crazy Powell's tantrums.

The official prison orientation finally came around after I'd been there for three weeks. I'd already been orientated by fellow inmates, but the class was mandatory, so I went. It was really nothing more than listening to the warden rattle off his superior credentials and a string of prison counselors trying to impress the warden. I'd seen and heard the dog and pony show before. During the class, a twenty-eight-year-old kid named Jacob sat next to me. He was from Des Moines, Iowa, and had arrived at FTC a few days after I had. Poor kid was on his first month of a seventeen-year sentence. He had sold $300 worth of pot to a federal undercover agent. The transaction took place at his parents' house while they were away on vacation. His dad, being an avid outdoor sportsman, had several deer hunting rifles in the house. That was reason enough to book Jacob for having firearms during the commission of a crime. Five years before that, the kid was busted for smoking a joint with some friends, so with his prior "record," plus the guns and the bag of weed he'd just sold, the feds enhanced their calibrations, and young Jacob got a seventeen-year stay in the federal pen. I don't know why they didn't just hang the poor kid. I'll bet that boy never salutes the flag again! I was wishing some of the politicians I'd seen that like to pose with their family in front of a church for their latest campaign brochure could come in here and spend a few years with Jacob.

During the orientation session, I got another break. While on a brief recess, a fellow inmate approached me and asked if I'd be willing to share a cell with him. His cellmate would be leaving the following week, and rather than take a chance on who the unit monitor might stick with him, he'd much rather have the Gov for a cellie. Although I'd seen the kid around the pod, I didn't know him that well, but anything would beat bunking in a locked cell with Powell.

Moreover, the kid had only ninety days left himself, which would present me with prospects of a bottom bunk and move me up to "cell boss." We shook hands and made the deal. Turns out deals were made in prison much like they were done at the state capitol. I was a master at that!

I had always heard that prison was a revolving door, but the term took on a new meaning from the inside. FTC was truly a revolving door, with inmates constantly leaving, making room for a new one. It was not so much the same guys coming back as new faces appearing. Cadre unit wasn't designed for long-term stays. Guys who came there were either beginning a lengthy sentence and would soon be on their way to a designated facility, or they were coming there for the final two years of a long sentence. Either way, cadre unit was a constant turnover of federal inmates. Very few stayed there more than two years.

I had been an outdoorsman all my life. Even as a child, I was indoors for only two reasons: eating and sleeping. Of course, some of that wasn't my own choice. Dad kept my brothers and I hooked up in the two-acre cucumber patch or cutting wood, bailing hay, fixing fence, and doing a myriad of other farm chores. When we weren't doing that, which was rare, I'd spend time picking blackberries or catching bass in Grandpa's pond with a good Calcutta cane pole. Even while serving time at the state capitol, I'd go home on weekends, put on my overalls, and stay busy outside. Whether I was following a redbone hound in Gaines Creek bottoms or running my garden tiller, that's how I kept my mind at peace. If I wanted to keep my sanity within the restricted confines of mortar and steel for the next two years, I had to find a way to stay busy.

It didn't take me long, however, to figure out that I was one of the very few lucky ones there. In fact, my fellow inmates would jokingly say they'd done more time on the "shitter" than I'd have to do during my whole prison stay. Most of them were kids with very little family support, and most of them had a background of addiction. All of them had been hit hard by a two by four when they could have been handled with a switch. A Christian nation that wallows in the trough of forgiveness had little to give these kids. As I got to know these young men, my disdain for pandering politicians like myself only grew. Knowing how that first day in prison had rattled my senses, I couldn't help but wonder what it felt like to a twenty-eight-year-old facing seventeen years or a twenty-three-year-old facing ten.

Law and order legislation serves as a reelection tool for most politicians. Cloaked in an otherwise cushy political environment, it makes them appear tough. Moreover, who can argue against law and order? My childhood preacher, Brother Ronald used to quote a favorite passage: "For all have sinned and fallen short of the glory of God." The trouble is, some fall a little shorter than others, and society loves making examples of them.

While in my dual role as party chairman and representative of a conservative rural house district, I often found myself casting votes in an effort to please both the left and the right. It didn't take many liberal votes to disgruntle my right-wing constituency either. To fix matters, I filed a "chain gang bill." I knew both sides would love that, and they did. Of course, the bill was impractical and stood no chance of being signed into law, but the folks back home loved it. It also covered up a multitude of liberal votes I'd made. I was sure hoping my buddy's in cadre didn't find out about it!

In the early sixties, Dad decided to go into the hog business. I, along with my older brother and sister, had been showing hogs in the local 4-H and FFA contests. Dad was purchasing the young pigs we'd raise for various stock shows from a neighbor. At the time, a prospective young show hog cost every bit of twenty bucks. Considering gas was only twenty cents a gallon back then, twenty bucks was a pretty good lick out of a large family budget. Dad would raise our own show pigs. He purchased a large red Duroc sow, had her bred, and, with me and my brother's help, built a small hog house, complete with a good farrowing stall. As time grew near for the birthing, he had my brother and me keeping close watch on the old sow. The farrowing stall was designed in such a way as to keep the old sow from lying on the newborns. With Dad working the night shift at the Army Ammunition Base, my brother and I would trek to the hog house every night as birthing time grew near. Finally, the moment came, and it couldn't have come at a worse time. On a frigid November night with sleet blowing like pellets of steel, the old sow began to deliver the infant piglets. My brother and I were peering through the pine boards of the farrowing stall with a dim flashlight, shivering from the cold. As each little pig slid out of the womb, we watched with amazement. One, then two, then three, and more—many more! Seventeen beautiful red baby piglets. Frozen in our tracks from both the sight and the weather, we were taken by surprise when the old sow stood up and whirled toward the newborns. In an instant, she began a feeding frenzy—on her own babies. Both panicked and frightened at the sight, there was little we could do. What she didn't eat, she stomped to death. The youngsters in this federal penitentiary were no different than those little red pigs. They were swallowed in the bowels of a nation that birthed them.

The fun-filled dining, twenty-dollar cigars, and unlimited drinks at the state capitol were a far cry from the way I was brought up, much less the social life I found in the federal pen. I was raised in the "spare the rod, spoil the child" era. I feared God and trembled at the sight of Dad! Before you conjure up images of abuse, let me clarify. My seven siblings and I weren't beaten with fists by a drunken loser. We simply got our asses whipped by a father who had too much work on his plate and not enough time to hold counseling sessions with eight children. He used a belt, and we could hear every loop in his britches pop when he took it off! We weren't any different from most family's back then in the area of child discipline; that's just the way it was. If you lied, you got a whippin'! If you tattled, you got a whippin'! If you disobeyed, you got a whippin'!, and if you dared to be disrespectful to an adult, you got a severe whippin'! You would be amazed at how a forty-five-minute counseling session could be accomplished with one stern look. We had absolutely no illusions of Dad being our best friend or counselor. He was Dad, and that was that! One "no" was all you needed!

Although Dad only stood five feet, eleven inches tall and weighed less than 190 pounds, it was clear as crystal who the head of our household was. He wore a short-brimmed black

Stetson hat, a well-trimmed black mustache, and had biceps that were groomed by a double bit ax. So far as I could tell, he feared no one and, even having only an eighth grade education, was intimidated by no one. He read the daily newspaper religiously, as well as Zane Gray paperbacks. He was both insightful and decisive but never espoused his views or personal beliefs on anyone. The philosophy he lived by was one of "mind your business, and I'll mind mine!"

So far, as we kids were concerned, there was little room for fun and games. That went for the family pets as well. A dog that wouldn't tree a squirrel wasn't welcome around our place for very long. The fun and games would be reserved for Christmas and the Fourth of July, at least in his presence!

In the mid-1960s, he borrowed the money from one of his close Italian buddies and purchased seventy-nine acres near the rural community of Higgins just off the old Indian highway. The acreage was seven miles east of our home place and farther out in the sticks, which suited him fine. Being mostly rock and timber, most folk couldn't have raised hell on it with a gallon of whiskey, but that was no deterrent for Dad. Making good use of an ax, a grub hoe, and my older brother and me, he managed to clear two acres of it for farming purposes. He then signed a contract with a pickling company that was located some forty miles west in Calvin, Oklahoma. They would provide the seed, we would raise the cucumbers, and the pickling company would buy them. The farm, as we called it, would pay for itself.

Didn't matter either that he had no modern tractor, cultivator, or the wherewithal to hire field hands. A walk-behind tractor with a five-horse Briggs and Stratton motor, a couple of sharp hoes, along with brothers and me, were all he needed. My older brother was sixteen, I was thirteen, and my younger brothers were ten and seven. We would do the cultivating and the picking! Mama would pick right along beside us and, most of the time, ahead of us. My older sister, Donna, who was fifteen, would stay at home with the three youngest siblings. She was required to fill in as Mom while she did the cooking and cleaning, as well as the babysitting.

Picking time came right on the heels of the school's summer break, which worked out great for Dad. Killing two birds with one stone, he'd keep our idle hands busy and get two acres of cucumbers picked. Wasn't any worry of the field hands showing up late either, as the four of us boys all slept in one room.

At 4:30 a.m., he'd open the bedroom door, flip on the light switch, and we field hands would hit the floor. Mama would whip up a quick breakfast of fried eggs and oatmeal, and by daybreak, we'd all be stationed at the beginning of a long row of cucumbers.

From a distance, the long rows of vines were a thing of natural beauty—lush and green, sprinkled with bright yellow blooms. What lay beneath them, however, could at times be very ugly, as well as very deadly. The dense vines not only concealed the ideal cucumbers but, at times, also the black widow spider and copperhead snake. Dad's brief instruction and warning would be repeated at the beginning of each day's work. "Be gentle with the vines," he'd say, "and watch under them good before reaching in with your hands!"

By noon, we'd have the truck loaded with burlap sacks full of cucumbers, blackened hands, and aching backs, and Dad would have just enough time to write out our list of afternoon chores, as if we hadn't done enough already, grab his lunch bucket, and head out to his regular job at the McClain Naval Ammunition Base.

While our time belonged to Dad, our hearts belonged to Mama, and she made well sure there was going to be room in our hearts for the Almighty. While Dad's roots were buried deep in Catholicism, with his parents coming here from Italy and being devout Roman Catholics, Mama was a Protestant's Protestant—a "speak where the Bible speaks and be silent where the Bible is silent" Protestant; a no dancing, no drinking, and no public bathing Protestant; a twice on Sunday and once on

Wednesday Protestant. We didn't miss a service. Nor did we miss the spring and fall revivals.

The church building was a modest white wood frame building with four classrooms, an auditorium that held slightly over one hundred people, a baptistry, a pulpit, and a blackboard. It had a wood floor and large wood frame windows and no air-conditioning. Attendance on a good Sunday rarely exceeded sixty people and, on Sunday and Wednesday night services, about half as many. In the wooden brackets attached to the auditorium seats were the songbooks and cardboard fans. The fans were for the adults.

The people who attended there were mostly country folk of meager means, just like we were. They were some of the finest people I have ever known—hardworking, God-fearing, family-loving, and selfless. Some of my fondest memories center on that old church. Not that as a kid, I liked going to church. I liked it the same as I liked going to school. To me, the best part of both was when they ended! But I did love the folks there.

Church was Mama's big deal, not Dad's, and, although he rarely went with us, he made sure we honored Mama's rigorous routine. He'd bring my brothers and me in from the fields every Saturday evening after a hard day's work either in the hayfield, the cucumber patch, or, in fall and winter, cutting wood. He worked us good enough that nothing was on our minds Saturday night but laying our heads on a pillow. We didn't even want to watch TV. Besides, that was Mama's "Lawrence Welk" TV time. But before we could lay our heads on a pillow or slouch in a chair, she would start in on us about polishing our shoes and getting our Sunday clothes laid out. That was worse to me than working the fields all day. So every Sunday morning, shortly before 10:00 a.m., Mama had the eight of us loaded in our '60 model Chevy station wagon and on our way to church! Any ears that hadn't gotten clean enough in the tub Saturday night, she would take care of on the way to church, and believe me, that was the hard way to get your ears cleaned!

You addressed the adults at church by prefacing their last name with either *brother* or *sister*—that is, if they'd been thoroughly washed in the blood or in the baptistry. The preacher's name had a different twist. *Brother* preceded his first name—Brother Ronald.

When we were kids, Brother Ronald was at that ripe age that was right in the middle—old enough to be respected by the old folks yet young enough that his merry-go-round functioned like a well-greased machine. He could quote most of the New Testament and a lot of the Old Testament from memory. He was self-taught and didn't have much use for so-called Christian schools, seminaries, or colleges. They were too far out in left field for him. He could paint the best picture of hell you ever saw but not so much about heaven, and he loved to debate the Bible. Back then, religious debates were held quite frequently. I'm pretty sure that's where "our side" was pointing out all the scriptural reasons as to why everyone, except our church, was going to hell, most assuredly the Catholics. They really seemed to put a burr under his saddle. I remember him preaching that it would be a sin to vote for John F. Kennedy because he was Catholic. The very rare occasions that Dad came with us to church—and that was probably twice—Brother Ronald's sermon would be an all-out assault on Catholicism. But for some odd reason, Dad never tried to turn us kids away from "the church." Although we sensed he didn't have much use for Preacher Ronald, as Dad called him, he maintained his vigilance in support of our church routine, according to Mama. The times that Mama was sick or for some other reason couldn't go, Dad would take us to church, let us out of the car, and return to pick us up after services.

Dad's family was just as devout to Catholicism as Mama's was to the Church of Christ. In fact, out of Dad and his seven siblings, his mate was the only one who didn't convert to the

Catholic Church, and when one of my uncles showed up to take the firstborn, my older brother, Danny, to get him sprinkled into the Catholic Church, Mama let it be known there would be no Catholics among her brood! Dad was caught in a religious vacuum, so until many years later, he attended no church at all. As we kids grew older, he quietly started attending Sunday morning mass at the Catholic Church, all by his lonesome.

It was pretty weird growing up under those two very different religious cultures. Mama's Church of Christ family was far away in West Texas, but Grandma and Grandpa Mass lived just up the country road from our house. We grew up very close to Dad's family, especially our cousins, and, of course, any family gatherings would be at Grandma and Grandpa's place. There were always the typical Italian foods of spaghetti, meatballs, Italian sausage, the homemade Italian cheeses, and, naturally, the various wines and cold homebrewed beer. The crucifix and Grandma's rosary beads hung prominently on her living room wall, and a little statue of the Virgin Mary was glued to the dashboard of Grandpa's pickup truck. Of course, neither Brother Ronald, and certainly not Mama, ever looked at us kids square in the eye and said, "Your daddy, your grandparents, and the whole Mass family are going to hell," but the implications of the Scriptures, as we were taught, made it quite clear! Kids have built-in coping mechanisms for the disturbing, so for me, those condemning thoughts were seared over into the farthest reaches of my mind especially where it concerned Grandma, Grandpa, Dad, and all my cousins. I loved them dearly and could not cope with thoughts of them in Hades.

Moreover, Catholics weren't the only ones on the fast track to hell, according to Brother Ronald's teachings. So were the Baptists, Methodists, Jews, Assembly of God, and any other place of worship that didn't display the sign "Church of Christ." Most of them he considered liberal because they had fellowship halls, gave money to orphanages, or gave financial support to what he considered liberal Christian schools.

There were a number of unforgivable sins too, adultery being the most prominent. There were several different ways one could commit adultery. Being immersed in water was essential to salvation, so naturally, I grew up thinking Billy Graham and all those other TV evangelists were wolves in sheep's clothing. The teachings were so rigid that by the time I was fourteen years old, I was convinced there was no way I was going to heaven! There was no dancing, including the school prom; no public bathing, meaning no swimming in a public pool; no musical instruments in church services; and no eating in the church building. Moreover, the King James Version of the Bible was the only Bible version that held the truth.

The basis for this "sound doctrine" comes from the last chapter of the book of Revelation, verses 18 and 19. As paraphrased by most leaders in the Church of Christ, "Speak where the Bible speaks and be silent where the Bible is silent."

That being said, Brother Ronald was a good man, and he sincerely believed what he preached, as do most clergy. He certainly didn't preach for the money. The offering in that little church barely kept the utilities paid and the lawn mowed. He held down a full-time job, aside from his preaching and teaching. He wasn't in it for the glory as he was willing to step on everyone's toes equally. He taught us kids to recite the books of both the Old and New Testament while we were preteens, as well as teaching us to memorize scripture. He always visited the sick and shut-ins, and, to this day, I truly believe he lived the life he preached so fervently.

Nonetheless, and regardless of sincerity, the teachings made for a horrible religious bubble, a very awkward bubble for a child to grow up in. It was a religion that had an answer for every question and a doctrinal reason for every action.

Adding insult to injury was the teaching on the sins of omission, as well as the sins of commission. As if there weren't already more than enough reasons to get you thrown into the lake of fire, "where the worm dieth not, and the fire is not quenched" for all of eternity, you could also go to hell for the things you didn't do. The basis for this teaching came from what was called the Great Commission—"Go ye into the entire world and preach the gospel to every creature," one of the more important "memory verses" in our arsenal of scripture that had to be memorized. That meant it was not only Brother Ronald's job to preach, we had to do it too! So periodically, we would have some good old-fashioned "door knockings," go house to house, knock on the door, and, with knees shaking, try to relay the plan of salvation before they sic their dog on you or slam the door in your face! The only door I have a vivid memory of knocking on is the one when a shirtless potbellied man opened the door with beer in one hand and scratching his hairy belly with the other and told me to beat it. This meant, "Get the hell outta here!"

I grew up with an extreme sense of guilt. With every move I made, God seemed to be pointing me out "guilty as charged." I couldn't save any souls. I was continually doing the naughty little things boys do. I cussed a lot. I even sometimes sneaked a peek at the women's lingerie section in Mama's Sears catalogue. I also sneaked into a burlesque show at a local carnival with two of my cousins. We crawled under the tent to get in. Once we were in, the adults there seemed to get a kick out of our wide-eyed response to the strippers: Minnie the Mermaid and Jodie Baby.

We sang a song at church entitled, "There's an Eye Watching You." It went, "Every step that you take, this great eye is awake, there's an all seeing eye watching you." That particular hymn seemed to get stuck in the wheels of my merry-go-round often.

Strange as it is to fathom, Brother Ronald became a sort of role model to me. And although he was preaching my soul to hell three times a week, I never took it as a personal thing. Ronald never made eye contact from the pulpit. He had an odd way of staring over the heads of his audience, so it always left a slim notion that perhaps he was talking to someone other than me. I'm sure everyone else had the same notion. As a child, however, he was a very impressive figure. I even wished I could comb my hair like him and was convinced he was the only man on the planet who understood the Bible.

The plan of salvation as taught by Brother Ronald and "the church" as a whole is relatively simple. It is referred to as the five step-plan of salvation: hear, believe, repent, confess, and be baptized. You must do all five, or your ticket to the pearly gates is void. You were expected to complete the salvation plan once you reached the age of accountability, or you risked having your soul eternally damned. So as a youngster in the church, not only are you going through puberty, you're also going through those years of wondering if you've reached that age of accountability. This in itself was scary as hell. It was that tender age when you think you know, but you're not quite sure. I can remember those invitation songs that seemed so gripping, so frightening. "Oh, why not tonight? Oh, why not tonight? Wilt thou be saved? Then why not tonight?" I stood through countless invitational hymns, petrified with fear, mainly petrified at the thought of walking down that aisle in front of all those people. When the song ended, I was then stuck in that real fear that I'd die before the next week's service rolled around. That meant the lake of fire and brimstone. You were literally playing with fire!

I will never forget that Sunday night when I finally summoned up the courage to let go of the pew in front of me and begin that frightful yet relieving walk down the aisle toward Brother Ronald while knowing all eyes in that building were fixed on my every step. Brother Ronald took my hand and seated me on the front row while the congregational hymn was being completed. I remember him whispering the questions. Do you repent of your sins and believe that Jesus Christ is the Son of God? And are you ready to be immersed in water for the remission of your sins? Of course, I responded with an affirmative. The only step left now was the baptism itself, and I was afraid of the water, which was a direct consequence of not being allowed in a swimming pool. I had never had my head held underwater, yet here I was, with Brother Ronald holding my hand as he led me down the steps into the water-filled baptistry. I held my nose and my breath as he recited, "Having repented of your sins and confessing with your mouth that Jesus Christ is the Son of the true living God, I now baptize you in the name of the Father, the Son, and the Holy Ghost!" With that, he gently leaned me backward into that watery grave. I was saved—and extremely relieved!

Unfortunately, the real fear of Hades didn't end there for me. Once saved, always saved is not in the Church of Christ doctrine. To me, that meant if I died between sins I had committed, or a good deed I omitted and hadn't ask God for forgiveness, my soul was still in jeopardy.

The borders of our physical world were almost as limited as the spiritual. Eating out meant eating on the porch or out in the yard because it was too hot to eat in the house, and except for the rare trip to see Mama's family in West Texas, we didn't do vacations. Dad's idea of a good vacation was either getting Grandpa's hay baled and stacked in the hayloft or building a new fence. He kept us busy right alongside him too.

Less than a quarter mile east of our home place was a small two-room shanty that was part of Grandpa's original eighty-acre homestead when he purchased it in the mid-1920s. While older brother and I were stuck in the incorrigible days of our youth, Grandpa rented the old shanty to a semiretired carpenter who went by the nickname Huck. The nickname suited his appearance to a T.

Although Huck rarely worked, save for a remodeling job now and then, he maintained a steady vigil of wearing his pin-striped carpenter overalls, mostly void of a shirt beneath the straps. For the most part, he kept his false teeth in a mason jar half filled with water, which left little room between his large nose and his chin. Huck entertained himself with a bottle of Old Charter and a collection of nudist magazines. He reeked of alcohol and Pall Mall cigarettes.

Even compared to standards of the day, the old shanty was less than desirable for living purposes. It was made of pine slabs, had a tin roof, and sat on a foundation of sandstone rock. In the small living room of the shanty, the walls were covered with pages ripped from his old nudist magazines, all sporting naked women, of course. Amid the sprawling array of these gaudy images hung a crucifix, complete with Jesus, his robe, and a crown of thorns—a memento that was left in the old shack by Grandma Mass.

The front porch of the shanty was supported by cedar poles hewn from native cedar trees that were decorated by a half dozen goat skulls, all sporting large curved horns. He told brother and me he hung them there to keep evil spirits away. Between the goat heads, the homemade wallpaper, and Huck's colorful stories, the place was a natural draw for two eleven- and fourteen-year-old boys like us. Consequently, sneaking off to hang out with old Huck became a favorite pastime. When we weren't inside gawking at the walls, we were quizzing old Huck about the bad spirits the goat heads were holding off. The education we received from Huck was quite a contrast to that of Brother Ronald and Mama and much more interesting!

My older brother, Danny, however, just couldn't stand prosperity. Always pushing the envelope, he could never let a good thing last for long. Being three years his junior, I had little choice but to reluctantly follow his schemes. One night, he decided it would be a good idea to try and wake up those evil spirits Huck talked about. So on a moonlit night, we positioned ourselves in the tall sage grass across the Indian Highway and opened fire on Huck's tin roof with our BB guns. The sound of the BBs pinging off the roof was thrilling for a little while but didn't seem to be waking up any spirits. It wasn't long before we were chucking rocks, and with a loud bang, they would land on the tin roof and make a good portion of noise as they rolled back down across the porch roof. I can only imagine what it sounded like on the inside of that old shanty. From where we stood, however, each loud bang provided a thrill, along with a good ole belly laugh, as we each tried to "outbang" each other!

We came to find out ole Huck wasn't near as drunk or oblivious as we thought he was. A few days later, he ran into Mama at the East Side market in Hartshorne. "Mam," he said, "youins' boys been throwin' rocks on my house, and it sounds like thunder." He went on to tell her that we rattled the old house so bad that we broke all the windows out. We weren't too scared of Mama, but all hell would break loose if old Huck decided to tell Grandpa or, even worse, Dad. I guess ole Huck could see just as good in the moonlight as we could.

Mama's wrath only served as a warning as to what was to come if Dad ever found out, and that we understood. My brother came up with a plan that would cure it all. He opened a can of Mama's biscuits, cut a hole in each one, fried them in a large black skillet, and made the prettiest doughnuts I've ever seen. He sprinkled them with sugar, put them in a paper sack, and off to Huck's we went. My brother was still convinced that we were a lot smarter than ole Huck.

While Huck sat on the porch beneath the goat skulls eating one doughnut after the other, my brother was busy explaining how he had seen some dastardly looking boys walking up toward his house late one evening with a pocket full of rocks. I guess my brother thought that he would frame some other poor kids who lived close by. After all, Huck wouldn't know one of them if he saw them, and anything was better than us taking the rap.

Satisfied that Huck appreciated our doughnuts and our intelligence, we figured we had beaten the system. We were certain he had bought our goods when he finished the doughnuts and invited us in to gawk at the wallpaper. We giggled all the way back home with much relief at the thought of washing our hands of the crime! Our relief was short-lived, however, as that very afternoon, Grandpa Mass summoned us both to meet him at the shanty that ole Huck rented from him. That's when we fully realized that ole shack belonged to Grandpa, not Huck. Ole Huck ate our doughnuts and told on us anyway!

Fortunately for us, there weren't any broken windows. Huck had done a little embellishing of his own. That eased the tension some but not fully. While inspecting the damages reported by Huck, Grandpa couldn't help but notice the makeshift wallpaper. Of course, my brother and I acted like it was the first time we had ever seen such a thing. I guess we thought Grandpa was dumb too.

Grandpa put us to picking up rocks and cleaning up Huck's yard. He then told Huck in his best broken English, "Hey, Hucka, either you takea the pictures down, or you takea Jesus down." I guess for convenience's sake, old Huck removed the crucifix. As for brother and I, we learned something that day—throw a rock at someone, and one will be coming back at you in one form or the other. Unfortunately, that subtle life lesson, like so many others I'd learned the hard way, seemed to roll off me like rocks off a tin roof.

# 5

My first run for political office of any sort was in the summer of 1990. At the time, I had no job, no money, and four kids in school. I had no campaign organization, only a vehicle with bald tires. My immediate family was all like deer caught in the headlights. Some of them thought evil had befallen me while others just simply didn't know what to do or how to help. So in early March of that year, I set out on a quest in unchartered and daunting political waters.

The question often asked of me was, "Why do you want to run for office?" or, in a more sinister tone, "Why do you want to get involved in politics?" For me, the answer was quite simple although a bit corny. I had a sincere desire to help our little corner of Southeast Oklahoma. Growing up in the fifties and sixties, small towns in our area of the state were vibrant communities. Businesses and retailers filled every store front in our hometown, and jobs were plentiful for anyone with a desire to work. Over the course of the next two decades, however, small towns fell victim to the super stores that began cropping up in the larger towns, leaving small-town Oklahoma reduced to a bedroom community. By the late 1980s, 90 percent of my hometown, as well as many other small towns in Southeast Oklahoma, were boarded up. I was naive enough to think I could change this for the better, plus

I needed a job! My plan was pretty simple. I'd just ask everyone in Oklahoma's House District 17 for their vote and hope they didn't have any clever political questions because I sure didn't have any clever answers!

At the onset, I learned that House District 17 had been "Jerry-mandered" after the last census was taken in our state, which occurs every decade. That's when all 101 House District boundaries are redrawn or reapportioned in order to maintain an equal number of people in each district. The adjoining district's representative at that particular time, who happened to be in a "leadership" position, had redrawn the boundaries not only to accomplish even numbers in the district but also to carve out any suspected opposition to him personally. It's sort of like chunking a rock in a pond and creating ripples, and the ripple effect he created by drawing out opposition left HD 17 in a mess. That's why they call it "Jerry-mandering." As a result, HD 17 was left a very large rural and awkward land mass in Southeast Oklahoma, at least for the next ten years. It was spread out all over the Jack Fork and Kiamichi Mountains, swallowing up almost four counties, and all very rural. It was the only HD in Oklahoma that didn't have a Walmart or a car dealership in it. It was all "country" and spread out for miles and miles! This was literally dozens and dozens of small country hamlets and communities.

Making matters worse, HD 17 was not an open seat. It was currently held by an entrenched three-term incumbent who had no plans of retiring or stepping down by any other means. He was college-educated, a former school superintendent, chairman of the House Education committee, a self-proclaimed Christian, and had no obvious looming scandals that would even remotely put his incumbency at risk. His campaign war chest was well financed, and he knew everybody who was anybody in the district. He was certainly well acquainted with every school teacher and administrator in the nearly two dozen schools spread throughout the sprawling house district. As if that weren't advantage enough, he had kinfolk in my hometown—an uncle who was a former county sheriff and his wife, who was a political machine all in herself. Then there was the guy who ran one of the last of the Texaco service stations in our hometown. The incumbent had made his acquaintance while stopping there for a fill-up on his way through Hartshorne to the state capitol. So the gas station attendant, who naturally came in contact with lots of the locals, fancied himself as a friend of the incumbent! Besides, the uncle and aunt traded with him as well! In the early stages of my candidacy, the three hometowners were busy telling folk that although I was a pretty good ole boy, I really didn't stand a chance in this big-league political race, and a vote for me would be a wasted ballot!

I didn't know the incumbent from Adam's house cat and certainly couldn't have picked him out of a lineup! I didn't know anything about him at the time, much less what his voting record was or what he stood for. All I knew was that I had the burning desire to help my little part of Southeast Oklahoma and that I needed a job! I sure didn't have sense enough to know you were supposed to be running against someone.

Although the filing period wouldn't open until the first Monday in June and the primary election wasn't until August, I started my campaign in early March. My campaign war chest consisted of a worn-out vehicle and handmade posters. My campaign adviser was the former Hartshorne postmaster, a decorated World War II veteran and longtime stalwart of the hometown. His name was Bill Morgan.

I spent those first three months scouring the countryside, nailing my homemade posters to trees, telephone poles, and fence posts. I'd leave the house at daylight every morning and get home after dark after hanging posters, knocking on doors, and asking anyone that would hold still long enough for their vote. Really, about all you could make of my posters from the road was a tacky white sheet of paper, and after every rain, I'd have to replace them. I did this so relentlessly that word soon got around that those flimsy white posters belonged to that "poor Mike Mass campaign." I spent every day driving country roads, in and out of the car, shaking hands, replacing flimsy posters, and picking up every tick and chigger in Southeast Oklahoma! I'm pretty sure that by 2:00 or 3:00 p.m. every afternoon, I looked like death warmed over. I know I sure felt like it! Early goings of the campaign were literally like hand-to-hand combat in the trenches.

"Hi, my name is Mike Mass, and I'd really appreciate your vote. I'm running for state representative." Generally, I would get a scowl and a "Yeah, what you gonna do for us, and who you running against?" followed by a three- to five-minute commentary on those low-life politicians. So I'd stand or sit quietly, acting as though I welcomed the humiliation. I didn't have a canned speech or even a promise to make. I'd never been to most of those backwoods communities before and didn't have a clue of their local issues, but it didn't take long to figure out that most of these yahoos didn't vote anyhow. In fact, the majority of them weren't even registered to vote, and out of the ones who could vote, there was only a small percentage who knew anything at all about the political system. Most didn't know, and I'm sure it's true even now, the difference between a state representative and a US congressman. There were a lot of folks in my district who had voted for me repeatedly and who assumed I was in Washington, DC, and one time, while door knocking after my fourth term in office, I asked a woman who was out weeding her garden for her vote. She looked me square in the eyes and responded, "Well, you got my vote, that son of a bitch we got in there now ain't doing a damn thing!" Of course, that son of a bitch was me, but I graciously accepted her support and moved on.

The first few months of that first campaign literally wore both me and my car out. It was not only physically exhausting, but mentally as well. All the while, the incumbent was still in session at the state capitol and acting as though I didn't exist. By the time session ended and the filing period opened in late May and early June, most people around that massive district at least knew I was running for something! Post–filing period, the campaign season was in full swing. Nearly all the county offices, as well as state and federal, were up for grabs. Newcomers came out of the woodwork. Challengers seemed to line up for sheriff, county commissioners, DA, and county and court clerks, and a couple more entered the race for HD 17. The miles I had traveled and doors I knocked on the previous three months were well worth the misery. Not only had I gotten all the grunt work out of the way, I had the field all to myself. Now it was crowded!

Not many candidates in our area of the state had the access or the means to run an automated campaign with computerized calls and mail-outs. Most campaigning was done via public speaking, pie suppers, door knocking, and limited newspaper ads. Of course, everyone had the placards and small handouts. HD 17 was particularly difficult in using media. There was not either a newspaper or radio station that would cover that large an area. The largest newspapers were in McClain, Poteau, and Idabel, but even the three of them wouldn't suffice. At that time, there were also weekly papers—one in my hometown, two in Wilburton, one in Talihina, and one in Wright City, all of which had to be used.

With the help of my campaign adviser, we organized our own pie supper in the hometown and raised a little over fifteen hundred dollars to officially kick off the "I Like Mike" campaign. From there on out, "Adviser Bill" would accompany me to most of the political speakings, along with his son Larry and my wife. While I was speaking, they would work the crowd.

The two other candidates who entered the race were a godsend. Figuring the incumbent was the man to beat, they antagonized him at every event. Both their speeches were designed to point out all the bad votes and lack of sound representation for the good folk in HD 17. So while the three of them continually sparred and fussed, I would simply tell a homespun story and humbly ask for the crowd's support.

Both Bill and Larry were good at raising campaign funds, which allowed me to purchase some bona fide blue-and-white campaign signs. They didn't melt in the rain either! We were also able to buy ads in the newspapers across the district. Of course, we couldn't compete with the incumbent's war chest, but at least it kept us visible. We also managed to purchase blue-and-white "I Like Mike" T-shirts and caps.

By the Fourth of July, political campaigns had taken to the streets, literally! Parades, rodeos, Little League ball games, political rallies—pretty much wherever a crowd was gathered, you could count on the campaigners to be there! And the "I Like Mike" campaign was no exception. By then, most of my immediate family had become involved—my mother, my siblings, in-laws, and, naturally, my wife and four children. All of them had the T-shirts! That was our secret weapon—a large family! When we showed up at an event, it was overwhelming, I'm sure, to our opposition. It appeared as though I was amassing a political army. And for some of the little Mass youngsters, the "I Like Mike" shirt was the only new shirt they had, so they wore them everywhere.

Finally, about three weeks before the primary election, which was held in August, the buzz around the district was all about Mike Mass. Some of the who's who in Southeast Oklahoma politics began calling. They were getting their foot in the door, however late! The incumbent's camp was suddenly in panic mode, so they began looking for dirt. My hometown detractors were in charge of that. The Texaco man and the retired sheriff had discovered that the precinct I was registered to vote in didn't match up with where I was living and quickly alerted their friend, the incumbent. When he attempted to have my name removed from the ballot because of the technical infraction, the county clerk informed him that the official protest deadline had passed, and he was too late. He was so upset that when leaving the courthouse, he ran a red light and broadsided a van full of people pulling out of Braum's parking lot. Fortunately, no one was hurt, but ice cream went everywhere, and I'm pretty sure no one in that van voted for him. Now that monstrous district that was once my nightmare had become his!

The incumbent and his mainstream support, who were mostly school officials throughout the district, seemed to be in shock. In a last-ditch effort, one of the Le Flore County school superintendents organized a large political rally. It was to be held in the cafeteria of his school, no less and Le Flore County was the largest county in the district. Usually, at a political rally or public speaking, a coin is tossed to see who gets to speak last because the last speaker definitely has the advantage. This particular event, however, was not your normal rally. It was designed to make me look like an ass and the incumbent look like a hero! The ground rules were that we'd each be given unlimited time, but we were to contain our comments only as to what made us qualified to be a state legislator, and in this case, there would be no coin toss. The incumbent would speak first, leaving me obviously intimidated by his credentials. There was standing room only, as the school superintendent also included a free feed. The crowd was also stacked in the incumbent's favor, but it wasn't without a good smattering of those blue T-shirts. They needed as large a crowd as possible to see the incumbent, surrounded by every affluent educator in Southeast Oklahoma, as compared to this good ole boy who had no business being in the state capitol, much less in their circles.

The incumbent took the floor first. He gave his pedigree, which started with who's who in high school, his grand champion steer, and the various fraternities he belonged to in college. Then on to his chairmanships at the state capitol and the assortment of complicated legislation he'd pushed through that literally saved our county schools. He meticulously orated how his education, political expertise, and God-fearing approach to problem solving would better serve the district. He spoke for what seemed like an hour. The school official who was mediating had a smug look of approval and would glance at me every so often as if to say, "You're sunk." My main man Bill Morgan, as well as my whole family, had that "we're sunk" look on their faces! As for me, their strategy was working. I was definitely intimidated and for the first time at a loss for words.

As I walked toward the microphone, I elected to just tell the truth, as I in no way could even make up credentials that would compete with that. My response was one of the shortest but most defining speeches I ever gave:

"Folks, I didn't go to college. In fact, I was probably lucky to have graduated high school. I've never held any kind of office, much less had any dealing with important legislation. All I can say is that, I was raised right here in the hills and hollers of Southeast Oklahoma, along with my seven brothers and sisters. Most of my experience growing up was bailing hay and picking cucumbers alongside my brothers, but I can lay claim to this: I was the lead picker!"

The crowd erupted with a mixture of good ole belly laughs and even applause, the kind of laughs and applause that brought out the disdain in the incumbent's circle of sophisticated friends. It even surprised me, in that I noticed some people applauding when they probably shouldn't have been. The incumbent's father jumped to his feet, obviously frustrated, and shouted "What's picking cucumbers got to do with serving in the legislature"? With that, Mama, bless her heart, rose to her feet and let the old fellow have it! She gave him a scolding and made him like it! By then, it was all out of control and an unlikely victory for the "I Like Mike" campaign.

Rumors of that event spread like wildfire and was certainly embellished by the expert politicians in attendance, but all to my favor. I went on to pull out the largest percentage vote in the primary and soundly defeated the incumbent in the September run off.

That first campaign was not without its consequences, lessons, and trials. The nearly two months of the ten to fourteen hours a day of grueling work had drained me both mentally and physically. By November of that year and prior to being sworn into office, most of my hair had fallen out, including my eyebrows and mustache. Just getting our four children back into a solid family routine and catching up on all the home front issues I'd neglected for the better part of a year was a challenge.

I had learned a lot about politics and the people drawn to it. The counterfeiters, the hangers-on, the snoopers, and even the solid, quiet voters like my friend Bill Morgan.

About midway through that campaign, an elected official in the Le Flore County courthouse sent word that she wanted to visit with me the next time I was in the vicinity. She fancied herself a political heavyweight, wore the gaudy framed 1980's eyeglasses, and was anybody's dog that would hunt with her. When I met with her in her second-floor courthouse office, she vowed her support and even predicted the amount of Le Flore County votes she would bring with her. At the time, I was thrilled to have such an astute and obviously schooled politician in my corner. I also knew that if she ran her gums to everyone else the way she did to me, she could certainly spread my name fast! After that meeting, she called me on an almost daily basis to find out how I was doing and who the latest converts to the Mass campaign were. I thought I'd struck political gold in the Le Flore County courthouse. She was also very interested in knowing what events I'd been to and where I was going next. Not more than a few weeks later, I changed my plans on a whim. I'd got one of my brothers to attend a pie supper on my behalf and decided instead to take my two young boys along with a pocket full of brochures and go to the Talihina rodeo. As we approached the rodeo entrance, there was my newfound political heavyweight alongside the incumbent. She was wearing his T-shirt and hat and helping him pass out his literature. After winning the election, she was one of the first congratulatory callers and even had the audacity to try and convince me she infiltrated the incumbent's campaign just to keep an eye on him!

There was also the nice man I met in a café while campaigning. He introduced himself and related how he'd been hearing good things about me and wanted to join the Mass campaign. Before leaving, I left him a stack of my brochures, along with a T-shirt and cap for both him and his wife. She was an elementary school teacher. In less than a week, he called needing more campaign brochures and signs. Heck, he even volunteered to work some remote areas in Le Flore and McCurtain counties. Both he and his wife spent their entire weekends dedicated solely to my campaign. He had been working on my campaign for almost a month when I got a call from a good friend who asked if I knew this guy was wearing my T-shirt around everywhere. When I responded in the affirmative, my friend told me I didn't need that guy's help, that he would hurt me more than help. My friend wouldn't tell me why, so I didn't think much more about it. Besides it was pretty common in most communities that it didn't matter who was helping you, there was always someone who didn't like them. My thinking was, "How bad could this guy be? His wife is an elementary school teacher, for crying out loud."

After the election, the volunteer insisted that I bring my two boys and stay one night at his cabin located near Winding Stair Mountains. He would have a dozen people there who he got to support me and wanted them to meet me. He also had two ATVs he would make available to my boys. Although I was completely exhausted from the campaign, my wife and I agreed it would be fun for the boys and a chance to show our appreciation to this guy by acknowledging all his friends.

This guy's cabin was literally so far back in the woods, you would have to go toward town to squirrel hunt! When we finally arrived, sure enough, there were the two ATVs fueled up and ready for the boys. There were also a couple of dozen vehicles there. I believe every hillbilly within fifty miles must have showed up to see the new representative. My friend greeted us as we parked in a special place he'd saved right next to the cabin porch and had a wide grin as he handed my boys the keys to the four-wheelers. They were on them and gone down the mountain roads before you could say *scat*. I could tell that I'd not only made the boys' day but had also made our host extremely pleased. He put his arm around my shoulders and whispered, "Come here, dude, I got something you need to see before we go in the cabin." He led me down a dim path a hundred feet or so up the hill from his cabin. As we approached a large clearing, the grin on his face seemed to widen. Next thing I knew, I was standing next to an acre of marijuana! It was like walking up on a dead body. I was numb, shocked, and caught completely off guard. At the time, there wasn't a day that went by that the news headlines weren't about the latest bust on an illegal patch of marijuana, and here I was, the newly elected representative, miles away from anywhere in the company of God knows who and scared out of my wits!

After that, I was so numb, I couldn't tell you who any of the people were who came to see me. But somehow, I managed to stay composed, as if this was just the finest damn thing I'd ever seen! The boys and I even stayed the night as planned, even though I didn't sleep a wink. I was never so glad and so relieved to leave a place as I was to leave there. I now knew why I'd been advised to stay away from this guy!

That man was just one of the many characters I met during that first race. There were a lot of phonies, like the hometown school superintendent at the time. She was new to our school system and acted as though she was the greatest gift Hartshorne had ever received. She was way too sophisticated to be associated with that cornpone Mass campaign. In fact, the first time she ever spoke to me was when she came parading into our watch party well after I'd been declared the winner. She was fashionably late, had a small entourage, and wore an "I Like Mike" T-shirt. I have no idea where she got it.

After that first term in office, I was sure of three things: First, it was the best job I'd ever had; second, I could actually help folks in my district; and lastly, there was plenty of Crown Royal!

# 6

The people I represented expected a lot. They didn't put much distinction between a freshman legislator and a veteran politician, partly because most of them didn't have a clue about politics at the state capitol but mostly because they were spoiled. In Southeast Oklahoma, I was following in the footsteps of giants—politicians who built highways and water navigation systems, like the late Bob Kerr and former US House Speaker Carl Albert; politicians who could get you out of jail or get you a job, like the veteran senator Mr. Stokes; politicians who were born in the sticks but certainly didn't fall off of the turnip wagon. These were well-educated men, some who had studied abroad and some with law degrees. These were politicians who could get their point across to presidents yet still sit comfortably in a small-town café and chew the fat with Joe Six-Pack.

The very first political event in Southeast Oklahoma's Little Dixie that I knew anything about happened on my tenth birthday, October 29, 1961. My older brother and I stood at the edge of our gravel driveway, watching as the caravan of cars and pickups headed east on what was then called the Indian Highway.

They were all headed to a small community with a big name, Big Cedar. The president of the United States, John Fitzgerald Kennedy, would be there too! Since Dad would rather be tending his chores or squirrel hunting than rubbing elbows with the politically charged, my brother and I were as close to the event as we were going to get.

Big Cedar was only thirty-five miles east of our house, smack-dab in the middle of nowhere! The closest metro to Big Cedar was Talihina or Heavener, neither of which had a population much over a thousand people.

The president was coming at the request of Robert S. Kerr, a former Oklahoma governor and now a powerful US senator. Kerr loved Southeast Oklahoma and had almost single-handedly gotten blacktop put on what was once a mere logging trail through the Ouachita Mountains. It would eventually connect Heavener to Broken Bow and extend south to Texas.

Kerr's reason for summoning the president was quite simple. He wanted to have a ribbon-cutting ceremony to dedicate the work he had completed on US Highway 259. On that day, the population of Big Cedar grew from a handful of country folk to an estimated twenty thousand people. When news of the president's scheduled arrival to the sticks of Southeast Oklahoma reached Governor Howard Edmonson, he called the president to find out the real reason for the visit. The president said, "I'm going there to kiss Bob Kerr's ass!" From that time on, Little Dixie has had more than its share of powerful Oklahoma influences.

While I could certainly talk the talk of my constituents, my pedigree consisted of a high school diploma, and I got that because of personality, not brains! So whatever I accomplished for my district would have to come from hard work and personality. Oddly enough, most of the calls from my constituents weren't about where their tax dollars were going. Their calls were on far more personal levels. I'm not talking about two or three calls a week either. I'm talking about two or three *dozen* calls a day! They didn't give a hoot about the several hundred pending House and senate bills, committee deadlines, or anything else that seemed to be a big deal to House leadership. They wanted a good state job, a kid out of jail, or a ticket dropped. They wanted their electricity turned back on after it had been cut off because they couldn't pay their bill. They needed to see a doctor and didn't have insurance or couldn't afford the co-pay. Most of them could care less about going through the proper channels. If they had an issue with little Johnny and his school teacher, they called me and not their school board. The only highway they were concerned with was the one in front of their house. There was the guy who owned one of the weekly newspapers in my district who wanted me to stop airplanes from flying over his house. He was convinced they were leaving chem trails that were surely poison and expected me to get it stopped. People called me when their roof was leaking or their porch fell in. They expected me to be their lawyer or preside over the funeral of a loved one. As farfetched as some of this may seem, that's just the way it was.

With the freshman term behind me, I'd also learned the difference between House leadership and regular House members. Regular House members couldn't get their own kids out of jail, let alone anyone else's. They weren't putting people to work, and they for sure weren't getting any roads built! What regular House members got was "good government." We got sent home with a big press release prepared by the House Speaker staff that pointed out how we'd saved all the schools and fed all the hungry. We even received a packet of talking points so we wouldn't appear dumbfounded when asked a question by a hometown reporter.

The leadership, on the other hand, could do specific things for their constituents. They could do magic tricks, like making legislation disappear or a speeding ticket vanish. They could pull a new bridge out of their hat and make jobs appear out of thin air. I was like a kid on the front row of a circus. From the stories I'd heard from old John to the tricks I could see, these were the acts that I wanted to perform. These were the politicians who got top billing in all the daily newspapers and, more importantly, could help their people.

Being a regular House member was not without its own perks, however. It required little and sometimes no effort at all. You might have to hold your nose for a vote now and then, but leadership would always provide you a positive spin. They would also help raise money for your next campaign and even make cameo appearances in your district to demonstrate how much "stroke" you had. Moreover, it didn't require much use of your brain because leadership was more than happy to tell you how to vote. It was really the best job a person could ever wish for! Just stay low key, enjoy the ride, and someday you could go home with a good retirement and maybe even a state job! If you stayed in line really well, leadership might even consider giving you a good title, such as assistant majority whip or assistant floor leader. They would even make you chairman of a made-up committee! What's more, you could become a sponsor of major legislation without even reading the bill. Just sign a slip of paper entitled "CoAuthor," hand it to the House clerk and, presto, you were author of big-time legislation! Most legislators were well satisfied to ride the leadership train, and I'm sure that most do even today. After all, not everyone can be the leader.

Being a regular House member, however, was not my cup of tea. I couldn't get by with a dog and pony show in my district, or at least I didn't think I could! From the history of politicians who preceded me in Southeast Oklahoma, my folks demanded results. Secondly, there was that personal desire to achieve top billing at the circus, to read my name in the daily newspaper and do the magic the big boys were doing!

Working my way into a position of power was not an easy proposition, especially in light of the fact that term limits had been imposed by a special referendum at the beginning of my second term. The term limit imposed was twelve years, and that meant that I or any other ambitious legislator didn't have the time to simply wait for seniority to carry us into the center ring, as had been a long-standing custom. There were legislators who had been in office a lot longer than I had who were still waiting for their turn to chair a committee of importance. So you had a couple dozen second termers like me, a handful of freshman legislators, and several members of our majority party who had nearly two decades of service.

Term limits was the clever idea of some right-wing Oklahoma enthusiasts who couldn't beat majority party incumbents at the ballot box. Although these enthusiasts bleed red, white, and blue and love democracy, the democratic system just wasn't working quick enough to suit them. Their clever idea struck a fancy with Oklahoma voters too. Who wouldn't like to kick an old politician out of office? It was a way to reach out halfway across the state and yank someone else's "old politician" out of office that you otherwise never had a chance to vote against!

At any rate, term limits put added pressure on already ego-filled legislators like me who had little time to work our way to the top. It also created jealousy and paranoia in the majority.

There are only two ways to get yourself into that leadership circle. One way was to kiss the House Speaker's ring enough so that he appointed you to a chairmanship of some real meaning. You also had to get along well enough with your other colleagues in the House so they wouldn't threaten the speaker with mutiny when he did appoint you! The other way was to be obstructionist enough so the speaker would give you a good assignment to shut you up! At that time, the speaker already enjoyed a solid three-fourths majority in the House, so you had to be one hell of an obstructionist to cause him any real grief. Also, the line to kiss his ring was literally a mile long. That line was filled with lobbyists, heavy political hitters from all across the state, his own constituency, reporters, staffers, and every state agency head there was.

Although I never viewed myself as an obstructionist, I had no problem challenging my own party, whether in a closed caucus or debating on the House floor, as was often the case. It just seemed to me that we never did anything to benefit what I called the real people. There weren't many real people who had the time or the money to wait in the ring-kissing line! The system, to me, was no different than slopping the hogs back home. Tall hog at the trough got all the feed! It was a natural and comfortable thing for me to challenge leadership in regard to these types of issues. After all, they were the only issues I understood. I often saw the CEO or the lobbyist of a utility company in the line but never the poor ole couple that could barely afford to pay their utility bill. There were the doctors and the optometrists but none of their patients. There were the college presidents but none of the moms and dads who paid the tuition. So I found myself more and more debating issues for the folks in my district who I knew would never see the inside of the Capitol building, much less get in the ring-kissing line!

Lucky for me, neither the leadership nor my house colleagues viewed me as an obstructionist either. I never debated or challenged my caucus in a malicious way, and they knew it. I did it the only way I knew how, with humor and sincerity. The lobbyists and other heavy hitters didn't seem to take offense either, as I was still welcome to eat their steak, smoke their cigars, and drink their whiskey. There were times that my passionate views aligned with theirs, and they loved having my debate on their side!

My break came early at the beginning of my second term, when the speaker appointed me to the subcommittee of Appropriations on Natural Resource and Regulatory services. That's when we got our allotment of the state's money to divvy up between the agencies I actually knew something about such as Department of Agriculture, Conservation, Forestry, etc. We were also responsible for some agencies I knew nothing about, like Consumer Credit, Banking, and Department of Environmental Quality. The first session I sat on that committee was a learning experience. The House staffer did most of the work while the various agency heads appeared before us stating their dire case for more money. We committee members would then decide which agency needed what the most. The real eye-opener came, however, as our committee deadline arrived, and I thought we'd already distributed what funding we had. That's when the senior member and committee chair looked at us and said, "Okay, guys, what do y'all want?" I didn't know what he was talking about. I assumed he was going to order us some lunch! No, the "what do you want?" meant "how much money do you want?"

I came to find out that a lot of agencies under the jurisdiction of our subcommittee generated funds of their own. This was aside from the allocation we got from leadership. These funds came from various fines and fees and were no small amount. Of course, I had no idea at the time just how much it was. That was private information between the House staffer and the committee chair. So at the end of each fiscal year, those funds were relinquished back to the state coffers for redistribution. Agencies had no chance of hiding funds from those clever House and senate budget analysts.

The money Mr. Chairman was offering was not cash to put in our pocket and take home for personal use. It was cash to take home to our district, and it could be used for whatever we wanted, as long as it was within the guidelines of the state constitution. Furthermore, it was intended only for the privileged few on that committee. I thought, "Wow!" I had arrived!

There were fewer than half a dozen of us on that particular committee, and a couple of them rarely attended the meetings and weren't at that one. That just left me and a couple of others to divide the spoils, but being completely surprised by the question and somewhat ignorant of the amount available, I didn't know what to say! My brain was accustomed to dealing with a lifetime of payday to payday, which involved a few hundred bucks, not millions. Aside from that, I was never good at asking for anything, much less money. At the same time, this was money for my district. This was "bring home the bacon" time! Being both ignorant and naive, I blurted out, "Fifteen thousand!" A big lick, I thought, and it was a big lick compared to what most of my colleagues would take home. By the chairman's quick "okay," though, I knew I had severely lowballed my request.

After session was over, the staffer had my fifteen thousand sent to an economic development entity of state government located in my district. It was earmarked for Representative Mike Mass. I later had the agency director divide the small amount among several rural fire stations in my district. At the time, the volunteer fire departments in Eastern Oklahoma were getting a whopping allocation of two hundred dollars a year.

The state capitol building and surrounding capitol complex was, in itself, a world far removed from the patchwork of small frame houses, trailers, and shanties sprinkled throughout my sprawling district. The capitol grounds and gardens were manicured on a daily basis, with numbered parking spots for all 101 House members and 48 state senators. The circle drive was reserved for the House Speaker and his leadership team. Inside there were marble staircases with polished brass rails, the breathtaking artwork that adorned the cathedral ceilings, and the plush high back chairs on the House and senate floors. They called it the people's house, but it didn't look like any of the houses where I came from.

The cosmetics in my district hadn't changed much for the past forty years, with the exception of a new roof or an add-on here and there. Main streets in most of the small communities had been reduced to unsightly, boarded-up ghost towns with maybe a convenience store or two as a source of city revenue. The streets were filled with potholes, complete with culverts and drainage canals left over from the Works Progress Administration of the 1930s.

The people and faces I saw in that state capitol building, for the most part, were far removed from the vast number of folks I had seen living at or below the poverty level in my district. You won't see many poor people roaming the halls of the state capitol. You sure never saw such a thing as the "association of the poor folk" putting on a reception with finger foods and cocktails or taking a group of politicians to the Petroleum Club for dinner and drinks.

Oh, I'm sure a lot of folks made the capitol rounds with their various associations and considered themselves poor. I'm also sure a lot of them were struggling from paycheck to paycheck, just as I had done most of my life. The cost of living was ever increasing, and their paycheck was ever decreasing. They were robbing Peter to pay Paul and mad because their insurance premiums went up and their benefits went down. However, beyond those poor folks are lots and lots of *really* poor folks!

In 1965 we got a brand-new 1960 model Chevy station wagon with overdrive and a radio that worked. All ten of us could fit in—Dad, Mama, me, and my seven siblings. Dad figured he was killing two birds with one stone. It could be used to haul the cucumbers we picked, which amounted to several dozen burlap sacks, to the brine vats in Calvin, Oklahoma, some sixty miles away, and Mama could also haul us kids to church comfortably. The day, Dad pulled that Chevy station wagon into our driveway is the day I thought we'd gone from poor folk to plain folks.

I believe kids grow up with a pretty good sense of their own status in society, and I was no different. We didn't wear new clothes; we wore hand-me-downs. New shoes and boots were also a rarity, so we visited Leonard Fain's shoe shop frequently for stitching and new half soles. Mama had a Maytag wringer washer and hung our clothes on a line to dry and rarely had enough clothespins. We lived in a small two-bedroom frame house on two acres one mile east of Hartshorne on a gravel road. We four boys slept in one bedroom, and the four girls slept in the other. Mama and Dad slept in a room Dad had converted from an outside porch. There was one bathroom and no air-conditioning, and our water came from a well with a pump house.

Mama canned most of our food: green beans, beets, tomatoes, and whatever else her canning jars would seal. We ate a lot of fried potatoes and fried squirrel. On Sundays, we'd have chicken. Mama had to cut the chicken into so many pieces you couldn't identify any of them. She always claimed she liked the neck.

Although we lived only one mile from town, we considered ourselves country folk. Dad had three milk cows, a pig, some white and brown leghorn chickens, several goats, and a large garden. This garden was aside from the two-acre cucumber patch on land he'd purchased six miles farther out of town. Every animal on the place had a name, except for the chickens. We did, however, name the rooster Baxter. The pig was a large red sow we named Viola. The milk cows were Molly, Pet, and Rose. It was brothers and me who did the milking and daily chores of feeding, gathering eggs, tending the garden, and keeping the yard mowed and the wood split. On weekends, Dad kept us boys with him for the major work, which was usually bailing hay for Grandpa or building a fence or cutting wood. The hay bailer we used was an old International stationary bailer. Dad fed it hay with a pitchfork while my older brother and me hand tied the bails. Up until I was a freshman in high school, we used a crosscut saw and a double bit ax to cut our wood.

At the beginning of each school year, it was customary for the teacher to have each of us tell what we did on our summer vacation. When it came my turn, I'd make something up that at least sounded similar to what the other kids were saying. We didn't take vacations, nor did we go to the movies or eat out. If you would have asked me, I would have said we were poor people.

There were some kids at school who seemed peculiar to me. They were more withdrawn and seemed to always wear dirty clothes. They didn't even make up a vacation story. Looking back, I'm sure they didn't know what the word meant. They'd just remain silent until the teacher skipped on past them. They weren't the kind of kids anyone wanted to play with at recess either. They pretty much kept to themselves. One group of these "self-isolated children" were all of one family. Their last names didn't even match, much less their clothing. They were half brothers and sisters. At school, they were made fun of and were referred to as the Shag-nastys! They called the boys Papa Shag and Baby Shag. The girl was called Mama Shag. They were all the same ages as my older brother, sister, and me.

When school let out for summer break, we were back to our chores and summer routine on our two-acre farm. By mid-June, the blackberries were ripe and would consume a lot of our time after the morning chores. There were gobs of blackberries across the dirt road from our house, growing along Grandpa's fencerows. Braving the chiggers, we'd pick the berries as long into the summer as Mother Nature would allow them to put on. After Mama took her share to can and made blackberry cobbler, we were free to sell all we wanted for ten cents a quart!

One day, while heading up our favorite fencerow, we noticed strangers picking our berries on the opposite side of the fence. As most kids would, we approached them cautiously but with much intrigue. It was two of the Shag-nastys, Papa Shag and Baby Shag. It was the first time we'd ever been close enough to actually talk to them, and with no other kids around, we were free to become their friends. Neither of them wore socks, and each had on some really outdated wingtip shoes that obviously were some their stepfather or grandfather had quit wearing. Their clothes were tattered and had an odor, even in the blackberry patch. The youngest wore a short-waisted army coat. In fact, it was the only article of clothing between the two of them that didn't have a hole in it.

That summer, my older brother, sister, and I became blackberry patch friends with the two boys. It wasn't long before the five of us would meet up on the dirt road and walk together down the berry-filled fencerows. It didn't take long before we could tell that these kids came from a whole different world than we did.

The boys would often stand in that gravel road and stare at our small frame house as if it were a mansion. It was with those two boys that I learned the difference between poor and really poor.

When school took back up in the fall, we all went our separate ways—the Shag-nastys to themselves and the rest of us with our friends. I really don't recall the last summer we all spent in that blackberry-filled fencerow, but I'm sure that was the last time we ever befriended the Shag-nastys.

After his high school graduation, the oldest boy in the clan joined the army. I'm sure it was the first time he ever had matching clothes and clean socks.

Many years later, while on a tour in Washington, DC, I looked his name up on the Vietnam Veterans Memorial wall, where over fifty thousand names are inscribed. I wept quietly to myself.

A few miles further from where we lived on that same gravel road was another poor family. They had a pine slab house with a tin roof and a couple of old farm trucks scotched up on rocks with weeds growing up around them. They didn't have a lawn; they had a yard. Wes and Maxine Baxter resided in that shack, along with a slew of kids, and Wes was pretty much an alcoholic, so it was left to Maxine and her older children to make a living. A couple of the older boys broke horses and did odd jobs on a neighboring ranch. Maxine did house cleaning and other odd jobs whenever she could hitch a ride to town. They raised a patch of field corn in the bottoms below their shack and ran a few horses and a cow or two. Just enough to keep the rest of Maxine's brood busy.

When cucumber-picking season rolled around, we passed by the Baxters' little shack both to and from our cucumber patch, and we would always see Wes passed out in an old armchair on the front porch, with an empty whiskey bottle and a few empty beer cans strewn around his feet. Whenever we saw Maxine and the kids, which was usually after we got the cucumbers picked, we'd stop. Dad had much affection for poor people, and it bothered him to see Maxine and those kids fending for themselves. He would always give whatever change he had in his pocket to the kids and ask Maxine if there were any chores we could help with. My brothers and I didn't understand it, and we sure didn't like stopping. He never put any change in our pockets, and we had plenty chores of our own to do! Besides, you had to watch where you stepped in their yard because of the weeds and broken glass.

We stopped there one time along toward the end of pickin' season in early August. We were always in the cucumber patch by daylight, so it was about midday when we pulled up into Maxine's driveway. It was hot and humid, and we were already tuckered out, but Maxine insisted we come in for a bite of lunch and a cold glass of ice tea. I guess Dad didn't have the heart to say no, and that cold glass of tea did sound good, even amid all the junk!

Maxine held the screen door open as Dad, my brothers, and I all filed in. Through the cracks in the floor, you could see the chickens scratching under the house. Wes was passed out on a bed that was visible from the kitchen table. The odor inside was similar to that of our blackberry-picking friends. Daylight poured in through several holes in the tin roof where Wes had shot a few rounds out of his old pistol while on one of his binges. Maxine had a pot filled with ears of field corn and a bowl of homemade butter on the table. Flies were swarming both the corn and the butter, but it didn't seem to slow their kids down. They were hungry! I was too, but I had lost my appetite. Then came that glass of ice tea that sounded so good; however, it wasn't in a glass. It was in a tall plastic cup that came out of a box of oatmeal, with the rims gnawed off from a lot of use by those Baxter kids. She only had enough ice to put one cube in each of the tall containers, and it melted before she ever set it on the table. That was my first glimpse of how poor folks ate. After the corn disappeared, without my help, the little Baxter kids swarmed around Dad as if he were Santa Claus come early. I didn't understand how Dad could be so benevolent and kind to those kids and never hand me and brothers so much as a thin dime. He was the farthest thing from St. Nick to us.

Another neighbor of ours on that gravel road was a small-time rancher. He wasn't poor by any means, but he wasn't wealthy either. Both he and his wife attended the little church that Mom herded us kids to. He had fell victim to a broken leg when a horse fell on him just as his hay was bailed but not yet hauled off the field. One hot Sunday afternoon, when we came home from church and before we could get to the fried chicken, Dad loaded brothers and me up in his '53 Chevy pickup and took us with him to the rancher's hayfield. We stayed there until we had every last bale of hay stacked neatly in the guy's barn. Dad wouldn't take a nickel of pay, nor would he let us.

# 8

I had long since learned that staying busy made prison time go quicker, so I found ways to keep busy. We had a good crew in laundry fold and were kept busy there from 6:30 a.m. until 2:30 p.m. After work and being escorted back to E pod, I'd shower and head to the rec deck over in D pod. They kept a washer board out there. The washer board was a small wooden platform with a hole drilled in its center just large enough for a heavy washer to fit in. Playing washers was basically the same premise as horseshoes. You got so many points for tossing a washer inside the hole and so many points for the closest to the hole. Each player had six washers. The game could be played with partners or one on one. Being an old-school horseshoe pitcher, I took to the washer board like a duck to water. Usually, I'd pitch washers until the 4:00 p.m. count. After count, it was supper time. We were usually back in the unit by 5:30 or 6:00 p.m., leaving about three hours before the 9:00 p.m. count. We were locked in the cells for count times—once during the week and twice on weekends. In the hours between supper and the 9:00 p.m. count, I would play spades prison style, which means you play for pushups, or else the losers have to walk around the pod quacking like a duck.

My first spade partner was a young man named Griff. Griff haled from Fort Worth, Texas. He was a very bright and polite young man. He would always offer me the most comfortable of plastic chairs when we played cards. And although I was usually the one who cost us the card game, he always took it in good stride and adhered to whatever penalty was imposed. One night while my knees were a little banged from the hours of standing on concrete in laundry fold, he even made the duck walk in my stead.

Griff was winding down his last eighteen months of a six-year sentence. Naturally, dabbling in the drug scene led him there. Despite whatever shortcomings got him in prison, he was one of the nicest kids I'd ever been around—hardworking, generous, and always respectful. Being a self-taught artist, Griff even volunteered his services to teach an art course in a small conference room located between D pod and E pod. The prison graciously supplied pencils and paper, and Griff supplied one hour of his time each evening. I often thought to myself what a really good legislator Griff and a lot of the other guys in there would have made. Very few of them were snitches or patronizing puppets.

On the eve of an inmate's departure (whose bunk I would soon claim), Griff and some of the other guys hosted a farewell party for a young Native American from North Dakota named Max. He had spent prison time with Griff previous to the stay at FTC. The two of them had become pretty close buddies, so Griff spearheaded a going-away celebration. I would discover later the going-away ceremonies were quite common. I don't know why, but it came as a surprise to me that inmates would show such hospitality. Maybe I'd watched one too many prison movies. The party would feature a "jailhouse nacho." Most of the inmates in E pod would pitch in a bag of nachos they had purchased from commissary. A generous portion of freezer-burned ground beef, cheese, onions, and bell peppers would be smuggled up from the cafeteria. Guys who worked in the mess hall would smuggle it out of the kitchen and hand it off to laundry workers, who'd carry it up the elevator buried beneath cadre laundry. The operation wasn't without its risks. A shakedown at any point of the cart's movement would result in inmates doing time in the SHU, otherwise known as the hole, a special housing unit where you were locked down 24/7. While an inmate watched for patrolling officers, others would cook the ground beef and melt the cheese in the unit microwave. Others would be busy dicing the onions and bell peppers. After stretching a trash bag over one of the unit tables and taping it down, the donated nachos were piled generously across the table. The ground beef, onion, and bell peppers would then be added, followed by pouring the melted cheese over the entire configuration. I couldn't help but think, *All these kids in here doing serious time, yet thoughtful enough to show this kind of hospitality.* Of course, Max was the first to dig in. It was a fitting good-bye to a young man leaving prison. After the treat, Max got a good dousing of iced water!

The next morning, I was quick to claim Max's bunk and say good riddance to old man Powell. Some other sucker could take that space, and it wouldn't be for long either. That very evening, after 5:00 p.m. chow, in came the new guy. He was easy to spot, wearing the sagging T-shirt, brown khaki pants, and canvas shoes and looking miserable and disoriented, just as I had only a few weeks before. Knowing how he felt, I approached him, introduced myself, and showed him to his new home with old man Powell. I felt a little bad for him after the bunk switch I'd made to get away from Powell, but not bad enough to go back. The guy's name was Fitz, a sixty-year-old, worn-out hippie from El Paso, Texas. His hair was long, his mustache untrimmed. He had a week-old growth of whiskers and smelled as if he hadn't bathed in weeks. Old Powell was likely going to run out of medicated powder tonight. I couldn't help but ask the old hippie-looking fellow what he was in for. Turns out he'd been homeless the past couple of years. He had no family, no job, no connections, and no means of help. Alcohol and gambling had turned him into a bum's bum! When I asked what his crime was, he said he'd tried to rob a bank in downtown El Paso. He looked like anything but a bank robber, so I asked him how he tried to rob it.

"Just slid the teller a note," he said, "with directions to empty her drawer."

I had to literally pump the story out of him, so I asked what the teller did after he handed her the note.

"The bitch started chewin' my ass out and told me I'd better get outta there before she called the cops."

I said, "No shit, she wasn't afraid of you?"

"Hell no," he said. "She just kept chewing my ass until the cops came and hauled me off to jail."

I couldn't help but laugh. It was the first good laugh I'd had in years. He went on to tell me he'd already figured he'd probably fail in his attempt, but he had nothing to lose. He said he couldn't find help from DHS or anywhere else, and the worst he figured was happening, sure enough. He said, "Hell, man, at least in here I'll get three squares and a cot. They only gave me two years, and after I get out, I'll be eligible for my social security." I really think Fitz was pleased with himself. He might rethink it, however, after a night with Powell.

Fitz was a brand all to himself there at the FTC. I didn't see many homeless street people there, although it seemed most were of meager means. I recalled old Senator Stokes quipping that you wouldn't find many people in prison who had money. "If they did, I'd have it all before they went."

As time went on, I was truly amazed at the number of quality young men in that place. They weren't whiners, and seldom did I hear them blaming someone else for their demise. It seemed like such a waste of humanity.

One of my favorites in the cadre unit was Gage. He was a thirty-seven-year-old black kid from Hugo, Oklahoma. Gage was an All American standout on Hugo's varsity football team the year I first ran for office. He was raised by a single mom, and she finally married while he was a senior in high school.

His adopted dad died of cancer just a few months before Gage was sentenced to prison. The feds made an example of Gage for dealing drugs. Without having resources for an adequate defense, Gage pled to a ten-year sentence. He'd been in prison since his twenties. As Gage put it, "Shoot, Gov, it wasn't just me against the district of Hugo, Oklahoma. It was me against the United States of America. It's just a wonder they didn't give me life."

Having been shipped from one facility to another like a piece of federal freight, he had recently been sent from Texarkana to the Transfer Center for his final year in prison. One Saturday morning, while I was sitting out in the pod having a cup of instant coffee, I noticed Gage coming out of his cell a little earlier than usual. When I asked why he was up and around so early, he said he wanted to call his mother and wish her a happy birthday. I asked him how old she was, and he said with a grin, "I don't know, Gov, I think she's fifty-something." Gage also had a ten-year-old son back in Hugo but had only seen him on a handful of occasions. Like so many others with limited family support, visits were few and far between. Having someone put money on his books for commissary was out of the question.

Gage had every reason in the world to hate the government, but I saw no hate in him. When I looked at the handsome, well-built young man with the bright eyes and wide grin, all I could see was the high school All American from Hugo, Oklahoma.

FTC wasn't without its share of the mentally ill either, including my new cellie. He was the total opposite of Gage, as far as his demeanor went, and more like a younger version of old man Powell. This kid would stand at our cell door in the middle of the night and cry, and I don't mean sob. He would cry loud enough to wake the dead. His name was Arlan, a thirty-year-old kid from Kansas City. His job as a cadre inmate was garbage detail, and it suited him just fine. Escorted by a guard, he and two other inmates emptied trash cans throughout the entire facility, which included offices of the nearly 250 civilian employees there. A few of the offices were evidently occupied by folk who liked to keep a good dip between their cheek and gum. Arlan would find their spit bottle in the trash can and strain the remnants of tobacco from it and somehow smuggle it back upstairs. I didn't bother asking him how he concealed it for the trip back upstairs. It was gross enough knowing he would use someone's already chewed tobacco! Just before the 9:00 pm count, he'd put the spent snuff on a paper towel, stick it in the microwave, and dry it out well enough to roll it into a cigarette.

Arlan had a pretty rough childhood, and I don't think he ever quite got over it. He was raised in OKC, where his mother worked at the GM plant. His father, who was a Vietnam veteran, turned into an alcoholic and often beat not only the kids but the wife as well. He passed away when Arlan was nine years old. By the time he was thirteen, both he and his ten-year-old brother were staying out all night roaming the streets. He said if they ever came home before midnight, his mother usually had some strange dude there and would give him and his brother some money and tell them to go back to town. Both of them were doing drugs and practically living on the street before they were sixteen years old. He quit school in the ninth grade. The poor kid was fascinated by letters I'd get from family during mail call. He'd been locked up eight years and had never received a letter much less a visit. I was as glad as he was that he only had ninety days left to do, but if there was ever a prime candidate for a return visit, it was him!

It really didn't take an expert to figure out that a lot of people with mental illness were housed in the federal pen. I was far from a mental health expert, but even I could spot them in the FTC. When I was a kid, they put those people in insane asylums, but society finally rose above that cruelness. Now we put them in a good penitentiary.

One of Arlan's running buddies at FTC was a kid from the San Francisco Bay Area. He didn't look right out of the eyes.

One of the boys I worked with in laundry who celled with him told me the kid woke him in the night while talking to himself in the mirror. Later, while I was pitching washers out on the rec deck on Saturday afternoon, I noticed the Frisco kid working out with some makeshift weights. He was shirtless, with the numbers 51–50 tattooed prominently across his chest. I asked him what the numbers signified. He said it was the California penal code for the criminally insane. When I asked if he'd spent time in a California prison, he said no, but that was the penal code assigned to Charles Manson. I had no idea if the kid knew what he was talking about, but he was awfully proud of the tattoo.

In the summer of 1966, my uncle Pete Mass bought a 1951 GMC truck in Oklahoma City and had restored it to mint condition. He brought the old truck to Grandpa Mass's farm, so my elder brother and I could use it to haul Grandpa's hay. It was a heavy-duty, three-quarter-ton flatbed, with a six-cylinder engine and a low-geared four-speed transmission. Uncle Pete also gave us permission to use it to haul hay on the side for others, so we could earn an extra buck or two, as long as we took good care of it.

Within a week, my brother and I got a job hauling fifty tons of hay for one of the local ranchers. We could easily stack forty bales of hay on that old flatbed but were soon stacking sixty on it. Didn't take us long to figure out a way to make more money with fewer trips. The only drawback was the strain it put on that six-cylinder engine. We were hauling the hay from a meadow in Gaines Creek bottoms across Gowen Mountain to the other side. Gowen Mountain was steep, and the road was narrow and winding. Going up the mountain was a slow proposition, especially toting sixty bales of hay behind that little engine. Seemed as though we'd never reach the top. We were naturally hot and sweaty, with hay stuck to every crevice of our body. We couldn't wait to top that mountain, pick up some speed, and get some air circulating in that suffocating cab. It may have been slow going up, but with two tons of hay pushing instead of pulling, going down was a breeze.

Naturally, the longer we hauled, the hotter and sweatier we got, and the faster we'd go down the other side. The air whistling through the open windows against the sweat was good air-conditioning!

By the time we'd picked up our last load, all we could think of was reaching the top of that mountain. Waiting on the other side was lots of cool air and a payday! I don't know if brother was more anxious for the cool air or the rancher's check, but he topped Gowen Mountain with a vengeance! Before we reached the second curve, however, the weight of the hay and the speed made the bend impossible to negotiate. We ran off the road, hit a big oak tree, and rolled one and a half times. Typical of a couple of wiry country boys, we crawled out of the wreckage with only a few bruises.

Near the end of my third term in office, politics for me was cresting a peak of its own. A lot of turnover in the house, combined with more friends and a little luck, had landed me chairmanship of the Appropriation Sub-Committee on Natural Resources. Now I had the budget analyst, along with some purse strings. Although I wasn't on the Speaker's leadership team, the slices of pie I could take home to my district were getting much bigger. I was also able to carve out a little pork for some of my colleagues, assuring myself of some votes on the House floor when the occasion arose. The budget analyst assigned to my committee was one of the smartest in the entire capitol complex. He knew the agencies and where they hid every nickel well. If I sent him to find an extra hundred thousand, he'd find it and more. He and I met several times a day, constantly digging for hidden cash in the state agency's coffers.

The bureaucrats and agency heads who had to report to our subcommittee hated us but didn't dare show it. They didn't show it because they were afraid we would take more! I also discovered that we could redirect a lot of their funds, even if we didn't take it, which happened quite frequently. The first time we redirected some funds was for the volunteer fire departments who were receiving only two hundred dollars ($200) a year. We fixed it so they would get two thousand dollars ($2,000) a year and, even at that, didn't seem to cause a ripple in the Department of Forestry's budget! However, it did cause a ripple back in my House district. The redirection of funds, combined with other cash we were earmarking for them, was making an obvious difference. They began building new fire stations, which also served as community centers in the more rural areas. They got better trucks and modern equipment. The result was better fire protection ratings, which drastically reduced fire insurance premiums for the locals. Other rural legislators were also noticing the difference in their own areas and liked it, so their backlash for me was positive. I was beginning to feel the breeze.

Some of the House turnover during that period of time had caught my old friend John, who I had roomed with. "Out with the old" got him again and this time for good. The last trip I took with John was to western Oklahoma in that old, ragged white Lincoln. He somehow got the notion that he wanted to run for statewide office of Labor Commissioner. He sauntered into our hotel room one evening with a paper sack and a big grin on his face. He dumped the sack out on his bed and out rolled ink pens, lapel buttons, and fingernail files, all with the campaign logo "John Meeks, Labor Commissioner." On our way to his first campaign outing, a pothole in the road caused his glove box to fall open, and inside was an old handgun. John said, "I'll be damned. I wondered what I had done with that pistol!" He had taken it from one of his fellow House members earlier who had pulled it out on the House floor with intentions of using it! That trip was about the extent of John's run for a statewide office, as enthusiasm soon fizzled out, as did his House seat. John was one of the last of his kind and was a true warrior for men and women who carried a lunch bucket. It's a shame most of them didn't realize it, but the days of really knowing your elected politicians were all but gone. Campaigns were becoming more of a media event. The politician had to appear on their TV or in their mailbox. Most politicians were beginning to do just that, and when they did appear, they were certain to have a Bible in one hand and a gun in the other. Most of them couldn't hit a bull in the ass with a bass fiddle, much less shoot a gun! Moreover, the Bible they'd borrowed was returned when the election was over. That sort of campaigning wasn't for John. He wasn't above dirty campaigning, but he sure wasn't going to use the good Lord to get himself elected. He was a Korean War veteran, a man of his word and refused to kiss anyone's ass!

His last stand for working class came in the form of taking personal privilege on the House floor. Early that morning, the "elite" state chamber, who bemoaned labor and their evil labor bosses, had delivered some fancy coffee mugs to every legislator's office. Under each mug was a note that said, "Thank you for your service and remember Oklahoma businesses." Old John examined the mug carefully and discovered on the bottom, in small print, "Made in China." When the speaker recognized him for his personal privilege, John rose with the microphone in one hand and the coffee mug in the other. "Mr. Speaker and fellow House members, you all got a nice coffee mug from the state chamber this morning asking you to support Oklahoma business. All of them were made in China. If the state chamber wants to help Oklahoma businesses, I suggest they start buying their cups from Oklahoma businesses and send these back to those Chinks, where they came from."

The Speaker cringed, but John didn't care. Before session ended that day, every Asian in Oklahoma was picketing the state capitol. Although I myself wished that John had picked his words more carefully, I knew he meant well. The state chamber didn't buy anymore trinkets that were made in China either!

With John gone, I went in search of a more fitting place to call my home away from home. I was sick of the hotel life and wanted a place where I could whip up a home-cooked meal and brew my own coffee. One of the capitol secretaries had a friend who happened to own a two-story white frame house just a couple of blocks south of the capitol on Lincoln Boulevard and Thirteenth Street. It was less than five minutes from my parking space at the capitol. The upstairs was equipped with all the amenities for one suitor, and the downstairs was big enough for two. It was all furnished complete with cookstove and refrigerator. The old house had to be a hundred years old but was in plenty good shape to live in. It had linoleum floors, painted cabinets, and the old-time wood-frame windows. Best of all, the rent was less than $400 per month! A couple of my buddies, one of whose district joined mine in the southeast, went in with me, and that became our new OKC home. The only drawback was the fact that, in order to keep it every session, we had to pay rent even during the months we weren't in session.

During this time, a new governor and first lady had taken over the governor's mansion, which was located just a few blocks north of the state capitol. Being of the opposite party affiliation as the previous governor, they accused him and his family of leaving the mansion in a less than desirable condition. Accusing people came naturally for the new governor, as he was formerly a lackey for the US Department of Justice. Their claims of a run-down mansion soon became headlines in all the states' daily newspapers. With momentum from the statewide media, the new governor and his wife asked the good people of Oklahoma to help restore this state treasure to its once prominent stature, whatever that was. I found it amusing that the governor's mansion wasn't good enough for them to live in while most people in my district would have killed for such digs. At any rate, the governor's wife established gift registries at various high-end furniture stores, chandelier shops, and other quality art and antique shops. These were places where the people of Oklahoma could go purchase something of high quality for the mansion in their own name.

The governor wasn't of my party affiliation either. I thought he was a pompous jerk. Furthermore, I was well acquainted with the former governor and his wife. They had been especially good to this Southeast Oklahoma hillbilly and my constituency. They had also sacrificed far more than any other public servants I had known. Suffering deep personal loss and relentless attacks by the far-right media, they maintained their dignity and grace while pressing on with a progressive agenda for a sometimes backward state. I had been to the governor's mansion on many occasions when they lived there and knew good and well they didn't trash the place. They just chose to use their power and influence to help the people of Oklahoma rather than spruce up the mansion.

Shortly after securing the deposit on the rent home with my buddies, I pulled an "Old John" and ask for my own personal privileges on the House floor.

"Mr. Speaker, members of the House, and distinguished guests in the gallery. I rise today to announce a housewarming at a mansion of my own. I got the first month's rent paid, but my roommates and I are in dire need of some furnishings. We have gift registries set up at Walmart, Kelch's Farm Supply, and Dollar General, so those of you that have a little less money in your pocket can also become a part of mansion restorations!"

The entire house, gallery, and even the press gallery all erupted in some good ole belly laughs, including the governor's own party affiliates. By 4:00 p.m. that very day, two Oklahoma City news stations were at the rent house with their broadcasting towers erect and looking for an interview. I gladly gave them and their cameras a tour of the old house and fielded all their questions. I had to wing it, of course, but my last thought was that this wouldn't go any further than the House floor. Evidently the media found it both entertaining and newsworthy. They asked what we wanted people to purchase and what date had been set for the housewarming. I just went along with them! I told them we needed paper plates, toilet paper, lawn chairs, etc., and pulled a date out of the air for the actual housewarming. Naturally, they wanted confirmation that this wasn't a spoof of the new governors attempt to raise funds for the real mansion.

From there, it took on a life of its own. People were actually buying gifts, everything from toothpaste and toilet paper to chairs and lamps! The housewarming was on, whether we wanted one or not! The evening of the event, there were cars parked around two square blocks, and it was standing room only in the old house. People had a hoot that evening, and not only that, the gifts they came bearing were valued at around $10,000, which posed a slight problem according to the Oklahoma Ethics Commission. We solved that by donating it all to the university's hospital hospitality house. They were delighted!

The old house wasn't an old house anymore. It was now the Mass Mansion and was known as such statewide. Funny how a little humor could cause such a stir!

Along about that time, there were a series of articles in one of OKC's major news outlets about legislators being possibly influenced by lobbyists. To put it more bluntly, were they buying politicians votes with cocktails and dinner? Several prominent legislators were bushwhacked in the halls of the capitol by investigative reporters looking for a juicy story, but what politician in their right mind would admit to that? And what doctor would admit to pushing a pharmaceutical companies drug just because they were being furnished season football tickets and goodie baskets?

After nearly four years of the dinner scene, I was growing tired of it and couldn't wait to get to the old mansion, kick my shoes off, put on my overhauls, and whip up some home cooking. Besides, the lobbyists knew where the Mass Mansion was and kept it well stocked with libations. Before long, my roommate and I were doing lobbying of our own. I'd put a big pot of pinto beans on early in the morning, and after our work at the capitol was done, we'd have guests at the mansion, with cocktails included! Soon we were wining and dining the freshmen legislators just like the big boys did. The only difference was they could enjoy the old mansion much more. There they could laugh, let their hair down, and speak their mind without offending someone at a nearby table or the leadership team. At least two nights a week and many times three, we'd have a group over for drinks and dinner—legislators from different areas of the state, various state agencies, bureaucrats, House staffers, senate members, law enforcement groups, firemen—and, of course, we didn't exclude the lobbyists. It was ideally suited to garner votes in support of, or against, the many legislative issues. After all, it's hard not to be with someone who shows you such a good time!

With a full session of mansion lobbying under our belt, we were ready to test the waters. Even though I was already adept at securing a few hundred thousand a year for various projects in my district (most of it for senior citizens centers and volunteer firemen), I wanted to do something big. I was gliding downhill with two tons of hay!

My roommate and colleague was sharp as a tack both mentally and physically. Coming from the same area of the state, his issues aligned perfectly with mine. His name was Randall Erwin. He was college educated and a whiz with numbers. His pastime was calf roping, and he dressed accordingly. While I wore overhauls, he wore the starched white shirt, jeans, and a white straw cowboy hat. His cowboy grin was infectious, and he was a master at hiding his disdain for a few, which weren't many. He could glance at the sources of state revenue and tell you within just a few million dollars how much surplus or shortfall we'd have for the coming fiscal year. Whenever there was a surplus, House and senate leadership, along with the governor, would decide for themselves where the extra money would go. From there, they would begin their process of getting their troops in line. My thinking was this—If I, being an elected representative, didn't get a say in where the surplus money would go, I knew the likes of Papa Shag were way out of the loop.

At the beginning of our second session at the mansion, Randall gave me his projections of a sizeable surplus, and I went to work drafting a bill that I thought would help folks in the poorest areas of the state. The legislation was given the name REAP (Rural Economic Action Plan). One of the brilliant House staffers came up with the name. REAP would carve over 20 million dollars out of the state budget, and it would be earmarked for towns and communities with a population of less than 2,000 people. I came up with that number because the largest town in my district only had a population of 1,800. The money would be used to replace the local revenue lost by those small communities to the larger cities in order to keep their streets and other infrastructures maintained. I thought this would at least slow down the hemorrhaging of small-town Oklahoma, if not turn it around completely.

I insisted that my buddy Randall become principal author of the bill, and I would be a coauthor. We needed every rank-and-file vote in the House to get this done, and I knew that Randall's name at the top of the bill would be less of a lightning rod than my own. I knew of at least two rank-and-file members who would not have supported it with my name as author. I didn't like them, and they didn't like me. Randall didn't like them either, but they couldn't tell it!

I assured Randall that if he agreed to carry the bill, both in committee and on the House floor, I'd do all the legwork. As the bill progressed throughout the session, leadership allowed it to wind its way through the process, figuring that on the eleventh hour, they would send it to a conference committee where they'd insert their own language, "When funding is available," meaning *never*!

By session's end, both leadership and the governor, realized just how much influence that old mansion had generated. The votes had been well secured and the bill passed along with the funding! So as not to appear as though the tail had wagged the dog, the governor held a special bill-signing ceremony in a small town in west central Oklahoma, where one of his own party affiliates would be having a close race for an upcoming election. REAP was their baby too.

Post–REAP, the mansion took on a life of its own. Everyone who was anyone wanted to be there. It was a place where some of the state's past and present political icons could spin their tales with a built-in audience, all of whom were political junkies. No one had to look over their shoulder for an investigative reporter. The bar was always stocked, and there were hors d'oeuvres a plenty. We had long since quit inviting groups. People just showed up, invited or not. Both Randall and I had a hospitable personality that made everyone feel welcome. Most people came for the relaxed atmosphere away from the structured process of politics at the capitol, and even the somewhat pointed dinners hosted by lobbyists at the fine restaurants. Some came for the free drinks and food. Others came with a wandering eye to fill their curiosity and carry tales.

What was once an asset was now becoming a liability. There were curves in the road ahead, and the weight of that hay would make them hard to negotiate.

In the home area newspaper, both the REAP program and I were getting a lot of praise, and like a fool, I was beginning to believe my own press. A quip on the House floor or a simple observation to a reporter would make front-page news. I'd come a long way from that small-frame church and the cucumber patch, and I seemed to impress everyone, except my Church of Christ brethren. My reputation as proprietor of the mansion was in itself enough to ostracize me from the church, let alone the embellished rumors and innuendo, of which there were plenty.

Hordes of songbirds gravitate to our quiet country home in the spring, from colorful finches to scissortails and woodpeckers. The huge pine and pin oak trees around our house make for excellent nesting and the garden provides an assortment of butterflies and other insects that keep my winged friends a steady buffet.

I love spending time pointing out various birds to my grandkids and explaining the features that help identify them. Most birds, however, are subtle and quiet as they flutter from tree branch to garden. They would rather not be seen, at least not for a long period of time, so the patience required for such teaching is usually more than a youngster can bear.

Not so for the mockingbird. He seems to love the attention. Flying straight up and back down atop our utility pole, he does his sky dance while mocking every bird in the countryside. When his beak is not in full throttle, which is rare, he is off chasing a crow or dive-bombing a cat, as if he could whip either of them. The grandkids still can't distinguish one bird from the other, but they can all point out the mockingbird!

On one of our Bossier City gambling trips, my wife and I got a cheap motel room just off Interstate 20 near Longview, Texas. The quaint motel was an equal distance between the casinos and a village of antique shops we wanted to spend time at.

After spending the better part of the afternoon and night on the gambling boats, we returned to the motel where we had planned to sleep in a good portion of the morning before hitting the antique shops. No sooner had I gotten to sleep than I was rudely awakened by a mockingbird swooping up and down from atop a streetlight and squawking at the top of its lungs. The outside walls of that cheap motel room did little to muffle the racket. I loved the mockingbirds around our house, but this bird had to go! In pajama bottoms and untied shoes, I ran down the inside stairwell and out to the parking lot, where I chucked what gravel I could find in hopes of scaring it off. No sooner had I gotten back upstairs and in bed than he was at it again, swooping up and down and squawking to the top of his little lungs. If I'd had my old .22 rifle, I would have shot him.

During my political career, I was a lot like the mockingbird, always seeking and getting attention. Most of my attention came via my country-spun humor, a trait I inherited from my Grandpa Mass. It was the kind of humor that usually left a barb in someone. The humorous barbs weren't just limited to opposing party affiliates either. I had plenty to go around for everyone. My homespun brand of humor seemed to always hit its mark, as far as laughter and jeers were concerned, but I'm sure it left its target in a quiet seethe.

Outside my comedic routine was the overexuberant politician ever fending for his constituency. Combined with my berating some uncooperative bureaucrat, challenging the House and senate leadership with a colorful debate, and compounding my insatiable appetite for attention was the unavoidable and constant association with my infamous senate counterpart, who for decades had gotten his own share of attention. That in itself was enough to keep a spotlight glowing. Be that as it may, my own personality and the inability to keep my mouth shut was such that left folk either adoring me or wanting to shoot me with a .22 rifle.

Adding to my already self-inflated ego, I was elected as chairman of the state's Democratic Party and appointed by the House Speaker as chairman of the House Appropriation Committee. I now held the purse strings to the entire state budget and was a part of the leadership team that I had dealt so much misery. These were the Bill Clinton years. In fact, being Oklahoma's ranking Democrat, I joined our former Democratic governor in welcoming President Clinton at Tinker Air Force Base. He had come there to speak at a memorial service for the Murrah bombing victims. But along with the prosperity brought on through the Clinton years, he'd also brought issues of morality front and center.

It gave new life to Oklahoma's arm of the so-called Christian Coalition! They were after every Democrat in the House, but not for smoking cigars and drinking Crown Royal. That would have spilled over to the other party. Their issues were abortion, homosexuals, and taxes. Being schooled at the feet of Brother R., I could understand the first two but always wondered what taxes had to do with Christianity. Although the Christian Coalition wasn't my favorite group, I certainly wasn't afraid of them. I could still quote the books of the Old and New Testaments as well as the book, chapter, and verse on the plan of salvation. Not only that, I had become an ordained minister! Some years earlier, my baby sister was getting married and wanted me to perform the ceremony. She assumed, as I did, that being such an important politician would be all the credentials I needed. When I checked with the county courthouse, however, they informed me that only a judge or ordained minister could do the job legally, but to my surprise, all I needed was to sign a document that gave me a book and page number at the courthouse! I kept the fact that I was ordained away from my colleagues. I sure didn't want them to feel uncomfortable when having a cocktail with me.

On the home front, I had hit one of life's mile markers that really gave me a sense of autonomy. I was in my early to midforties and had become a grandparent. I was Grandpa to an energy-filled boy who I immediately nicknamed Little Man. Little Man was conceived out of wedlock, which in that day and age wasn't all that out of the ordinary, but my religious upbringing hadn't prepared me for such an event. It certainly would not sit well among the church brethren from whence I came.

When my daughter (who was my firstborn) informed me that she was pregnant, I reacted in a way that seemed perfectly normal to me. I demanded that she marry whoever the father was. The only problem was that the father didn't want to be or plan to be married, and I'm quite sure my daughter may have felt the same.

As the months passed before Little Man's birth, it became quite clear and evident to me there wouldn't be a marriage, so I slowly and begrudgingly accepted it. What I wouldn't accept, however, was the notion that this guy was planning on showing up at the child's birth. When I found out about it, I blew a head gasket and threatened to throw him out of a hospital window. In my narrow view of the world, I'd be damned if he was going to be some part-time daddy. The fact that my daughter may have had something to say in the matter never entered my rigid mind.

The day Little Man arrived, I was there, front and center. It was one of the proudest moments of my life. When my own firstborn had arrived, I was a kid myself and didn't comprehend the full gravity of such a miracle. Now as I looked at my first grandchild, Little Man, I understood the miracle, and from that moment on, he and I were joined at the hip!

From the time he was born, I would be the male figure in his life. The old state auditor who was nearing retirement at the time told me that grandkids are the good Lord's reward to you for not killing your own! My sister told me that our children and grandchildren are equivalent to the Old and New Testament; the first was governed by law, the second by grace. As far as I'm concerned, they are both right.

Little Man's first toddling steps would be his last because every step following would be at a dead run. He was wired for high speed, and it was the only gear he knew. Keeping up with him was a chore, but he single-handedly kept me in stories that I would share at many a political event. By the time he was eight years old, he was certainly savvy beyond his years, having spent a good deal of time with me at political gatherings and campaign rallies. He had also been exposed quite well where the Almighty is concerned, as his mother had his little feet planted firmly in the First Baptist Church. Before his eighth birthday, he had caught on enough to express his faith and would stop nothing short of the full cure for becoming a Christian. He wanted to be baptized, and he wanted Papa as his witness and, more importantly his lifeguard, should the preacher hold him under longer than necessary. So on a Wednesday night following a brief Bible study, I accompanied Little Man and the Baptist preacher as we made our way up the staircase to the second floor, where the baptistry was filled and ready. After the ceremony, Little Man picked up a handful of the preachers calling cards. He was ready to spread the Word!

I was spreading the Word myself, as I was in the midst of a campaign for reelection. Several days later, the grade school custodian, who also served as a deacon at the First Baptist Church, ran into my wife at the grocery store. He had a Little Man story of his own. While doing his routine janitorial work at the school, he noticed Little Man in the hallway between classes, passing out the preacher's cards. He would hand a card to his classmates and tell them to "Repent, be baptized, and vote for Mike Mass!"

In political circles and around the Capitol, I was referred to and introduced as Mr. Chairman. I was consumed with politics and was impressed with my title. Like a man full of political wine, I thought I was bulletproof and invisible. My new office as A&B Chairman was huge! I had a receptionist, two secretaries, and a full staff of budget analysts. Behind my office was a large conference room with a long table surrounded by a dozen high back leather chairs, and in the foyer, people were waiting to kiss the Chairman's ring. I thought they all loved me.

Although full of myself, I never forgot about the folks in my district. Whatever they needed, I did my best to accomplish. I was able to help folks get a job or get their grandkids out of jail. I helped bail some of our rural hospitals out of debt. I made funding available for new senior citizens centers and vehicles to haul their meals in. I helped enhance our rural industrial parks and even some rural cemeteries. Absolutely no one's call was ignored.

Serving in the Oklahoma legislature was a remarkable and eye-opening experience. It was there I met some of the most interesting and colorful people I had ever spent time with. One such character was a longtime House member who was also a part-time minister back in his rural home district. Happily married and preaching the Word, he served a combination that was reelection proof. Away from home and at the capitol, however, was a different life, one that entailed lots of good timing, good dining, drinking, dancing, and a pretty young mistress—a mistress who for several years had taken his facade of being single and his promises of a future life together hook, line, and sinker. Secrets like his weren't all that easy to uncover, but as fate usually rears its ugly head, it eventually found him out.

On a sunny Sunday morning, midway through one of his sermons, the young mistress burst through the church doors, walked down the aisle, and unloaded a pair of his boots, along with various other clothing items he had left at her apartment back in the city. With a few choice words in front of the congregation, including his wife and kids, she stood firmly awaiting his reply. Not missing a beat, he hurriedly began praying for this poor disturbed woman who obviously had him mixed up with someone else. The brethren bought it, but the boots looked mighty familiar to his wife.

The mansion, by now, had gotten out of hand. Not only were uninvited guests showing up, there would be a half dozen or so there helping themselves to all the amenities before Randall or I ever got home from the capitol. Every night, there were those who overstayed their welcome well into the night. Some were rowdy and obnoxious and should have been run off, but we were too congenial for that. Even various groups from our home districts would show up and use it as their resting place after making their rounds at the capitol. I'm sure there weren't many days that passed without some political wannabe spouting off about the party they'd been to at the mansion. They were there to ride the old mansion's coattail!

There were a couple of legislators in particular who wouldn't have given either Randall or myself the time of day yet would show up at the mansion with their own entourage. They delighted in using our place to show themselves. One night, the two of them brought a potato gun and shot potatoes across Thirteenth Street into the confines of Oklahoma School of Science and Math. Randall and I found out about it after the school officials left a note on our door. Both of these characters had a jealous streak a mile wide and weren't at all concerned about the mansion's reputation, let alone mine or Randall's. We had acquired reputation enough without their help.

Nevertheless, things were sailing right along in that big budget office with the high back chairs and the big conference table. If Maxine Baxter would have had a table like that, she could have put the whole corn crop on it.

The big office brought new friends, people I hadn't ever seen at the mansion. The Chancellor of Higher Education and one of Oklahoma's major college university presidents came bearing gifts—a box of cigars wrapped with a little red bow. Neither had ever spoken to me, but now I could add them to my list of new best friends. I soon figured out that most of these new best friends were not only in dire need of large chunks of the state's budget but were also concerned about my well-being. I got flashbacks of that first campaign, when the hometown school superintendent showed up at my watch party late wearing one of my campaign T-shirts. I'm sure these folks loved me all along. It just took them a while to drop in.

The CEO and delegation of board members from one of the large hospitals in Tulsa also came by to check on my well-being. They needed a ten-million-dollar vaccination of the state's money to inoculate themselves from bankruptcy. While they were there, I had them sit in the big chairs around my big table. I was anxious to tell them of something I'd seen in the health care community that I was quite sure they were unaware of. This was the first "house call" I'd ever seen a doctor make. I proceeded to tell them how one of my sisters had been turned away with a couple of sniffling kids because she didn't have a co-pay. I was sure that sort of thing never happened at their facilities but thought they ought to know about it. I told them about my father who had been sent home from the ER with a handful of nitro pills because, according to the attending physician, the insurance companies were complaining that they were admitting too many people who probably didn't need admitting. I told them also how my father collapsed and died of a massive heart attack on the way back to the ER that following day.

These fine gentlemen gasped at the thought! Why, they had never heard of such things! They were so nice they had a brand-new clinic built in my hometown the following spring and furnished it with two doctors and full nursing staff. They also got their ten million!

At home, things weren't going so well. My wife and I had been together well over twenty years and were feeling strains on our marriage we never dreamed of when we were sailing down the highway in that red 1963 Ford. Spending more and more time in OKC while she was trying to corral our four teenage children wasn't helping either. Although I had become a whiz at math with the state's budget, my finances at home were a wreck. I was upside down on both vehicles. We had refinanced our home more than once, and creditors were swirling like vultures. Bankers were covering bad checks and extending notes that they wouldn't have done for ordinary folks, but Mr. Chairman wasn't ordinary folk. On weekends, I began to moonlight at the casinos in Bossier City, Louisiana. All I needed was a couple of good hits, and I'd be back in the game! After all, that was the poor man's stock market.

Weekends at home were becoming more and more a dread, and I couldn't wait to get back to that artificial world at the state capitol. The closer I'd get to OKC, the more that old Merle Haggard tune would play in my head, "Eatin' rainbow stew with a silver spoon underneath those skies of blue. We'll all be drinking that free bubble up and eatin' that rainbow stew!"

When it rains, it pours! Just as I was settling in and getting comfortable with my new role as Mr. Chairman, rumors began swirling like a dark funnel cloud around the capitol complex, rumors of an investigation and rumors that involved me. The rumors were soon confirmed when a couple of dreaded investigative reporters showed up at my big office. It was then I recalled that old hymn that went, "There's an all-seeing eye watching you."

# 11

There was a time that I was invincible. My heroes were Hopalong Cassidy, the Lone Ranger, Cassius Clay, and John F. Kennedy—the latter two I held secretly. Those were the days of Molly, Pet, and Rose, the days of the blackberry patch and stuffing cardboard between the worn-out soles of my shoes and my feet, back when Dad, chigger bites, and a long Sunday sermon were all I feared.

Hartshorne was a town back then, and people filled its streets on Saturday. We had two movie theaters, two drugstores, a five-and-dime, several department stores, an Otasco, shoe repair shops, grocery stores, an icehouse, three feed stores, two lumber yards, and a half dozen full service stations. There was also a Dairy Bar, two cafés, a diner, and two large hardware stores. In addition to the town's chief of police, a watchman walked the sidewalks at night checking the storefront doors. On the side streets were radiator shops, mechanic shops, and Jimmy's Garage, where the owner could fix anything from a garden rake to a diesel motor. There were dry cleaners and Laundromats, Danny's Pool Hall, and Teen Town, where kids who didn't go to the Church of Christ could dance, and, of course, a big fire station and a city hall with its own jail and large post office. It was quite the contrast to today's Hartshorne with only a handful of businesses and an aging infrastructure.

Every Saturday, the town merchants held a trade's day at the west end of town between Fain's Shoe Repair and Powell's Hardware Store. There, in a vacant lot, old man Carshal would rotate a big hopper before pulling out the winning ticket. The tickets were given to customers by local merchants, along with any purchase at their store. The winning ticket holder would receive a brand-new crisp twenty-dollar bill! Gasoline was only twenty cents a gallon, and a quarter would buy you a deluxe hamburger, so twenty bucks was pretty big medicine! Public school teachers back then were earning slightly less than five thousand a year.

Because ours was the largest family of the local Mass clan, and I'm sure the poorest, relatives had saved their trade's day tickets and had given them to Mama. She put them in a shoebox and sent me to the drawing a foot. Living only one mile east of the city limits, I was in Fain's Shoe Shop in less than thirty minutes. We were rarely in town, especially on a Saturday, and just to walk down the big sidewalks past all the stores was a treat to me. Sitting on a bench in the shoe shop, I signed every ticket. The shoebox was full, and I had to hustle to the big wire basket outside as the drawing was soon to get underway. After dumping the tickets, I sauntered to the back of the huge crowd of people. I didn't know any of those town folk except for a black kid who was on my Little League ball team. He was a couple of years older than me and seemed to fit into the big crowd of people just fine.

Old Carshal was a trader and knew everyone in town, except for me. He dealt in antiques and traded horses and mules and such, one of the types who knew everyone's business. He wore glasses that appeared to be made of pop bottle bottoms, a straw hat, and kept his pants tucked inside his cowboy boots. He looked to me like a real person of authority the way he talked through the megaphone, quieting the crowd as he turned the wire basket.

Although motionless and quiet on the outside, I was brimming with anticipation on the inside. He pulled the ticket and held it up as if to get the name in focus, glared quickly, crumbled it, and dropped it to the ground. Claiming he couldn't read the name, he began churning the wire basket again. While he was churning, my Little League baseball teammate, whose name was Gary McClendon, picked the ticket off the ground and shouted, "This is Mike Mass's ticket!"

Carshal, as well as everyone else in the crowd, ignored him. Gary ran to me with the ticket, and it was mine, but even with my buddy's encouragement, I was too petrified to approach the large crowd and Mr. Carshal.

Carshal drew again and once more held the ticket up, with squinted eyes glaring through those thick glasses. Just like the one before, he wadded it up and dropped it to the ground. My friend, being young and athletic, squirmed through the crowd and fetched the ticket. "Mike Mass!" he yelled, "this is your ticket too!" This time, with a lump in my throat and shaky legs, I approached the crowd and Mr. Carshal with both tickets. He was already cranking the basket for a third time when I confirmed to him that the tickets were mine. With a glare I'll never forget, the old man said, "Well, they should have been signed in ink." The third ticket he could read fine, but it wasn't Mike Mass. I was so backward, I didn't find it strange at all that out of that entire crowd, only a fifteen-year-old black kid would speak up for me. The lump in my throat and shaky knees stayed with me on the long walk home.

By the time I was a sophomore in high school, I had lost the shyness and grown out of that awkward stage boys go through. Although I still wasn't considered a Hartshorne insider, I certainly wasn't intimidated by the townsfolk. I was active in sports, loved to hunt and fish, and got along well with just about everyone in school. Other than wrestling a kid in second grade, I'd never been in a fight or any other kind of trouble. It was hard to get into trouble when your dad kept you hooked to a hay bailer or a double bit ax. I did, however, love to cut up and pull harmless pranks. To get a good laugh, I could easily imitate an old teacher or just about any other colorful character we kids knew. I'm pretty sure it was early stages of the politician coming out in me. I rarely cracked a book but managed to pass each school semester by getting along with the faculty and using a little wit. It's hard to flunk a kid when you like them.

Be that as it may, my wit and humor managed to land me in a serious investigation and my first brush with the law. Dad had a fishing partner whose name was Sam. Sam was considerably older than Dad, and when I was much younger, Dad and old Sam did a lot of "trot lining" together on Gaines Creek, and occasionally, Dad would even take Sam on a deer hunt in the fall. The last outing they made together was on a deer hunt at Limestone Gap in Atoka County. Sam became somewhat disoriented while out hunting, and it took Dad a good while to find him. Unbeknownst to Dad, Sam was in the early stages of Alzheimer's. By the time I was in high school, old Sam had been reduced to a babbling old man who sat on the various benches along Main Street talking to himself and anyone else if they'd listen. Back then we called it senile. As folks walked by, Sam would show an old hunting license, as if it were his identification as a secret service agent. In his mind, he thought he was. Everyone in town knew old Sam and just went along with his imagination as if he were a child.

I thought old Sam needed some real credentials and knew just how to get them. A buddy of mine had an older sister who was in a high school office class where they used typewriters, so I drafted a letter to old Sam and had my buddy's sister type it up in professional form. "I, Mike Mass, a member of the FBI, authorize you, Sam, to bring Mr. Carshal in dead or alive. Mike Mass, Assistant to Director." I signed it and put "J. Edgar Hoover" as director. I had a signature for him as well so that the letter looked authentic. The letter got a real chuckle out of both my friend and his sister. I used Carshal as the bad guy for obvious reasons, although I certainly meant the old fellow no harm. We gave old Sam the letter, had our laugh, and forgot all about it. Sam didn't.

A few days later, senile Sam was taking his new credentials, along with a 10-gauge shotgun, and going in search of Carshal. Fortunately for both me and Carshal, some fair citizen intercepted Sam and the letter. Unfortunately for me, however, they didn't think the joke was funny, and I soon began hearing rumors that authorities were looking for me. School had dismissed for the summer by then, and I was back to doing my chores and picking cucumbers. I didn't dare mention any part of this to Mama, and especially not Dad. I just went about my chores with that God-awful knot in my stomach, hoping it would all go away.

At that time, my older sister was dating a guy who smoked no-filter Camel cigarettes. She'd often take them away from him in attempts to make him quit smoking. I'd get them out of her purse and smoke them myself on the sly, and while the rumors continued, I smoked more of them.

The dreaded day of reckoning finally arrived. I was sitting on a bale of hay under a shed located on the east end of our two acres, getting high off of one of those short unfiltered Camels. Peering through a nail hole in the tin siding, I was keeping a close eye on Dad when beyond him and into our driveway pulled in the Hartshorne chief of police. Behind the chief, the county sheriff rolled up, followed by a state trooper, and behind the trooper, a suspicious-looking, unmarked black sedan pulled in. My heart felt like it was trying to jump out of my body, as if it sensed that I was in serious trouble. I lost my buzz as the entourage of lawmen approached my dad. When he turned to look toward the old shed, I felt as though he could see me right through the small nail hole. He was the one I feared, not the law!

I didn't dare run. The long arm of the law wasn't even a thought. It was Dad's long arm that could have reached across two acres and snatched me up! I was in double jeopardy because just a couple of days before, Dad had heard the same rumor I had, only from different sources. When he confronted me, I lied and pled ignorance. I was just too dadgum afraid to tell him the truth. Now I had to face the devil. And I knew it was going to be hell to pay!

As for that entourage of peacemakers, the best thing they could have done for me would have been to haul me off before Dad got ahold of me. But in my mind, I knew they wouldn't. It was a joke gone wrong, for crying out loud! I just wondered how all those grown men and peace officers hadn't figured that out long before now. They had to have been working on this major case for at least a month! Or at least that's how long it had been since my buddies first tipped me off.

In the black sedan were two FBI agents. They did all the talking while the chief and sheriff stood there looking dumbfounded. The trooper looked like he knew what he was doing, even if he didn't say anything. Turned out that the old shotgun Sam was wielding didn't work. It was a relic, rusted over and frozen up. There weren't any bullets in it either, but old Sam didn't know the difference. The letter I had drafted was bona fide, however. The agents claimed that the way I signed J. Edgar Hoover's name was eerily close to that of his own penmanship, and they were thinking mighty strong about booking me for forgery! I was thinking, *Please book me!* But they didn't. They just stayed long enough to put Dad on a slow burn, gave me a stern warning, and left. Lots of firepower, I thought, to catch a sixteen-year-old country boy who had pulled a prank on a senile old man.

The wheels of justice have always struck an odd chord with me. Like Brother Ronald's sermons, what I was taught and what I witnessed just didn't seem to jive.

I was twelve years old when President Kennedy was assassinated. As did millions of others, I watched the circus of events unfold in the aftermath. A spectacle of unbelievable proportions put on by every level of law enforcement in the land. It was plain as black and white, like the television we watched it on. As a young boy, I knew at any moment someone would ride in like the Lone Ranger and bring real law and order. After all, this was my hero, the president of the United States of America.

It also disturbed me deeply when the authorities reduced my hero Cassius Clay into public enemy number 1. His crime was refusing to participate in the Vietnam War, a war that was primarily fought by the poor and underprivileged, like my poor blackberry-picking friend. I think it made them mad, mostly because he changed his name to Mohammed Ali.

Only six short months after the federal government was called in to help sort out my dastardly deed, there was a double homicide in our little hometown. This investigation, however, would only require the local police chief and county sheriff.

November 29, 1967, was a cold dreary day with a steady downpour of rain. Hartshorne schoolteacher Ms. Pearl had made a shopping trip on her way home from school. At 6:30 p.m., she pulled into her driveway, grabbed her shopping bags, and hustled through the rain to her front door. The door was slightly ajar. Pushing her way through, she discovered her teenage son sprawled dead on her living room floor. He had been beaten severely, shot once in the back and once in the head with a 12-gauge shotgun. His name was Patrick. Only a few feet away in a narrow hallway lay his sixteen-year-old sweetheart, Sharon. She had been shot in the abdomen at close range by the same gun.

In shock and disbelief, Ms. Pearl could only think to call her son's best friend. Poncho was a close friend of her son's, and the two hung out together frequently. All she could say to Poncho was, "Something's wrong with my boy. I need you to come as quick as you can!" Poncho sprinted the few short blocks to her home. When he arrived, Ms. Pearl was standing among the carnage holding her phone. On the other end of the line was the local doctor. In the meantime, Poncho's sister, who had actually answered Ms. Pearl's call and had handed the phone to her brother, alerted her parents that something was dead wrong over at Patrick's residence. Within minutes, the rumors were spreading like a wildfire throughout the small town.

The first officials on the scene were the doctor and the undersheriff, both longtime Hartshorne residents and well respected among their peers. On their heels, however, was a steady stream of onlookers, busybodies, and otherwise concerned citizens. My future father-in-law, who lived across the alley from Patrick's house, had just come home from work. He commented to my future wife and his teenage daughter, Suzanne, that "there must be one heck of a party at Ms. Pearl's house. Cars are parked plumb around the block." Soon, another high school friend called Suzanne and informed her of the tragic event.

It was a Wednesday night, so naturally I was at the midweek Bible study with Mama and my siblings, completely oblivious to it all. At the crime scene, Poncho's parents had arrived and were doing their best to console their son, as well as Ms. Pearl. Soon after, the young lifeless bodies of Patrick and Sharon were taken away. Several curious townsfolk were casually touring the awful scene, pointing out bullet holes in the wall and carelessly picking items up that were strewn about the house.

Not long after arriving at the scene, the undersheriff had noticed that Patrick's body had been searched in a possible attempt to get his car keys. His 1962 Ford Falcon and his 12-gauge shotgun were both missing from the residence. An all-points bulletin was issued for the vehicle. Along with the coroner's help, they were also able to determine that the two had been dead for a good period of time. The probable time of death was believed to have been during the school's lunch break. They were both still wearing their jackets and appeared to either have just entered the residence or were preparing to leave when they were so brutally murdered.

The APB that was put on Patrick's car was responded to almost immediately. It had been driven to Ada, a town approximately fifty miles west of Hartshorne, by nineteen-year-old Ed

Burns. He abandoned the car there when he was identified by a woman who saw him exit the vehicle. From there, he made his way south to the city of Purcell via another stolen vehicle and turned himself in as being AWOL from the army. A state trooper, being aware of the APB and linking Burns to the stolen vehicle, held him in the Purcell city jail while he notified the Pittsburg County Sheriff. Both the Pittsburg County sheriff and undersheriff, who knew Ed Burns, drove to Purcell to take him into custody.

Back in Hartshorne, the rumors that night had switched gears by now to who had done it. Kids in town already had a pretty good idea, especially the ones who were in Patrick and Sharon's circle of friends. Poncho knew it, but not because he witnessed it. He just had that gut feeling. He knew that Burns was AWOL. In fact, he also knew that Patrick had even let Ed hide out in the family cellar. It was the third time he'd been AWOL in less than a year. The evening prior to the murder, Burns had come calling at my future father-in-law's house. He wanted to speak with Suzanne. When she came to the door, he asked if she knew where Patrick was. She said it was the first time she had ever seen anyone with glassy eyes. But the authorities didn't question any of the two victims' friends or neighbors. This was going to be a slam dunk, and they sure didn't need the help of kids! Late that night, the sheriff and undersheriff drove to Purcell to take Burns into custody and return him to the Pittsburg County Jail. According to news reports, Sheriff Kendal read Burns his rights. He told him that anything he said could and would be used against him in a court of law, that he had the right to remain silent, and that an attorney would be provided by a court of law if he so desired. He allegedly read him his rights in the presence of the arresting state trooper. Afterward, he told Burns that there was a killing in Hartshorne. Burns replied that he didn't know anything about that. Sheriff Kendal then said, "We pretty much know who did it. We just need some answers."

At that, Burns said, "I need to talk to someone and would like to have an attorney."

A few minutes later, the sheriff left the room to take a phone call. While he was gone, the undersheriff told Burns that he was in a lot of trouble, more than ever before. He was a Hartshorne local, and he and Burns knew each other. Burns said, "Yes, I know I am" or something to that effect. He went on to tell the undersheriff that he'd abandoned the victim's car north of Ada after it ran out of gas. He also indicated that he'd entered Patrick's home through an unlocked back door and that he threw the shotgun away somewhere on a rural highway east of Hartshorne. They drove Burns back to Pittsburg County, where he would spend what was left of the night in jail.

At daybreak the next morning, Burns led the sheriff, the undersheriff, and a deputy to the spot where he'd thrown the weapon. The gun, along with some unspent ammunition, was recovered, as well as a Dr. Pepper bottle and a drinking glass from Patrick's stolen vehicle. It was all turned over to the state crime lab, where fingerprints were lifted and would later be positively identified as belonging to Burns.

Meanwhile, that same morning, school officials summoned my future bride, whom I was not yet dating, and a few other close friends of the victims and asked them to leave school, go to Ms. Pearl's residence, and clean the blood from the carpets, as well as blood splatter and bone fragments on the walls. Their purpose was to keep Ms. Pearl from returning to the gory scene. An unbelievably traumatic task for teenagers to deal with! The nearby *McClain News Paper* was no more sensitive, as their front-page headline that day included a close-up photograph of Patrick lying dead on his living room floor.

Within two weeks, the Hartshorne police chief had resigned under pressure from the city council. Everyone in town (well, all the high school students, anyway) knew that Burns was AWOL and hiding out in Hartshorne, but someone had to be a scapegoat. It had been rumored for quite some time that the small town chief was a little cozy with the glassy eyed Burns.

The deaths of seventeen-year-old Patrick and sixteen-year-old Sharon were a heart-wrenching tragedy for their families, as well as the students at school who knew them as well. They both came from families of meager means and were very popular at church. She was a majorette in the high school marching band and well-liked by everyone. Sharon was laid to rest in her prom dress and kept for viewing at the family home. They were buried side by side in the local cemetery.

The ensuing process of justice was tragic as well. From the opening preliminary hearing, where the judge mistakenly listed Patrick as the defendant, to the name-calling and violent objections hurled about among the prosecution, the defense lawyer, and the judge. Hearings and court dates were delayed and postponed. The defense asked for a demurrer since most of the testimony showed that the defendant had indicated he wanted an attorney but had not been provided one before he made certain statements to investigating officers. Then there was the court order sending the defendant off for a three-month psychiatric evaluation. The school fall semester had come and gone.

I believe the good Lord put a protective mechanism in the hearts of the young and innocent to keep them from carrying tragedy more than they could otherwise bear. The fiasco of justice finally ended with Burns being sentenced to two fifteen-year sentences to be served concurrently and being eligible for parole in considerably less time. Courthouse records are vague or missing today concerning how much time Burns actually served.

Most of my co-inmates at the Federal Transfer Center were there on account of firearm violations. Poor kids who got caught in close proximity to a bullet or a gun and had a prior felony record. Their prior felony wasn't anywhere close to being violent either. They were all casualties of gutless Washington politicians.

I was in a place now where I could plainly see the results of politicians trying to satisfy their constituency without losing their sugar daddy. It goes something like this: there are newsbreaks of another school shooting where innocent kids are gunned down by some crazy S.O.B with a machine gun, and then the news of the tragedy brings on that divisive debate of gun control. The simple question is, who needs a machine gun to hunt squirrels with? Most of the politicians know the answer, but they just don't have the guts to say it. Nobody does! If they did, the NRA would get them beat come next election. Instead, they come up with a lame solution that sounds good to the folks back home. "We don't need new laws on the books. We just need to enforce the ones we have!" The result is that federal law enforcement has to prove their point for them by rounding up all the poor kids they can and packing them like sardines into a penitentiary.

One of the felons in for possession of a firearm was a gentle giant we called Bro. He was a forty-two-year-old black man from Little Rock, Arkansas, who'd managed to get a felony on his record back in his youthful days, and even back then, it was far from a violent offense. He was eighteen years old when it happened. Having long since grown to be a responsible father and community volunteer, Bro gave little thought to his decade-old felony record. On the outside, he was very involved with the girls' and boys' club, where he volunteered as a referee and a coach. He had worked at the Firestone plant in Little Rock for fifteen years. His children were aged 11, 21, and 23. His oldest son had become an avid outdoor sportsman and owned a deer hunting rifle and, on occasion, would leave it at the family home. As fate would have it, a disgruntled parent who thought her child wasn't getting enough attention on the basketball court knew of Bro's prior felony conviction. She also knew that Bro's son would often leave his hunting gear at Bro's home. Being somewhat connected, the scorned gal managed to bring about a search of Bro's home, which produced a hunting rifle. Bro got an automatic sentence of thirty-four months in federal prison.

Most of the guys caught in similar circumstances would tell me their story and just shake their head in disbelief, as if not really comprehending the magnitude of injustice. I comprehended it. I had been on the other side. I knew what most lawmakers were made of. Throwing good people like Bro in the federal pen came about by politicians cowering to the likes of the NRA. The NRA is a powerful organization and one that makes most politicians tremble at the thought of their opposition. That's why you see a lot of political ads feature a candidate holding a rifle. Most of them like to display at least one good ad holding a gun and one good ad holding a Bible. As a result, most politicians, especially in Oklahoma, will cast their vote to please the NRA, whether it makes sense or not.

I'd had my own confrontation with the NRA when one of my good friends and House colleagues sponsored a concealed carry bill. I didn't support the bill for a couple of reasons, the first being I'd grown up seeing good folks carrying guns. There wasn't a pickup in Southeastern Oklahoma that didn't sport a gun rack full of guns in the back window of the truck. Why on God's green earth would we need legislation now when we could already tote our arsenal of weapons? Secondly, I thought it was a throwback to the Wild West, where everyone carried their own sidearm. Moreover, I was one of the few rednecks in the House who actually owned guns and used them frequently. Last thing I was concerned with was some organization being able to make me out as anti–Second Amendment rights. I found out differently, however, when I made my bid in the Second District congressional campaign. The NRA pummeled me with negative ads. By the time they got through with me, I looked like a bleeding heart liberal who wanted to dismantle everyone's right to own a gun! The culmination of this madness is politicians trying to figure out ways to satisfy both the NRA and a segment of their constituency who don't understand why an assault rifle is necessary to hunt squirrels with. Their answer is to keep guns out of the hands of those mean old felons, including the ones like Bro—a one-size-fits-all attempt to hide their own cowardliness.

Another unfortunate victim of felon in possession was a forty-five-year-old guy we called Ricky Ice. Rick hailed from Pennsylvania, where his family operated a dairy farm. By age 19, Ricky Ice had all the farming he could stand and joined the United States Army. He was soon stationed at a base in Germany, where he learned to become an avid beer drinker. After serving nearly a decade in the US military, he received a medical discharge and moved to Tulsa, Oklahoma, where he'd begun a new life. He wasn't in Tulsa very long until he received a DUI by the Tulsa Police. He paid a fine and got a one year suspended sentence. One year later, he was stopped again by the Tulsa PD for doing 35 mph in a 20 mph speed zone. Having a six-pack of Bud Light some time earlier, he blew positive in the Breathalyzer. They wrote him a ticket for DUI again and gave him a court date. Remembering the first incident and subsequent one-year probation, he was afraid to make his court-appointed appearance. Well, that was that. No one came looking for him, and after two years passed he figured all was well.

He was living in an apartment complex where he'd loaned a TV to a neighboring renter, a woman who evidently had druggies and thugs in and out of her apartment at all hours. As time went by, Ricky had tried several times, unsuccessfully, to get his TV back. A couple of months later, while visiting, Ricky's son decided he'd help his old dad get his TV back. Their plan was to knock on the door, and when she opened it, they'd rush in and grab their TV. When she opened the door, however, she was stronger than the both of them and managed to slam the door back in their faces. They stood outside her door shouting obscenities for a few moments, then went on back to Ricky's apartment, defeated and disgusted. I could see how Ricky could be overpowered; he wouldn't weigh 130 pounds soaking wet.

Unbeknownst to them, the gal called the Tulsa Police who soon showed up knocking at Ricky's door. They informed him that his neighbor complained that he'd tried to break in her apartment and had threatened her. He admitted to his failed attempt at recovering his TV, but while they were questioning him, they noticed a .22-caliber rifle leaning against a corner wall. It belonged to Ricky's teenage son. They asked for Ricky's ID and ran a check on him. It came back that he was a fugitive felon, so they booked him and took him to Tulsa County Jail.

After sitting in jail for 3 months, the state dropped all charges (mainly because there was no bed space left.) By the time the jailers released him, however, the feds picked his case up from the court clerk records, and Ricky was appointed a public defender. The two DUIs and failure to appear were used as violent offenses by the feds. Now having been caught in the vicinity of a firearm put him square in the crosshairs of the Armed Career Criminal Act. The offense carried a minimum federal penalty of fifteen years and maximum of life! This was notwithstanding the facts that the gun was purchased by the boy's mother as a Christmas gift and properly registered to the kid and that the neighbor even confirmed to police the gun was not used during their so-called break-in attempt.

Not willing to take a chance on getting life in prison, Ricky plead to one count of felon in possession of a firearm and received fifteen years in the federal pen. While in prison, Ricky met a former US prosecutor who was in prison for stealing drug money. The guy helped Ricky file an appeal to the Supreme Court. The court ruled that the DUIs should never have been used as violent offenses and reduced Ricky's sentence from 180 months to slightly less than 50 months. He grins when he says a six-pack of Bud cost him a third of his life and damn near all of it!

While at FTC, I also worked alongside a young man from Missouri named Billy. Billy appeared fidgety and always in a hurry, like he had somewhere to go. He had been sentenced to twenty-five years for an array of crimes, all stemming from drug addiction.

He and his younger brother were raised by his grandmother in southeast Missouri. Billy said when he and his brother were barely in high school, they were already smoking pot. He and his brother would hide in the basement of his grandmother's house, light up a joint, and exhale the smoke through a venting system in the basement. The smoke would end up coming through the vents into his grandmother's sitting room. He said his grandmother had no idea what the strange odor was but would sometimes get high herself! He said when she did, she was easier to borrow money off of. Billy still laughed about it.

By the time Billy and his brother were in their twenties, they were very adept at manufacturing meth, as well as distributing it. They also kept plenty on hand for their personal use. He said they managed to stay one step ahead of authorities for quite some time. In fact, there were several times when he lay in the brush close enough to watch the cops dismantle a lab and collect evidence. His younger brother got careless one day, which led to their arrest and inevitable conviction. Billy said, "Gov, I was wild as a March hare, both during and after my sentencing, I cursed the judge and everyone else within earshot, including my brother." He said the twenty-five-year sentence only dawned on him after nearly a year in the federal pen

Billy made no excuses for himself, as he said, "Gov, I guess I'm getting what I deserved." I remembered an AWOL soldier who'd gunned down two teenagers back in 1967 that only got a third of the time. Billy went in just shy of his twenty-ninth birthday. He will be well past fifty before he will go home—if he's lucky.

# 13

Political investigations begin with rumors. That's when the torture begins for the investigative target, and there's always a target! After a few weeks or months of the torturous rumors, the investigative reporters are unleashed. Investigative reporters are like busybodies on steroids. They love to pry and uncover those dirty little secrets. Most of them look the part too, and that's their job, to nose and pry into every facet of your business twenty-four seven. And believe me, they aren't looking for anything good! My friend and former governor David Walters once told me that if he were to walk on water, the headline would read, "Walters Can't Swim!" It finally becomes a feeding frenzy. The reporters feed off the rumors, the investigators feed off the reporters, and the combination fuels more rumors.

Already rattled by the rumors, the sight of those two reporters sitting at the entrance of my office was unnerving. Not that I'd done anything outside of the law, but the prospect of these sleazeballs digging into my business didn't sit well on my stomach. I already had a guilty complex, mainly from those old fire-and-brimstone sermons I'd heard. If there had been a back door to my office, I'd have sure used it!

Their questions involved a good number of folks I knew well, including my oldest daughter, and they all had one thing in common—they were all recipients of state jobs as recommended by Mr. Chairman!

The initial investigation was launched by an appointee to the state's health department by the governor who I had mocked with the old mansion housewarming. They were on the hunt for ghost employees and the people responsible for their hiring. The governor's appointee who spearheaded the "ghost hunt" was also from a law enforcement background. I don't know what he knew about health, but he was one hell of an investigator. As the old saying goes, he had blood in one eye and shit in the other. It would have been a stretch to go after politicians for simply helping people get state jobs, especially since it's been happening in Oklahoma since statehood. They had to find an employee who didn't exist.

My oldest daughter was a licensed practical nurse and a single mom. She had been working at various nursing homes for not much more than minimum wage. She never asked me to help her find a job, probably because she knew I got calls from people on a daily basis wanting help and didn't want to be a bother. Nursing home owners do pretty well, but most of the people who did the lifting, bathing, and nursing work for minimal pay. I took it on my own to call the director of Pittsburg County's Health Department. I told him of my daughter's situation and asked if he'd consider her for employment when he had an available position. He obliged, and the next job opening, he put her to work.

She hadn't been working there long when the ghost scandal broke, and the ghost police investigated her thoroughly. They questioned her supervisor, fellow employees, and the director. All of them had nothing but good things to say, and she had bona fide credentials. The story in the statewide newspaper didn't read that way. It just listed her name among the many ghost suspects. Just a good old-fashioned branding!

The ghost police were made up of a division of the attorney general's office, and wherever a good rumor popped up, there they were.

The state health department had been packed with political patronage jobs long before I came on the scene. A lot of them were sheer political hacks who were given a state job with all the benefits solely because they were part of a campaign machine for a powerful politician. Anyone in state government who wasn't blind could have pointed them out. They didn't need the governor's henchman and a full division of the attorney general's office to figure that out. All they needed was someone who could breathe, see, and point a stick at them. But that was old news. They needed a new revelation, something juicy, maybe even something that could bring down the old mansion!

Although I helped a lot of my constituents get jobs, most of them fell under the preview of my old subcommittee that didn't include the health department, but the governor sure didn't know that. I had only recommended three people that the Department of Health actually put to work. One was my daughter, and one was an old high school friend. Both of them were LPNs and both hard workers. The third, however, had no credentials in the field of health. He was simply a good friend, an older gentleman who had supported me from my first race on. He never asked me for anything, much less a job.

I met this fellow during my very first campaign. He was running a café in one of the more rural areas. A café that wasn't exactly a money-making proposition. It was the kind of café that old-timers like to frequent to buy a cup of coffee and visit with their old buddies for hours on end. There would be the occasional guests who ordered a hamburger with a side of fries, but the old café barely paid the utilities and left a little change in my friend's wallet. When I made my first stop there to campaign his patrons, we hit it off. He had his four-year-old grandson, who he was raising, with him. He'd take the boy with him every day.

From that first visit, every time I drove through the small community, I'd look him up. He was raised country like I was. His dad raised a big garden just like my dad, and I was comfortable in his company.

By the time I had become Mr. Chairman, my friend's health was faltering. He'd had at least three heart attacks and was unable to compete in the long hours of restaurant work. His wife was a schoolteacher, and they were living off her income alone while still raising a now teenage grandson.

I summoned the regional health department director to my big office and told him of my old friend's plight and asked if he had anywhere he could put him to useful work considering his age and health. After not hearing from him for a couple weeks, I summoned him again, and this time, I leaned on him a bit more. I reminded him of the political hacks that roamed the Department of Health and found it disturbing that he couldn't accommodate both Mr. Chairman and Mr. Chairman's friend in a useful and helpful way.

After being assured he'd find work for my old friend, I was anxious to call my buddy with the prospective offer of a good state job that I knew he needed. When I called him with the good news, he was excited and appreciative but also very reluctant. He explained to me that he knew nothing about the health department and that he was afraid he would not be qualified for the task. I assured him that they would fit him into a job well suited, one I knew he could handle. I told him it may be janitorial duties, answering phone calls, or inspections of some sort but at any rate, they'd surely provide sufficient training. I also reminded my friend that although the pay might not be that great, the state insurance would definitely benefit him. After our conversation, he was more at ease, and I felt like I had done something good.

The regional director, however, didn't take it so well. He was from the old school, and my remark about the old political hacks must have hit too close to home for him, and although he'd become one of the mansion regulars, it wasn't because he loved Mike Mass. He was there to ride whatever bus he needed to ride. So instead of finding a useful job for my friend, with a wink and a nod, he pushed him off on an underling who was director of one of the health facilities in Le Flore County. The local director was also resentful, so he stalled for another couple of weeks.

After a month or more of this runaround, I was fed up. The regional director wasn't hard to find. He'd be bellied up to the mansion bar at least three evenings a week. Coming in late from the capitol one evening, I found him there with several other hangers-on, eating our food and drinking our whisky and riding the mansion coattails. I must have had a bad day at the capitol because I lit in on him with a fury! I let him know that my friend would be worth more than all his old political hacks if he never lifted a finger. I also let him know in a roundabout way that if he couldn't live up to his word, he could find a new place to drink his cocktails and spin his old stories.

I was too embarrassed to call my friend again. He hadn't asked for a job anyway, and I was beginning to appear like a blowhard who couldn't deliver what I had promised. I still wasn't sure the health director would do what I asked, especially after that humiliating ass chewing I gave him. The next day, however, his underling called my friend and had him report to the local facility to start his new job.

Much later, I would find out that the local director let my friend know that although he was hiring him, he neither wanted nor needed him. His attitude was reflected by other employees there also. My friend had too much character to call and bother me with the way he was treated, but after a couple of weeks, I called to ask him how his job was going. His only complaint then was that they weren't giving him any kind of job assignment. He'd been voluntarily sweeping, mopping, and cleaning restrooms, but outside of that, he'd had absolutely no direction from the powers that be. It was a setup designed for failure.

I had way too much going on to babysit the situation and figured that surely after a month or so, they would have my friend either trained or put in a capacity of work to utilize his time. That never happened, though, and things only got worse. My friend thought he'd be letting me down if he quit but was becoming all the more aggravated by the continuous cute comments of some fellow employees. The snide remarks were being funneled down vicariously from his supervisor. One day, one of the busybodies who worked there, who obviously was no friend of mine, couldn't help but belittle him by letting him know he wouldn't have a job if it weren't for his political connections. Having been prodded enough, he responded by saying, "That's right, they pay me to go party with Mike Mass at the mansion," a comment that would come back to haunt us both.

The busybody wasted no time in contacting the ghost busters! The investigation had been ongoing for quite some time and was well publicized. Finally, here was something they could sink their teeth into!

Both Randall and I were hand delivered subpoenas by the AG's office to appear before an Oklahoma County grand jury, and we were swarmed by Oklahoma's finest investigative reporters. I asked a colleague of mine who was an attorney by profession what to expect in a grand jury proceedings. He advised me not to appear. "Look, man," he said, "a grand jury can indict a ham sandwich." I knew I hadn't broken any state laws, but I sure felt guilty. The buzzards were swarming, I was a nervous wreck, and needed a shoulder to lean on. I beat a hot path to the Speaker's office after receiving the subpoena, told him I had done nothing wrong, and asked that in the event that I were to be indicted, would he not strip me of my chairmanship? He was mute. That very evening, when Randall and I got to the mansion for some much-needed consoling, not a living creature was there. All our political friends and allies who loved us so much had vanished. The old house was eerily quiet for the first time since our housewarming.

All the advice and counsel I could get told me not to appear. The experts warned me that the grand jury was nothing more than a tool for prosecutors, a one-sided ass kicking where you're not allowed an attorney to be present. By not appearing, I was assured of an indictment, so against better judgment, I decided to go.

The day we were to appear, the AG's office was more than happy to send a couple of their investigators to the capitol to give Randall and me a proper escort to the courthouse. Randall was pretty relaxed and still had that cowboy grin on his face. Of course, he hadn't put anyone to work at the health department. You couldn't have driven a needle in my hind parts with a sledgehammer! The ride to the Oklahoma City Courthouse was giving me flashbacks of the walk from that old shed when the FBI came for me back in 1967. I was comfortable enough with what I had done and what I hadn't done but was horrified at the thought of what these ghost cops and a grand jury could do.

When we got to the courthouse, Randall was first to testify, which gave me even more time to sweat. Surprisingly, though, they didn't keep him a full hour, and when he came out, he looked as though he'd been fully entertained, like he'd just seen a good side show at a carnival!

They finally called me in, and I took my seat in front of the grand jury. None of them looked happy either, especially one guy in particular. He was a burly-looking fellow wearing a tank top. It looked to me like he had somewhere else he'd rather be and would just as soon fry him a politician than down a cold six-pack. Then through a side door came the prosecutor, and my heart sank. I recognized her! She had been to the mansion a few years back on one of the nights we were entertaining some of the more infamous Oklahoma politicians—political icons, if you will. Those were the nights when only the heavy hitters were recognized to spin a tale, and the wannabes were all but jumping out of their skin, wanting to take the stage. Back then, she was a fledgling in the AG's office and evidently felt as if she was overlooked in the recognition order. Now she had the look of a woman scorned, and believe me, hell hath no fury—well, you know the rest!

This up-and-comer may not have been properly recognized at the mansion, but the young prosecutor had center stage now and used every inch of it. Her spiked heels pronounced every step as she paced back and forth, grilling me like a Fourth of July hot dog. She was rather attractive, with a shapely figure, but the scowl on her face didn't match her looks. With every question, she looked at me as if to say, "It isn't any fun when the rabbit's got the gun, is it?"

Oklahoma has had its share of powerful political figures, but she certainly wasn't one of them. Neither was I, and oddly enough the two of us had a lot in common. We were both big ducks in a little puddle. Neither of us was good at hiding our emotions, and we were both overzealous in our work. I'm sure it was quite obvious to the jurors. She didn't like me, and I didn't like her! The grilling lasted just short of two hours, and the questioning seemed to have little to do with ghost employees. They were mainly intended as a character assassination and a lot to do with the mansion.

When she finished, I was afforded the opportunity to say whatever I wanted. There had been plenty said about the liquor, the parties, and my ability to "dole out" the money in my role as A&B chairman. There were some things about the mansion neither she nor a lot of other folk knew, however, so I did my best to enlighten them. I started with the ten thousand dollars in goods we took from the mansion and donated to the Oklahoma Hospital hospitality house. Then I told them of the three-year-old girl who'd been shot through both elbows and left in a house with her murdered mother for three days and how during one of those "mansion parties," we'd raised over ten grand to put in a trust fund for the child. I went on to describe how, through dinners and other mansion events, we were able to secure a quarter million dollars for foster kids statewide. The young enthusiastic prosecutor began to pace again, looking at her watch and obviously irritated. She interrupted to let me know the hour was growing long. I wrapped up by telling of the many cookouts for volunteer fireman held there, as well as wedding receptions and other events in honor of selfless Oklahomans. In closing, I told them there were both invited and uninvited guests too numerous to recall and that the rent was paid by Randall and I, not the state of Oklahoma. The last thing we needed to do was get someone a job just to get more bodies in that old house.

When the dust settled and the smoke cleared, the grand jury found no grounds to indict either myself or Randall. My good friend, who was only guilty of making a remark out of frustration, wasn't so lucky. He ended up paying restitution for a job he never even asked for. Had he the wherewithal to hire an attorney, I'm sure his outcome would have been different. A lot of good people were accused and made sport of. The ghost patrol and their investigators got lots of press. Most of the accused who could afford a lawyer beat the accusations handily but were left with scarred reputations. My old friend, who had to pay restitution, hasn't spoken to me since, and I can't blame him. During the course of this political version of "keystone cops," the media had questioned and interviewed me relentlessly. In one of the news articles, I was quoted as saying, "I can help people get jobs, but I can't do their work for them," or at least something to that effect. He evidently took the remark personal. I still miss his company.

# 14

The ghost employee scandal came right on the heels of a tumultuous beginning as state party chairman—a fiasco all in itself! In Oklahoma, you have to be either an idiot or passionately dedicated to a cause to want to be chairman of its Democratic party. I was both.

Republicans had been steadily gaining seats in the Oklahoma House of Representatives, as well as the state congressional offices. With help of the Christian Coalition, they were successfully branding the whole lot of us as national liberals. That's a mouthful, considering the religious upbringing I'd had, and it was chapping me to come out of Sunday worship service and find leaflets on the windshields of all the cars depicting me as pro-abortion, pro–gay rights, and anti-guns! Their theme of "God, guns, and gays" was working like a charm in a state where everyone has a dip in their jaw, a pickup truck, and a big ole gun. They were outsmarting and outpoliticking us Democrats at every turn. We couldn't talk about real-life issues. We were too busy trying to explain the difference between the left wing of the national party and that of Oklahoma Democrats. Their best and most effective line was to sympathetically shake their head and actually say that they admired the Democratic Party back in their daddy's day, but it just wasn't the same party anymore. They were partially right, but those clever jerks never admired the Democratic Party. What they were doing was patting people on the back while they pissed down their leg.

Although it scorched me to see those leaflets in the church parking lot, I wasn't too worried about them beating me at the polls. I had built too many senior centers and rural fire stations for them to get me. My democratic friends in other areas of the state weren't so lucky.

Even in the rural areas of the state, voters were changing. Gone were the days when democrats voted the party line when they went to the polls and "stamped that rooster till the feathers flew!" Those were the days when everyone knew the difference between a Democrat and a Republican. My buddy Randall said his father explained the difference to him at an early age. He told him a Democrat was like an old sow. She'd keep all the other pigs out of the trough until she got her fill, then she'd go lay in the sun while the others got what was left. A Republican, he said, was like an old dog. He'd keep all the other dogs away until he got his fill, then lay down by the trough and growl like hell if they tried to get the leftovers!

At the time, our party chairman was stepping down in an all-out bid for lieutenant governor, which was leaving the top seat in the party wide open. It was largely assumed the party's executive director, who ran the day-to-day operations, would step into the chairmanship uncontested since they normally had to beg someone to take the job anyway. Absolutely no one was anticipating a challenge for the thankless position. The party's executive director was a good guy, as far as I know, and I certainly didn't hold anything against him. I figured he wanted the job to use as a springboard to run for a real office someday, which is pretty normal in politics. Nonetheless, I threw my hat in the ring. I was out to save the Democrats!

Back in high school days, we didn't have all the technology kids have today. We pretty much had to invent our own fun. There was a tall, lanky, redheaded boy named Roy who was especially good at coming up with fun things to do! About a block down the street from the high school gym was one of those houses that always had a dog under the porch. That dog loved to chase cars, and it was good at it too! He'd lie in wait, hidden in the shadows, and bolt out in a fury just as a car would get even with him. He'd chase any vehicle for nearly a block, acting as if he could rip the front tire right off your car!

Everyone hated to drive past that old house. Not many people had air-conditioning in their cars, and most drove with their windows down. That dog would startle the daylights out of people, and then they'd have to drive on pins and needles, trying not to run over it. The dog fascinated Roy. He'd lean out his window, pounding the side of his old pickup, stirring the dog into a real frenzy! One day, Roy stuffed one end of a burlap sack inside the left front hubcap of his '60 model Chevy pickup. He wanted to give that dog something to catch. The dog caught it too but had a heck of a time getting loose from it. He got his canines hung up in that ragged burlap, and Roy gave him an extra block's ride!

When I threw my hat in the ring for state party chair, I ended up like that dog did when he finally caught Roy's pickup. I was in for a wild ride! For starters, no one had asked me to save the party, and it was déjà vu all over again, just like my first race for the House seat. Secondly, the party's executive director not only expected to step into the chairmanship uncontested, he wanted it bad and had party activists lined up in his support, including my own House Speaker! Finally, although I had friends in the sticks of Southeast Oklahoma, a large part of the state didn't know me from Adam's house cat.

I knew very little about the inner workings of the "party machine." The party was never actively involved in any of my campaigns. I knew there was a local county Democrat chapter with officers, but they rarely met and were really a moot point as far as any elections in my area. My timing was awful in that it was a presidential election year, when all the nutjobs came out. Unbeknownst to me, they came out in Oklahoma too, all wanting that ticket to the national convention. The politically affluent get involved so they can rub elbows with other delegates from around the country. It was a good time to hedge their bets on the possibility of bigger deals, like judicial appointments, should success find its way to the top of the ticket. Then there are the real activists that wear all the buttons and the funny hats. They didn't seem to be that passionate in the "off" national convention years, when their Democratic office holders were getting beat at the polls. At any rate, they were all fired up this particular year.

It wasn't long after tossing my hat in the ring (or putting my foot in my mouth) that I realized winning the chairmanship would be a long shot. My opponent had been running the party headquarters for quite some time. He already knew the process, knew who all the delegates were, and had established somewhat of a working relationship with most of them. I had been busy about my work at the capitol, and oddly enough, that's the last place you would learn anything about how the party functioned. I had been there several terms and never heard or seen anything of our party platform.

Being a long shot in any race has its advantages if you're willing to work, and I hadn't forgotten how to work! Right away, I got a list of the delegates from all seventy-seven counties. One of my House colleagues who lived in Oklahoma City went to work setting up a phone bank in a warehouse he'd purchased. He was for me big-time because he knew our House Speaker was supporting my opponent, and he was all for doing anything to get under the Speaker's skin. Several of our "mansion friends" volunteered to man the phone lines, and in less than a week, we'd personally contacted delegates statewide. Most of them were quite impressed to get a personal call.

My opponent ran his campaign mostly from the confines of his office in the party headquarters, e-mailing delegates and listening to the experts as they told him he had nothing to worry about. During the campaign, we only met once in a public setting, and I wouldn't have been there had he not been gracious enough to invite me himself. It was a privately held function in a large house in Oklahoma City, sponsored by the gay community. Brilliant me, however, didn't know that. I didn't know there was a gay community in Oklahoma. Oh, I knew there were gay folks in the state but had no idea that there was a formidable organization. No telling what these fine people had heard about this redneck from the sticks, but after fifteen minutes into the meeting, I knew it wasn't good. I may as well have been the leader of a white supremacy group because the reception I got was cold as ice! My Southern drawl was, in itself, enough to have me burned at the stake. Needless to say, I left there with about as much support from the group as I had before I went. It didn't help matters when the group's spokesperson asked what I was going to do, if elected, to further the cause of gay rights, and I said "nothing." Not that I supported bigotry, but my personal belief then, as it is now, is that government should help those who can't help themselves, such as the very old, the very young, and the very poor. Nevertheless, I was labeled a bigot and had stirred up a hornet's nest.

After that unpleasant meeting, the race became a little more personal with me. I didn't take kindly to being treated so inhospitably, especially by fellow Democrats, and I'd be damned if I was going to be intimidated. The state's six congressional districts would be holding their individual conventions a few weeks prior to the state convention where the election would take place. Most of them would be held on the same Saturday. With the help of my state senator, I secured a small single-engine aircraft and made a personal appearance at all but one of them. My opponent only managed to make a couple. My reception at the district conventions was much more cordial, which made me feel confident going into the state convention.

On the morning of the state convention, my opponent approached me with a noble gesture. He proposed that whoever came out as top vote getter, the other should rise and move to elect the vote leader by acclamation. He explained that it would show unity and put the good of the party above our personal differences. I wholeheartedly agreed and sealed the agreement with a handshake.

As delegates filled the convention center, my opponent's eyes seemed to widen. He knew the race would boil down to Eastern versus Western Oklahoma, and he was seeing way too many people from the sticks. It was an exceptional crowd for a state convention with over seven hundred delegates showing up to cast their vote. There was no secret ballot either. People had to stand up for their pick and be counted. After the tally, I had one vote more than my Democrat friend, but he didn't move to elect me by acclamation. He and his backers wanted a recount. My supporters would have none of that, and pandemonium ensued, with half the crowded hall shouting "cheaters" and the other half shouting "sore losers!" It really wouldn't have taken much more for a full-blown fistfight to break out. Finally, cooler heads prevailed as the outgoing chairman pounded his gavel. A recount was agreed to and order restored. The second vote tallied up to have me winning by two votes. Half the crowd screamed their disdain, and the other half cheered! Still, there was no noble move for acclamation as my opponent had suggested. Outgoing chairman Bobby Kerr pitched me the gavel and literally ran from the convention hall! Last thing he needed was to take sides in that brawl. Running for lieutenant governor was on his mind.

This wasn't at all like my watch party back home, where, after I was declared winner, everyone cheered—not by a long shot! Half the crowd was cheering, plus two, but the other half were mad as hell and didn't mind letting me know it. So there I stood in all my glory and the chairman's gavel, wishing I could disappear.

Some said I had split the party. Frankly, the party was already split, I just helped define it. Truth was, nobody outside that convention hall gave a damn either way. The press loved it. They had just been handed a golden egg. This was a story even they didn't have to embellish.

The gay wing of the party didn't stop there. They filed a petition with the National Democratic Council (DNC) suggesting I had fraudulently won the party chairmanship, and I spent the next six months fighting their attempt to have me removed from office. They didn't get it done, but it wasn't for lack of trying. Oklahoma Republicans seemed bewildered. They couldn't find a democrat to fight with. We were too busy fighting each other! It took the better part of a year for things to finally calm down. The gays figured out I wasn't the bigot they thought I was, and the press had ridden the story all they could. By the time the National Convention rolled around, we were all one big happy family again. At the Staples Center in Los Angeles, I proudly placed Al Gore's nomination for president on behalf of Oklahoma Democrats.

Although I'd been in office for nearly a decade, I was still learning just how vicious politics could be. The old stories my old friend John had shared were really starting to make some sense. There was a standard saying among politicians at the capitol. "We can either do it to you, or for you." My senate counterpart, the late Senator Stokes, was railing against a bill on the senate floor with all the passion he could muster. When he finished, a senate colleague pointed out that Stokes name was listed as a coauthor of the bill of which he was so passionately against. Without breaking stride, Stokes responded, "That's correct, and now that I've pointed out shortcomings of the bill, let me tell you about all the good points."

While sitting in the lounge of the Roosevelt Hotel in Los Angeles, my buddy Randall pointed out several of my "new" best friends. There was the lady from the Le Flore County Courthouse who I caught campaigning with my opponent at the Talihina rodeo during my first run for office. She was near the entrance to one of our meeting rooms, sorting out all the latest campaign trinkets handed down from the DNC. She was stuffing her pockets with the more limited items before disbursing them to the other delegates. Then there were those who had signed the petition to challenge my election as chairman only a year earlier, all scurrying about as if they were my first lieutenants, not to mention the top gun of Oklahoma's prosecuting office, who would later "haunt" us both with a ghost hunt, sipping the complimentary drinks and dipping his fingers in the salted peanuts at our very table.

I was a little behind the curve my whole life, a late bloomer if you will. I didn't wear bell-bottoms or long hair until a year before they were out of style. The political beat was no different. What most knew from the beginning took me a while to understand. It was a world far removed from the basic ethics I'd learned in the cucumber patch or picking blackberries with the Shags. This was a place where jealousy trumps friendship and pride trumps honor.

# 15

The year following my prank gone wrong with old Sam was less than pleasant around Dad. He had a low tolerance for liars. Neither the FBI, along with all the other local police, pulling into our driveway, nor the prank I'd pulled was the issue with him. It was the fact that I lied about it. He wasn't really the mean SOB I thought he was. He was simply a stern man whose yes meant yes and no meant no. If he told you it was fixin' to rain bowling balls, you'd better find yourself a steel umbrella.

By then, my older brother had gotten his draft notice and was stationed in Anchorage, Alaska. That left me as the oldest son at home and a sure lightning rod for dad's wrath if the chores didn't get done according to his specs. It was my final year of high school, and I wasn't planning on finding out what life on the farm was like without my brother.

My last day of high school came in May of 1969, and my plan was already in motion. On career day, I'd met an army recruiter who was more than happy to get me out of my dilemma. He got me a "free" round-trip bus ticket to Oklahoma City, along with a free one-night stay at the Black Hotel. That's where I'd take my physical for the armed services and get my ticket away from home. So on the last day of school, while my fellow seniors were taking class photos and mulling over plans for a senior trip, I was boarding a Greyhound bus headed for the big lights of the city!

Stepping off that bus and checking into the hotel was a real culture shock to this country boy. It was sort of like checking into a big house full of delinquents. The old hotel was chock-full of city kids with long hair and bell-bottom britches. I was a seventeen-year-old country bumpkin' with white sidewalls who grew up on gospel hymns, Johnny Cash, and Merle Haggard. That night was like sleeping in a zoo. Someone was blasting the new hit song, "Hair," by the Cowsills as loud as their radio could play it. Long-haired kids were running the halls and clanging beer cans all night. I was relieved when the sun finally came up.

That morning, along with hordes of other young men, I lined up to take my military style physical and get my official military orders. I passed with flying colors and received orders to report to Camp Polk, Louisiana, where I'd do basic training. Being only seventeen years old, however, meant I would have to face Dad at least one more time. He would have to sign off on my induction since I hadn't turned eighteen yet.

After the one night stay in the less than luxurious Black Hotel and the physical, I boarded the bus back to McClain, where the recruiter would pick me up and drive me back home. The recruiter was impressive to me with that uniform, shiny shoes, and all those stripes on his sleeves. I couldn't wait to approach Dad while escorted by such an authoritative figure. I felt like a man when we pulled into our old gravel driveway.

When we walked into the house, Dad was sitting at the kitchen table eating a bowl of pinto beans and a salad fresh out of his garden. He had on his sleeveless shirt, and his short brimmed black western hat was in its usual place when he was idle, which was a rare occasion. As we approached the table, Dad ignored us and went about his lunch as if we weren't even there. He didn't offer either of us so much as a look. I was beginning to feel a little uncomfortable, but the recruiter stood firm and erect. When

Dad finished his beans and salad, the recruiter laid the paperwork neatly beside Dad's empty bowl and pointed out the Xs where we needed his signature. That's when the shit hit the fan!

Dad gave the papers a swipe that sent them sailing over the kitchen floor, then he gave my "authoritative figure" a rather ugly undressing. "I've served my time," he said. "My brothers have all served their time." He went on to say, "That boy's brother is serving his time right now, and this boy [meaning me] can serve his time when he's old enough to sign those military papers himself!" Making his final point, Dad told the recruiter to get his papers and that green car out of his driveway and never bring either of them back!

My father was a patriotic man who had served his country while stationed in the Philippines. He loved the flag and taught us all to respect what it stood for, but he wasn't naive where the government was concerned. While he and his two older brothers were serving in the European and Pacific theaters during World War II, the government came and confiscated his dad's guns. Grandpa and Grandma were Italian immigrants, and it didn't matter that they had three sons abroad, with one listed MIA. Mussolini had thrown in with the Nazis, and that made them enemies of the state by proxy. Dad wasn't anybody's fool, let alone the government's fool, and although he never said as much, I'm sure he didn't approve of poor kids fighting a political war in the rice paddies of Vietnam. Moreover, he more than likely saved my life.

It was then I realized Dad didn't hate my guts, but I was still determined to leave home and make it on my own. Within the next week, I managed to muster up enough hay-hauling cash to board a bus on my own, this one bound for Denison, Texas. Dad's three sisters all lived in Denison, so I knew there was a place to stay until I got a job and could fend for myself. That didn't take long either. The very day I got off the bus, I landed a job at Spencer's Furniture store in downtown Denison. I would be making $1.75 an hour. Within two weeks, I had my own garage apartment at $75 a month and paid $35 cash for a 1957 Ford that was scotched up on blocks in an elderly lady's yard. With a few trips to the salvage yard, I had the old Ford up and running and was on my own.

By September of that year, the fellow I replaced at Spencer's Furniture had returned from his stint in Vietnam, and old Mr. Spencer had to let me go. Old man Spencer had taken a liking to me in those few short months, however, and used a connection of his to get me employed with Safeway's Brookside Division food processing plant. I started out there at $2.40 an hour. By then, I'd forgotten all about the military idea, and the draft was replaced by a lottery system. I was one of the lucky few who never got my number drawn.

After a year at the Safeway plant, I was well on my way with a steady income. I gave the old '57 Ford to my younger brother, David, and I purchased a real car—a shiny red 1963 model Ford Galaxy with bucket seats, an automatic transmission, and an eight-track stereo tape deck. Every weekend, I'd load the trunk with goodies to take home to my younger siblings and spend time with my high school sweetheart. Even Dad seemed to be enjoying my company.

In October of 1970, on a weekend at home, I married my sweetheart in the old Church of Christ building I grew up in. Our honeymoon was a one-nighter at Fountain Head Lodge on Eufaula Lake. We couldn't have been happier if we had spent a week on a luxury cruise liner! After the brief honeymoon, we were back on Highway 69 en route to Denison, where I had to be on the job the following day. Thirteen months later, Suzanne gave birth to our first little girl, Elena. Shortly thereafter, we purchased for $7,500 our first home—a modest three-bedroom frame house with central air in a decent neighborhood.

We settled into a routine that was pretty much standard for the next several years. Suzanne was a stay-at-home mom while

I did my forty hours per week at the plant. Most weekends, we traveled back to our hometown, where she could visit her parents and I could hunt and fish in the familiar Gaines Creek bottoms. It was during those years that our next two children would be born, another little girl we named Angie and our first little boy, Micah.

Politics was the furthest thing from my mind in those days. People my age had been disillusioned with it all since the assassinations of JFK, Martin Luther King, and Bobby Kennedy. I had long since been burned out on watching the news. The previous decade, news was nothing more than a nightly count of body bags from Vietnam. Besides, the sexiest thing going in politics of the '70s was the Watergate scandal. The price of gasoline had spiked from its meager price of 20 cents per gallon to over 50 cents during that era. The latest fashion in clothing didn't wear well with me. There sure weren't any heroes on the horizon, and the movies even had bad endings. We pretty much lived in a vacuum those days. We tended our little family, paid our bills, and stole a trip back home every chance we got. Watergate, *Saturday Night Fever*, and the death of Elvis Presley summed up the '70s.

Before we married, Suzanne was a "dancing Baptist," but to suit me, she'd converted to the sound doctrine of Brother Ronald. Her background in matters of religion differed from both Mama's Church of Christ doctrine and Dad's Catholicism. As a matter of fact, hers would have been much easier to deal with. Hers was the pure simplicity of faith—no list of do's and don'ts and no Hail Mary's. Be that as it may, neither of us settled in to a church routine. The big Church of Christ's in Denison had carpeted pews and floors, and I knew they surely had to be doing "unscriptural" things there! Suzanne was quiet about it all and dared not beckon me off to a Baptist church! With all the weekend trips back home, we were in neither place long enough to really participate in a solid church fellowship.

I was completely clueless about romance, love, or the reality of marriage, much less, rearing children. I was barely nineteen when our first child was born and was so enthralled with the upcoming deer season that I never gave a thought to all the possible complications of childbirth. I took all that for granted. After they were born, I'd hold them once in a while, gently kiss their sweet little head, take in the fragrance of the Johnson's baby lotion, and promptly hand them back to their mommy. I let her worry about the next feeding, the soiled diapers, and the sniffles.

So far as our marriage was concerned, it was a little like Tina Turner's version of "What's Love Got to Do with It." I thought I'd really stretched the boundaries of romance when I bought her a box of heart-shaped chocolates for Valentine's Day. After all, I'd certainly never seen Mama open a box of them. Oh, we got along fine. We rarely fought or argued, but neither of us knew how to share or discuss deep secrets of the heart. She was afraid to discuss her true feelings of faith because I already knew all there was to know about that subject. Outside of leaving the kids with my favorite aunt to get groceries and eat lunch at a local diner once a week, we never took time to spend with each other. From my strict upbringing, dancing and drinking were the devil's work, so we never even approached the subject. Except for the occasional Tupperware party or get-together with other couples our age, most of our social life was with family.

Financially, we lived payday to payday. When I did manage to get a cost of living raise, we'd charge something else at JCPenney or Sears. That pretty much covered the whole gambit of clothes and appliances. We always managed to keep a decent vehicle. I eventually traded off the '63 Ford for a later model Chevy. It wasn't a new car, but it was new enough—and within our means to make payments.

Despite our payday-to-payday existence, I felt like a rich man, and, for all practical purposes, I was! For the first time in my life, I had a bedroom with carpet, one I didn't have to share with three brothers. I had my very own shower. No more drawing water out of a well to fill a bathtub when the pump house malfunctioned. I was amazed that you could wake up in a warm room in the dead of winter and go to bed in a cool room in the heat of summer. The house I was raised in had no air-conditioning. In the winter, it was heated exclusively by a wood stove, and in the summer, we prayed for a breeze. The wood stove was good heat—if you could stay within four feet of it. The heat certainly didn't reach the bedrooms. Back then, I'd never heard the term *standard of living*, but my standard of living had definitely improved!

I had purchased my own chainsaw and found out I could cut more wood in thirty minutes than Dad, my brother, and me could cut in a week with the old crosscut saw. I bought my own pickup, as well as my own car, and both had AC. I was wearing shoes without the aid of cardboard inserts and, for the first time in my life, could have meat on my plate at least once a day that wasn't squirrel or venison. They say that when the Okies left the dust-ridden state for California in the dirty 30s, it raised the IQ for both states. It was sort of the same when older brother and I left home, only for different assertions. A smaller family back home was spelling relief for Dad, and a new home was spelling hope for brother and me. That being said, we may not have had a savings account or a college trust set up for our children, but we thought we were living high on the hog.

By mid to late '70s, however, I'd had all the city living I thought I could stand. Although we lived only a couple of hours' drive from the old home place and could go back every other weekend, I still felt as though I were a thousand miles away. I could just never fully wean myself from the hills and hollers of Southeast Oklahoma.

Since I'd boarded that Greyhound bound for the Red River in 1969, a lot had changed back home. All my siblings had left the nest by then, with exception of my baby sister, and she was about to enter high school. The old home place had been condemned to make room for a widened highway, and Mama and Dad had built a new brick home on the farm where we raised cucumbers back in the day. Dad was like a different man. I'm sure being unhooked from raising eight children lightened his load a bunch. Mama was no longer canning beets and green beans by the bushel or hanging laundry on the clothesline, not to mention feeding and cleaning up after a slew of kids. She had modern appliances and some central air of her own. She had also settled into a "worldly" job working as a clerk at Kakish Department Store in Hartshorne and, for the first time in her life, had her own spending money. Of course, she was still not missing a beat at the old Church of Christ. Dad had even found his religious rhythm and was attending early Mass at the Holy Rosary Catholic Church.

Suzanne and I had been discussing our plans to move back home for quite some time, but the only definite plan was to make the move before our oldest child started kindergarten. The closer that time came, the more I'd mention our idea to other folk. Absolutely *no one* thought it was a good idea. Dad said, "Hellfire, son, you can do all the hunting and fishing you want on the weekend. You don't need to move back here to do that." Mama didn't say much, but I could tell she cringed at the thought. Parents are like that, though. They worry about their children no matter their age. They knew I wasn't going to take their advice anyway. I'd already made up my mind. While at the Brookside plant one night, I told a coworker that I was going to tell the boss that I'll never come back here. He said, "You're damn sure right about part of that, because once you get back to Oklahoma, you will never have the money to make another move!" We both laughed, but it did ring a bell deep in my gut.

In the spring of 1977, we put a "For Sale" sign in front of our small frame house on Meadowlark Lane in Denison, Texas. I had put a fresh coat of paint on both the inside and out and had the lawn neatly trimmed. Within a week, our little house sold for just over $30,000, leaving us a profit of over $20,000. That very day, I drove to work and gave my two weeks' notice. I didn't tell anyone to take the job and shove it either. I got along good at that old plant with everyone from the janitors to the managers. They had all treated this Okie well since the day I picked up that old Weedwacker, and I believe they sincerely hated to see me leave. One of my coworkers, with whom I'd shared many a laugh in the break room, was a huge soul brother with a perpetual grin and lightning-fast wit. We called him Pinky! My last day at the plant, Pinky pulled a turquoise ring from his finger, placed it in my hand, and, with tears in his eyes, bid me farewell. Although the ring is twice my size, I keep it tucked away in a safe place to this very day.

Both anxious and excited to be back home among the familiarity of old acquaintances and the creek banks I hunted as a boy, we settled in quickly. With the "bonus" equity from our house in Denison, we purchased a house on a large lot. It had a free-standing garage and workshop and was just one block from the hometown elementary school. The man we bought it from was one of the old-time city fathers who ran the Ford dealership years earlier. He had converted the old dealership to an office building, where he dealt in oil and gas properties and Lord knows how many sections of land. He had his own attorney draw up the legal contract and bring the abstract up to date, which was fine with me. I didn't understand all that legal mumbo jumbo anyway. He laid the contract in front of me, which was several pages of legal-size paper, and his secretary pointed out the lines where I needed to sign. I didn't read a word of it. I handed him a check for $20,000 and signed my John Henry on every page. There was absolutely no reason to suspect this longtime Hartshorne businessman would do anything but right by me and my young family. We were home among friends now! The people in Texas I didn't know had treated me fairly, and I knew full well we would be treated fairly here.

We wasted no time diving right into the hometown life. The first Sunday, we were front and center in the old church I was raised in. I had grown up some, though, and was there because I wanted to be, not because Mama was dragging me. I was a man now, dragging my own little brood in so they could learn of the "lake of fire and brimstone." Brother Ronald's black hair had grayed some, but he was sharp as ever, quoting scripture. The old pews were the same, and except for a few of the old widowed women who had passed on, not much had changed. They had, however, managed to install a couple of AC units in the old frame windows. I sensed that they irritated Brother Ronald a bit, as he had to compete with the humming of their noisy compressors. I was soon taking my place as one of the song leaders and waiting the communion table.

The hometown had changed a lot while we were living in Texas. We hadn't noticed the gradual change all that much during those weekend trips home, mainly because we rarely stopped in town. We were always in a big hurry to get to our folks and pretty much kept ourselves isolated out at Mama and Dad's acreage in the country. I had too much hunting and fishing to catch up on to be concerned much with the hometown. We couldn't help but notice now that we were living in town, that at least two-thirds of the Main Street businesses had closed their doors. The old hardware store was boarded up, Rexall Drugstore was closed, the Grand Leader Department Store was gone, and a myriad of other businesses had vanished. Main Street looked horribly vacant on Saturday, with hardly a vehicle on the street. There was no trade's day, no shoe shop, and the downtown theaters had even closed. Even more noticeably, old Sam had passed on and was no longer there to show his credentials to the passing pedestrians.

I also soon discovered why all the grimacing faces and discouragement at my notion of moving back. Although there were jobs, they were all taken. There sure weren't any jobs in the hometown unless you were qualified to be a public schoolteacher. That meant you had to have a college degree and be kin to someone already in the system. I had neither. The army ammunition plant some twenty miles away where my dad had worked for over twenty years was considered the largest employer in the area. Getting work there took a veteran's preference or some political string pulling. I was also void in those two areas. Dad could probably have pulled the strings, but he was always adamant that we boys stood on our own two feet. I had put applications in everywhere possible, including the Oklahoma State Penitentiary in McClain. I probably could have gotten on there or with the highway department had I known any local politicians, but beyond the mayor of Hartshorne, I knew none.

Our nest egg was tied up in the house we purchased, so I did the only thing I knew how to do. I got in my three-quarter ton GMC pickup and hit the hayfields. I also put my name and phone number on a corkboard at the local lumberyard as a handyman. So for the next couple of years, that's what I did. I patched roofs, dabbled in small plumbing jobs, mowed lawns, hauled hay, and during winter months, cut firewood and trapped furbearers for the "hide" market. With exception of the annual week of deer season, which was not only a must but a longstanding tradition with Dad and my brothers, there was no time to enjoy the banks of Gaines Creek. I worked from sun up until sundown but managed not to miss a church service.

I was awful at the handyman work. My older brother was an ace carpenter and cabinet builder, but I didn't have those skills. I could swing a hammer and do some crude work but was severely lacking in any real skills. The calls I got were mostly calls that real carpenters or plumbers wouldn't touch with a ten-foot pole. They were jobs mostly for folks who didn't have much money to pay with, virtually impossible patch jobs. I was in no position to be picky, and, at the same time, I was so worried that I would charge too much that I'd end up either losing money or working for a penance. I was pretty good at replacing a roof or painting a house, but some of the patch jobs were ridiculous.

An old fellow who at one time operated Moore Bro. Cleaners in Hartshorne had called me about doing some plumbing in one of his run-down rent properties. He wanted a waterline run from the kitchen to a bathroom on the opposite end of the house. The old floor beams had long since sagged so that it was impossible to crawl under, so I soldered copper tubing around the inside walls in every configuration possible, making my way to the bathroom. About the time I finished, old man Moore walked in to survey my handiwork. While he was there, I went out back to turn the water on. When I came back in, a stream of water was shooting from one of my soldered joints, wetting a large circle on the baggy pant legs of the old gentleman. After coaxing him outside, I discreetly turned the water back off and went about redoing the entire job. Later, I got a call from another lumberyard that was still operating in the hometown. The roof of their facility was an old-style flat roof, and it had been leaking in spots for quite some time, so they wanted me to fix it. I took three five-gallon buckets of tar and spent a full day on that hot roof patching every crevice I could find and finished just in the nick of time. That night, the skies gave way to a deluge of rain. The next morning, I showed up bright and early to get my pay and was stunned when I walked inside. That place was a mess! Portions of the ceiling had collapsed from the weight of trapped water from my patch job. The inside displays of hardware, tools, paneling, paint supplies, as well as their countertop and cash register, were covered in wet Sheetrock and insulation. The owner and his wife couldn't help but laugh, partly because of my expression upon sight of the mess and partly to keep from crying. Luckily, they had already contacted their insurance agent, who affirmed the damage would be completely compensated. In fact, it compensated them so well that they gladly paid me for the botched job. After all, they knew I had done the best I knew how and certainly couldn't have found anyone else to make the attempt.

Of all those odd jobs, I finally landed one that paid off. The man at T. H. Rogers called one evening and said there was an elderly man who lived at the edge of town who needed a new front door. They had the right-size door in stock, and all I needed to do was fasten the hinges, take the old door off, and hang the new one. I could do the simple task in less than an hour and make a cool $20. When I got to the lumberyard to pick up the door and get the man's address, I couldn't help but notice the name scribbled about the address was that of Mr. Carshal, the trade's day man. All that went through my mind was that innocent country boy who had been denied his twenty dollars years earlier. Although the old man was barely getting along on his walker, I hung his door, then charged him a hundred and fifty bucks for the thirty-minute task. He wanted to argue, but I wasn't the innocent little country boy of long ago. I was six feet two inches tall, with calloused hands and weathered skin from the sun-ridden hay fields. He paid, and I didn't bat an eye. I didn't get any more calls from T. H. Rogers either.

Suzanne was having to juggle the bills and weekly trips to buy groceries, and eating out was out of the question, but I was undeterred. I continued doing whatever I could to make a few bucks, always with high hopes and lots of elbow grease. Although I worked continuously, there was nothing steady about the pay. A break finally came when I caught wind of a job opening at the local rock crusher. Dolese Bros. was supplying rock for some new highway construction and needed some extra swampers. I was hired on to work the night shift, where myself and the other new hires were to refuel all the heavy equipment, do a hodgepodge of maintenance, and routinely do hard-surface welding on the buckets of the large loading tractors. Right away, the job was an uncomfortable fit for me. There was no night supervisor or anyone else to help navigate new hires through the unfamiliar maze of conveyers and colossal machinery, and mechanic work came about as natural to me as did carpentry. The lead mechanic on the day shift was one of their kind who loved pointing out the shortcomings of other employees, and I was certainly not exempt. He was in charge of lining me out for the night's work before the shift changed. The other new hire was considerably younger than me and didn't give a hoot about nothing but stealing all the diesel he could cart off before the day crew came in. Even though I didn't steal any diesel, I just couldn't seem to fit in, and soon became the butt end of the lead mechanic's complaining. Just a little over a month into the job, I realized I was in a no-win situation. The old lead man would leave me with just enough instructions to keep me busy for maybe a couple hours, then complain to the plant superintendent that I wasn't pulling my weight. I also knew someone would have to be blind not to miss all the stolen diesel and that I was probably getting the blame for that too. It wasn't in my DNA to rat people out or complain about others on the job. Knowing there was no pleasing anyone there, I began going about my work with the same don't-give-a-damn attitude as my cohire. I just didn't steal any diesel. One night after a good rain, I cut some giant-sized feet out of some thick Styrofoam, wired them to the bottom of my boots, and made bigfoot tracks in obvious locations around the facility. I thought maybe I'd break the tension with a good laugh. The old lead mechanic was the first to discover the bigfoot tracks when he arrived the next morning and beat a hot path to the plant superintendent's office. That old guy didn't see the humor in it, and neither did the boss man. Dolese let me go one day before my ninety-day probationary period was up. The diesel thief got on full time.

Even though I was born and raised within two miles of that crusher, I was an outsider there and couldn't seem to fit in. The plant superintendent was a weasel who patronized some of the more senior workers, and getting rid of me was a feather in his hat as far as his head mechanic was concerned, so I was fired and felt every ounce of the stigma that went with it as I drove home that day. I just couldn't seem to find any rhythm back home. I was a true jack-of-all-trades and a master of none.

Word was getting around among the church brethren that old Mike was having a tough go at it trying to get his feet under him and support his young family. I'm sure the word started from Mama. By then, she was a matriarch in the church and was widely known among the brethren for single-handedly raising eight children in the church while rarely missing a service. She also had respect among brethren in the larger churches. Soon the church grapevine produced a tip of a part-time job in the Soil Conservation office, which was located on the third floor of the Mclain federal building. The district conservationist was a deacon in one of the large McClain congregations and was very amicable toward my hiring. Although the job was really designed to accommodate summer work for kids on school break and paid minimum wage, I was happy to get it. Moreover, it was the sort of job nobody could begrudge or be jealous of.

The decade of the awkward '70's was coming to a painfully slow end, but there were glimmers of hope on the horizon. We were catching glimpses of a long-awaited hero riding in straight out of the west. His name was Ronald Reagan, and he was coming to town with guns blazing and the colors waving! Shorter hair and straighter-legged britches were coming in with him. My new job, seeding watershed dams and staking out ponds in the quiet countryside of the area I loved, didn't pay much, but it was a comfortable fit.

Both Suzanne and I were completely and utterly ignorant of politics, politicians, or their so-called policy. Both of us were in our late twenties and weren't even registered to vote. We didn't care about any of that, though. We were just eager to vote for this hero we'd seen in the old westerns. Suzanne and my older sister looked up the local precinct chairperson so they could register themselves, as well as my brother-in-law and me. To be sure we'd all be able to cast our vote for our new hero, they registered the whole lot of us as Republican, even with the registrar trying to explain we could register as Democrats and still vote for him in the general election! When Dad caught wind of this, he embarrassed us all enough so that the girls went back and changed our registration to the D column. I had always wondered why Dad called squirrels Republicans. We squirrel hunted a lot, and every time we'd bag a squirrel, he'd comment "another Republican!" He didn't embarrass us so badly, however, that we didn't vote for our hero.

The conservation job was intermingled with local, state, and federal government resources. The fellow churchgoer who had hired me was paid by the federal arm through the Soil Conservation Service. The service was there to provide assistance, as needed, to the local conservation district board. The local board got their advice, direction, and some resources from the State Conservation Commission, a typical convoluted mess of bureaucracy. What it all boiled down to was that the local conservation board, which was made up of local ranchers, farmers, and bankers, was to set their own priorities in regard to soil and water conservation programs. The federal arm, headed up by the district conservationist, was to assist them in carrying out their goals.

I had been on the job there, steadier than not, for roughly a year, mostly helping the soil technicians lay out pond designs and seeding various vegetation projects. On weekends, I continued hauling hay, cutting wood, and doing whatever else it took to keep our little family afloat. The district's board was gearing up to do a pilot project, funded by the State Commission, which would allow them to hire their own district manager. The goal was to have someone who could acquire easements for their watershed construction projects and promote their various conservation projects in general. I thought the project would be ideally suited for me. I went straight to the district conservationist who had so graciously hired me because I knew he met with the board every month. I had high hopes that he would recommend me for the job but soon found out that the blood between these "spiritual brethren" ran a little on the shallow side where a meaningful job was concerned. Without saying as much, he let me know that I was way beneath the circle of brainpower the board was in search of.

Within a month, they hired an attorney to fill the manager's position. I could tell right off the guy didn't have sense to pour water out of a boot. Nevertheless, he was formally educated and came highly recommended by our district conservationist. He lasted only three months. With another opportunity at hand, I asked my fellow Christian if he would allow me the opportunity to approach the board since he was uncomfortable in recommending me. Once again, he let all the air out of me, assuring me that I was ill equipped to handle the level of skills required by the board. A few weeks later, they hired another formally educated ringer. This one was a former Ag teacher and also came highly recommended by my deacon friend. He lasted only six months.

That very day, I asked one of the technicians who the board chairman was and where he lived. The old gentleman went by the name of Doc. He was a very successful area rancher and former school superintendent. He lived on his four-thousand-acre ranch, about fifteen miles south of McClain. I was parked in his driveway at sunup the next morning. He was an early riser himself and was impressed that I would begin my day early like he did. We sat under a tree in his yard, and I listened while he talked. When the opportunity came, I told him I wanted the job of conservation manager. I assured him that although I had no formal education, I was adept at looking up land rights in the county courthouse and was no stranger to hard work. Before I left, old Doc assured me that he'd bring my proposition to the board at their next monthly meeting. Based on that off-the-cuff interview under the shade tree in his yard, Doc recommended me to the board, and I was immediately hired.

From as far back as I can remember, up until the day I left home, I could easily count the pairs of new shoes I'd ever gotten on one hand. One pair in particular stood out to me like the crown jewel in footwear. Mama took me to Curry's shoe store and let me pick out a brand-new pair of tennis shoes—within her budget, of course. I got a pair of white high-top canvas PF Flyers, the kind that made you run faster and jump higher! I'll never forget trying to run and look down at those new Flyers in action. I kept my eyes on them when I ran and when I walked and stared at them a considerable length of time when I took them off at night.

Landing the new job as the conservation district manager was every bit as good a feeling as wearing those new PF Flyers. I just wanted to stand back and look at it awhile! The job could not have come at a better time. We were at our wits end trying to keep our bills paid, our fourth child was on the way, and my morale had all but bottomed out. There wasn't any time to stand back and admire the accomplishment or celebrate. Along with my hiring came a stern warning from Doc, "We want you to hit the ground running, big boy, and do the best you can. If your best ain't good enough, we'll find someone else." Although the job came with a modest salary, it was far better than the minimum wage I was making, and I was determined that my best would be good enough.

Doc's pet peeve was the Brushy Peaceable Creek Watershed Project, which had come to a screeching halt. It was the district's responsibility to get easements signed for ingress and egress to the proposed lake sites, as well as the conservation sites themselves. They didn't have funds to acquire them, and condemnation was out of the question, as far as the district board members were concerned. Most of the proposed construction sites were located on land belonging to folks they knew, their neighbors. The last thing they wanted was to have angry neighbors. All the easy ones had been acquired, and they were down to the nut cracking. The project had been stalled for the better part of two years, and the inability of the two former managers to move the project forward was a large part of their demise.

My first day as manager, I picked out the easement that was considered to be the toughest nut to crack. In fact, there were other landowners holding out in lieu of our ability to get this one signed. The property was owned by the pastor of a small Assembly of God church there in McClain, a man of high moral character and also a man of high living standards. He wanted pay for his easement! I'd never met the man. I was knocking on his door by 8:00 a.m.

The old pastor came to the door much as I'd anticipated, with a welcoming smile and a big wooden cross dangling from his neck. His wife was one step behind him, with coffee and doughnuts on an oblong glass platter. Of course they both knew why I was there, but I made no mention of the watershed, much less the easement. We talked about family and faith. I bragged on the pictures of his grandchildren strewn about their mantle and told him of my own upbringing. I told him how my wife and I had struggled trying to keep our little ones in food and clothing. Within the hour, they were both kneeling and praying for my kids. I even let them lay hands on a banged-up knee I had! Before

I walked out their door, I had the easement signed and dated. I held my breath as I walked down their sidewalk to my pickup, praying they wouldn't change their mind. I dared not look back toward their house. Just as I was opening my pickup door, I heard a shout coming from the pastor. I was so caught up in my great accomplishment, I'd forgotten my banged knee was healed, and I had been slightly limping along their walkway. With a shout, he wanted me to jump up and down and stomp that old devil out of my knee. I did just that!

There was no looking back after that. Others in the watershed plan began to sign up, and Doc's pet project was off high center! Within the next few months, I had established a conservation education program in every Pittsburg county school and was organizing their first Banker's Conservation Awards Banquet. With every move, I'd send press releases to all the local media, crediting Doc and the district board. My credit came when the pilot project turned full time.

I continued to show up once a week and chew the fat with old Doc under his shade tree. I made a point to be there by sunup. Being a former educator, Doc delighted in the conservation education program and enjoyed being informed of our progress on a regular basis. He especially enjoyed the publicity. The chairman of the board was never satisfied with the status quo, however, and continued pushing and challenging me for bigger, better deals. I was more than happy to accommodate. It sure beat roofing, plumbing, and hauling hay! I soon organized a Conservation District Youth Board that mimicked the district board with their own monthly meetings and projects. I had also gotten the district involved in an Abandoned Mine Reclamation Project.

The 1980s had kicked off with a fever pitch. The gunslinger riding in from the west who we admired so much became president. Our fourth child had been born with no complications, a dark-haired, brown-eyed, little Italian. I felt as though I'd gone from the outhouse to the White House! For the first time in over a decade, I was actually enjoying my work without punching a time clock. I was even finding time to slip along the banks of Gaines Creeks for the spring turkey hunt. The oil-and-gravel odor of the Rock Crusher was but a distant memory.

I had made acquaintances with every prominent rancher in Pittsburg County, every school superintendent, and was on a first-name basis with everyone in the big Conservation Commission office in Oklahoma City. The big McClain Chamber of Commerce, of all organizations, had even recruited me to sit on their board of directors, as well as the Fairground Trust Authority.

The Farmers Home Administration had an office next door to mine on the third floor of the federal building, and I'd become well acquainted with those folks as well. One morning, the director of the program summoned me from the hallway into his office. He wanted to inform me of a 3 percent federal loan that was designed to help get young farmers and ranchers back on the farm. He thought the new loan program was a perfect fit for me. Although I didn't have a pot to piss in or a window to throw it out of, I certainly must have had the appearance of success. It didn't take much encouragement, and before the day was up, I was filling out an FmHA loan application! On paper, I looked good, especially with the equity I'd been sitting on in the small frame house near the elementary school.

At the time, there was a 233-acre plot of land that was tailor-made for this hillbilly. It was across the highway from Dad's farm and ran along the north bank of Gaines Creek for a mile. During the course of all the legal work with title searches, abstract updating, and loan processing, we discovered some rather unsettling news. The equity we thought we had didn't exist. Turned out all those legal-sized documents I'd signed for the old upstanding Hartshorne businessman were nothing more than a legal way for him to steal the twenty thousand I'd made from the sale of my home in Denison, Texas. It was immediately soaked up by the outrageous interest he'd so neatly tucked away in all those forms. Despite all that, we were approved for the big loan, and overnight, I became a rancher. After a few months, we untangled ourselves from the "expensive" house near the grade school and built a new but very modest frame house on our 230 acres. The loan not only covered the land and house but sixty head of cattle as well. Go figure!

By then, I was burning the candle at both ends and loving every minute of it! Our success at the conservation district had garnered recognition statewide, as well as nationally. Old Doc had been inducted into the Conservation Commission's Hall of Fame and was now sitting on their board of directors. I was making appearances statewide, sharing our success story with other conservation districts and making the convention circuits. We traveled to Hawaii, Tennessee, Colorado, Washington, DC, Louisiana, Alabama, and more. I had become a real socialite and was the life of the party in the hospitality suites.

In all reality, it was too much, too quick. I was more like a kid in a candy store. On the eve of Suzanne and my departure to Hawaii, I'd gotten my three-quarter-ton truck buried in eight inches of snow and mud and on it, a load of hay. It didn't matter, though. I called my brothers to bail it out of the muck. We left the kids with Mama, and we flew first-class to the Aloha State.

After losing our equity, which was the only real savings we'd ever had, we were mortgaged to the hilt, and although my salary was decent enough, we were still barely making ends meet. Suzanne was continuing her role as stay-at-home mom. Making payments on our ranch operation wasn't working out in real life, like it had on paper, so we were applying for one deferral right after another. The convention trips were courtesy of the conservation district, but outside of the travel, room, and meals that were comped, we were walking around with empty purses.

In February of 1986, we made a trip to Nashville, Tennessee, where the National Association of Conservation districts were recognizing our youth board. We stayed in the Opryland Hotel, and by the last night there, we were watching our pennies pretty close and opted out of our group to eat dinner on our own. The hotel dining was a little more expensive than we could afford.

A mile or so down the road was a small restaurant that one of the hotel workers referred us to. The Nashville Palace was a place that had burgers and fries at a reasonable price. The restaurant was small but clean, and the menu featured a hamburger basket that was priced to suit us. The menu also depicted a picture of a young man in the upper right-hand corner, and below it was a caption that read, "Randy Travis, appearing nightly." My wife claimed she'd heard one of his songs before, but I'd never heard of the guy. We sat down at a table right next to a small dance floor that joined a raised platform containing a piano and a less than extravagant sound system. While we were ordering our burgers, an elderly gentleman wearing pop bottle glasses quietly ambled onto the stage and sat down at the piano. A few minutes later, the young man whose picture was on the menu, strolled out of the kitchen area, took the stage, and began raising the microphone bar to suit his height. Right away, I was impressed with the old piano player. I'd never heard such runs as he was playing up close and personal like that. Then the young man began joining in with a country song that sounded better than Merle Haggard's! The burgers were good, the price was right, and the music was splendid! We finished our meal and stayed for every last tune.

After the show, I approached the young man, shook his hand, and told him how much we had enjoyed his singing. I informed him that Merle Haggard was one of my favorites and that I thought he was equally as good, if not better. He introduced himself as Randy Travis and was gracious enough to join us at our table while we finished our iced tea. During our conversation, I told him why we were in Nashville, where we were from, and I'm sure a lot of other stuff he wasn't interested in. Nevertheless, he was as genuine and polite as anyone I'd ever met for the first time.

I also told him about my role in the Fairground Trust Authority and how we were in the process of raising funds to complete the project. Then I asked if he'd be interested in coming to our area and doing a concert as a means to promote our Fairground, and possibly even raise some funds. He said he'd do it in a heartbeat but had just signed on with a new manager whose name was Lib Hatcher. He gave me her card and suggested I call her.

On the trip home, my wife and I discussed how that burger basket ended up being the highlight of our stay in Nashville! My wheels were already turning. In September of the same year, which was only seven months away, McClain State Penitentiary would be hosting their annual prison rodeo, which always drew a large crowd. I told my wife this Randy Travis fellow might be famous by then and that I was going to call this Lib Hatcher and see if I could get him to come do a concert around the prison rodeo time. When we got home, I did just that. By the next week, she'd sent me a contract to sign, complete with date and venue. The cost would be fifteen hundred dollars for two ninety-minute performances. I figured with a lot of hard work and pleading, I could sell enough tickets to cover it. Besides, I figured this guy might be big time in another six months.

I hadn't considered the fact that the venue was nothing more than a cow pasture since the fairgrounds had only been recently purchased. Nor had I considered how quickly six months would fly by. Having the contract secured, I began touting my new-found country singer to everyone I knew and some folks I didn't know. Everyone had the same response, "Randy who?" It seemed as though my wife was the only person in Pittsburg County who was up on country music. By May of that year, I started getting little feelings of panic. I couldn't find a soul who was the least bit interested in helping me organize a concert for an unknown country singer, and I definitely needed help! At the very least, I needed a platform built somewhere in that cow pasture that would accommodate a band. It also dawned on me that there wasn't even electricity there yet! If all else failed, I knew I could count on my brothers. That sort of stuff was right down their alley. Selling enough tickets to cover $1,500 for an unknown country singer was my biggest problem.

Then about mid-July, inspiration came subtly through the radio speakers in my car. Suzanne and I were headed to church with our four kids when the young man we'd met in Nashville was singing to us once again. We quickly shushed the kids and turned the volume up on our car radio and heard for the first time a song entitled "On the Other Hand" by Randy Travis. By mid-August, his songs were bouncing off the airwaves of all the local radio stations, and volunteers began coming out of the woodwork! Anyone will give you their coat when it ain't raining.

The owner of McClain Radio Stations and brother of a prominent and powerful state senator called me one morning and began gabbing like we were long-lost buddies. He was owner of the same stations that refused to give me a break on promotional ads for the event only a couple weeks earlier. He'd had a sudden change of heart and not only wanted to give me ad space, he also wanted half the action. He had evidently given this proposition some thought because he proceeded to tell me who *our* sponsors were going to be, what *we* were going to charge, and how *he* would handle it all. At the time, I was not only politically incorrect, I was politically dumb, so cutting my nose off to spite my face, I declined his late, however generous, offer and soon found out how politics worked.

That very day, the same Randy Travis hits that were climbing the billboard charts disappeared from all the local stations. A week later, another country music concert featuring a well-known artist named Steve Warner was blasting the airwaves every fifteen minutes, sponsored by none other than the most powerful radio station in Southeast Oklahoma. The event would be held at the very same time and date as the Randy Travis event, only five miles farther down the road in a large well-equipped roping arena called Ghost Rider's Arena. I eventually turned every radio I had to the off position. The senator's brother was making a statement, and I was getting it loud and clear.

Humped up like a mule in a hailstorm, I did my best to block his loud and professional promos out of my mind and went about my business hanging small posters of the Randy Travis concert wherever I could. I would have my concert, but on the other hand, I'd get stepped on like a bug.

The yet to be developed fairground property had no specific parking area and no main entrance that was designated as such, just several primitive access openings from the main highway. On one end of the property, there was a utility pole for electric hookups and a large gently sloping area that made sort of a natural site for an amphitheater, so that's where we put the makeshift stage. Knowing rednecks would pour into the site from every direction possible, I decided to station a couple of volunteers wearing nail aprons near the hillside overlooking the stage to collect the admission money. I guess I thought people would get out of their car, form a neat line, and wait their turn to file past my volunteers wearing the aprons.

On the eve of the event, I was sweating bullets, and with good reason. For starters, this wasn't the same Randy Travis I'd met nearly a year earlier. I knew there were a lot better places he could have been going other than a cow pasture in the sticks of Southeast Oklahoma. I also had heard he was making a lot more than $1,500 for a show, so I wasn't sure he would even show up. With the limited means of promoting the concert, I had no idea if a hundred people would come or a thousand, and if it rained, I was screwed! Finally, even under the best of circumstances, I was competing with a well-publicized professional event only five miles down the highway. The feeling was almost as dreadful as the day the FBI pulled into our driveway back in '67.

When concert day arrived, most of my fears were soon put to rest. The weather was fine, the stage was solid, and the utility pole was live with juice. I did have sense enough to hedge my bet by having an assortment of local talent front the Randy Travis show. I figured that at the very least, their families would show up. Among them was some guy that played piano, guitar, and banjo simultaneously. He called himself the "Piatrajarbo Man." I'd also arranged a Country Hoss contest for early in the day. It was an original idea I had come up with—having contestants split wood, huck hay bales, and other challenges you would encounter as a country boy. The only problem was that my apron wearers weren't yet stationed when these folks arrived. The big relief came when I saw a travel trailer and a truck pulling an enclosed trailer to the hillside. Sure enough, Randy Travis, his full band and his new manager were all on the scene!

As concert time neared, cars were pouring in from every direction, and we already had a sizable crowd that came for the prelude of homespun events. Hardly anyone, however, got in line to pay admission. There was so many people meandering about the hillside, my two kids in the aprons may as well not even been there. A handful of honest folk did look them up and drop money in their apron, but not very many. Luckily, I'd arranged for a friend of mine who was in the restaurant business to set up a concession with hot dogs and soft drinks. So every few minutes, I'd make a concession run, gather up change, and take it to the travel trailer. I'd dump the coins and small bills out on a coffee table, and Lib Hatcher would count! It took a while, but we finally managed to gather up the $1,500. I don't think Lib was all that impressed.

Randy Travis not only did the two ninety-minute performances, he stayed well into the night as he autographed hats and T-shirts for every hillbilly there! He was exactly the stand-up guy I'd figured him to be from our brief encounter back in Nashville.

Although I didn't make a dime from the event, it served to be a home run for the fairground. A state-of-the-art concrete stage, complete with a roof and professional lighting, was eventually erected in place of my makeshift stage. Moreover, talk of the Randy Travis fairground show overwhelmed any talk of the Ghost Rider's Arena event.

Life for me in the '80s was on the fast track. After the Randy Travis deal, everyone in Pittsburg County thought I was a real promoter, and I soon found myself involved in all kinds of causes that didn't pay anything. The fairground trust had me going from place to place promoting a temporary sales tax that would fund a real fairground facility. The conservation folk had me speaking at various banquets and events promoting conservation, and being a board member of the McClain Chamber was in itself time consuming—all this, not to mention the variety of new programs that I had undertaken in my role as conservation district manager.

On the home front, I was trying to keep up with all the perils that come with being a rancher with outdated equipment and run-down fences. Most weekends, I was bailing and hauling my own hay, doctoring sick cattle, or patching a fence with the help of my two small boys.

Both Suzanne and I, along with our four small children, were still front and center at the old church. Brother Ronald had even dispatched me to preach on occasions at a small country church in Haskell County forty miles from nowhere. So every other Sunday, we'd drag our poor kids off to this strange congregation of mostly old folk and make them sit there as though they enjoyed it. As if there weren't enough on my plate, my baby sister was soon to be wed and wanted me to perform the ceremony. Since I'd been preaching on and off at that country church, she thought I was well qualified. Delving into the legalities of signing her marriage certificate, however, we discovered that only a justice of the peace or an ordained minister could legally bind her in matrimony. Although I preached the Gospel some, I'd never been ordained. I assumed being ordained surely meant that some sort of special religious education or ceremony had to take place. I had none of that and figured I was off the hook. Instead of leaving well enough alone, my sis called the courthouse where she had gotten her marriage license and found out that being ordained was quite simple. All I had to do was show up, so the court clerk could assign me a book and page number in the county record book. It took me ten minutes to become an ordained minister! I dared not share my new credentials outside the family. They may not have played so well in the hospitality suites.

The older I got, the more difficult it became living up to Brother Ronald's far right standards, and going to church became a facade. Being brought up under such absolute truths where the Bible was concerned had led me more to a place of arrogance as a young man. When the subject of religion came up, I had all the answers and didn't even understand the questions. A co-worker back at the old Brookside plant who was much older and wiser than me had engaged me in a biblical discussion. It wasn't long before I was driving home a point with the vigor of a true know-it-all. While my gums were still flapping, the old gentleman interrupted and suggested I come back and talk to him after I'd been to a funeral or two.

The point he'd made came home to roost in March of 1984. The man in the black hat had succumbed to a massive heart attack. He was only fifty-nine years old. He was my dad and one of many the church had labeled a pagan worshiper. In all likelihood, he'd saved me from the horror of a war that claimed the lives of over fifty thousand kids just like me. He minded his own business and gave generously to the more unfortunate. With an eighth grade education, he'd fought a war and raised eight kids. When he died, he didn't owe a dime.

The funeral service was half Catholic and half Protestant. My little brother, Steve, delivered a heartwarming eulogy while the priest ceremoniously swung the canister of incense over his casket. Brothers and I staked out his burial plot in a country cemetery called Mountain Station. When they lowered his coffin into the ground, with teary eyes and using shovels, we covered him ourselves. I was thirty-three years old and had never uttered the words, "I love you, Dad."

Six months later, his dad passed and soon afterward his mother. They were Italian immigrants who spoke the Italian language far more fluently than English—Fidelas and Bonnie Rose Masciantonio. Neither of them had so much as a secondary education. They too had raised eight children, five sons, and three daughters. They were my paternal grandparents, and they were Catholic as Catholic could be. Grandma birthed her children at home. She made their clothes from flour and feed sacks and washed them on a rub board using homemade lye soap. She cooked their meals on a wood stove and baked their bread in an outside rock oven. Grandpa had cleared and farmed his land with a team of mules, turning eighty acres of timber and sprouts into a paradise of orchards and gardens. This was the very place I roamed as a child, picking berries and catching bass in his hand-dug ponds. I'd never heard either of them preach or debate the Bible, but then, they didn't have to. Their very lives were testimony of sacrifice, benevolence, and faith.

While I lived in Texas, I could hardly wait to stop by Grandma Mass's whenever we made the trip back home. Although she had slowed considerably from the days of making cheese in her woven baskets and sautéing wild mushrooms, she could still set a king's dish with a dab of olive oil and a pod of garlic. I pulled in their driveway one weekend with a pickup load of wood I was delivering to an elderly man. The old fellow only lived a couple miles from Grandma and Grandpa, but it was lunchtime, and I knew Grandma Mass would have a skillet full of something good! When I went inside, Grandpa asked where I was going with the wood, and I told him the old man's name. He then asked if he lived at the foot of Gowen Mountain, which he did. Upon my confirmation, Grandpa's disposition turned from inquisitive to agitated. "Hey, Mica," he said, "unloada the wood righta there, I'lla pay you for it." Grandpa hadn't had a wood stove or a fireplace in years, so I couldn't help but ask why. He didn't mind answering the question.

"I solda that sona-ma-bitch a load of cane in 1928, and he never pay me."

Grandma was quick to scold him for using such language and reminded him that he was supposed to forgive those who had done them wrong.

Grandpa shot back just as quick, "Hey, Mama, I can forgive the dirty sona-ma-bitch. I just no can forgets."

After that handful of funerals, the winds that fueled my spiritual sails diminished rapidly. My children were at the age where they needed sound spiritual guidance, but I had none to give. My answer was to continue a charade of churchgoing halfheartedly. Meanwhile, I buried myself deeper and deeper into my work as manager and promoter, pushing hard to outdo one accomplishment after another.

Dad's sudden and unexpected death had affected me far more than I realized. He was like a compass—an anchor. There was nothing frivolous about him, and I was really just beginning to know him. A simple expression on his face could tell you more than any hour-long sermon or counseling session. One brush by him let you know if your problem was a real problem or a mere bump in the road. All that wisdom and sound direction was gone. If only I could have dug him up and ask him some real-life questions. The day I was let go from the rock crusher, I so dreaded telling Dad. Not only had he disapproved of my leaving a good job in Texas, I knew he would worry about me and my young family. Nevertheless, I wanted to tell him first, just to get it over with. On the way to his place, I spotted his green Chevy pickup parked near the bridge crossing Gaines Creek, a favorite crappie hole he liked to frequent in the spring. I pulled over and forced myself down the creek bank, knowing I'd ruin his otherwise peaceful day. He was sitting on a bucket with his black hat, favorite Calcutta cane pole, and a good dip of Skoal. I really didn't have to say anything. He could tell by my body language something was wrong. I cleared my throat and told him I'd lost my job, which made me feel some better, just getting the words out. He leaned to one side, spit some tobacco juice, and said, "Are you gonna fish or just stand there? These crappie are bitin'." It was his way of saying, "You'll be all right."

Although my style of managing the conservation district was producing one success after the other, the venture into the cattle business was going south. A few of the cattle that I purchased at the local stockyard and unloaded crossed a washed-out water gap in the creek onto 12,000 acres of adjoining brush and timber. I never saw them again. Without Dad stopping by routinely to help out with fence patching and give me sound veterinary advice, it seemed as if no one really cared, except me. Adding to the drama, I'd purchased a dozen cow-calf pairs from an individual who was retiring his small cow operation. They were all fat and looked much better than anything I'd bought at the stockyards. They were gentle too. When I unloaded them, they mingled in with the rest of my herd as if they'd been there all along. Unbeknownst to me, however, they were all infected with a disease known as bangs. "Bangs" was a disease that caused sterility in cattle, and it was very contagious. The disease had become so rampant in Oklahoma that the Department of Agriculture had put a program in place to eradicate it. That meant that any animals testing positive for the disease would be branded with a "B" on the side of their neck or jaw and be sold strictly for slaughter. Within six months of purchasing those fat cows, my operation was quarantined, with a state vet showing up once a month to test my herd. Every trip he'd find "bangy cattle." After a few weeks of the harassment, my herd had become so spooky we could barely get them into the testing pens.

It didn't matter that the place was losing money hand over fist, it had become home and was allowing me to raise my children just as I'd always dreamed of—out in the country, with plenty of chores. I kept my boys right beside me whether fixing fence, feeding, or bailing hay. I was determined to teach them at least two basic principles: (1) the difference between right and wrong and (2) how to work. Try as I may, however, little boys sometimes have a mind of their own.

One afternoon, with both of them in the truck with me, a week-old calf jumped out of the tall grass in front of us. I said, "Look, boys, a little bull calf." The youngest boy, Lucas, asked how I knew it was a bull calf.

I said, "You see those little nuts dangling between his hind legs? That's how you know it's a bull." I went on to tell him, "Don't call them nuts when you are around other people. Call them testicles."

The following Sunday, we'd invited my mother over for lunch after the church service. As most grandmothers do, she was ooh-ing and aahing over my little ones and how well they behaved in church. When we got to the house, Lucas plopped down in the front yard with his knees folded outward, and our little terrier named JoJo scurried up and laid his head in Luke's lap. Mama leaned over to catch a closer glimpse of the adorable sight when Lucas, who was barely four years old, said, "Look, Nonnie, JoJo has his head on my test-tackles."

A few years later, while we had left the kids with Nonnie for our trip to Hawaii, she swabbed Luke's mouth with a bar of Zest soap for saying "dang it." Later, his brother Micah told me that when Nonnie had left the scene, Lucas had peered around the doorway, making sure she was out of earshot, and said, "Damn, that stuff tastes like shit!"

The 1980s were whisking by like boxcars on a two-engine freight train. They say time flies when you're having fun, but in all reality, those years were a series of highs and lows. In between my job as conservation manager, our small farm, church, and the kids, there wasn't time to slow down.

Never one to recognize prosperity, I made another life-changing decision that would assure the caboose of the 1980s rolled by on anything but a high note. After seven enjoyable and successful years of managing the conservation district, I accepted a new job as manager of the McClain Chamber of Commerce. I had been approached by the chamber board president about the new position, which thoroughly impressed me. He was a staunch republican, owned an advertising agency, and had taken notice of my promotional abilities. Hindsight being 20/20, I'm sure he had in mind Mike Mass bringing big events to town that would result in big advertising for his agency. I don't know what I had in mind. I was going from working for a five-member board of directors, all of whom were easy going and congenial, to working for a board of more than a dozen self-serving entrepreneurs. I was by then, however, too stuck on myself to realize that the success I'd had at the conservation district was due to the fact that I worked for a group of individuals who gave me the freedom and the confidence to explore my own ideas. I was beginning to think way too much of myself!

I soon found out that me and this chairman of the board would have *anything but* the relationship I'd had with old Doc! Although he had his own clever notions, he was held in check by fourteen other board members who each had their own ideas. Making matters worse, the manager I replaced was retained by the board to play a support role in my efforts. Her role, however, was anything but support. She resented being demoted and hated me from day one. There was an inside joke that said, "If a tornado's coming, call the chamber. They never let anything come to town!" Damned if it wasn't the truth! One year of that mess was all I could take. I resigned without any prospect of another job. I was like Jerry Clowers, a country comedian from that time who said he was hemmed up in the top of a tree with a lynx cat, when he hollered down and said, "Just shoot up here in amongst us. Somebody's got to have some relief!"

I was back to square one, hauling hay, patching roofs, and peddling crafts for my brothers, on occasion. Oh yes, we were broker than Cooter Brown! A new job was developing on the horizon, however—a job that required no education and no sanctioning by a board. It came with good pay, good benefits, and a prestigious title—state representative for House District 17!

# 18

As time in the federal pen crept ever so slowly by, we all became accustomed to seeing poor old Fritz exit his cell every morning covered in medicated powder. Convinced that he most assuredly had a bad case of gas, he signed up for sick call. He thought if he could solve his gas problem, old man Powell might go easy on the powder. He told the on-duty nurse about his problem and how it must be keeping his cellie up at night busy squirting powder. She said, "Well, go tell your cellie he shouldn't have come to prison." Fitz couldn't win for losing.

Aside from Fitz's visit and the subsequent cute answer, sick call was rather a joke. It was another of the many government mandates without adequate funding. Politicians love being tough on crime but rarely give pause to the cost. Sick call amounted to putting your name on a list and getting in line to see, at best, a PA. Outside of the usual stethoscope and blood pressure cuff, they were pretty ill equipped. I had developed a rather large boil at the base of my eyelid that started out much like a typical sty. By my third month there, it was the size of a large grape and beginning to blur my vision. I think it bothered the other guys in cadre as much as it did me. It concerned me enough that I signed up for sick call. The PA told me to keep a hot towel on it and read some scripture. I must have read the wrong scripture because it did nothing but get larger. My card-playing partner, Griff, had also signed up. He was having a lot of difficulty breathing. Just making the rounds while working in utilities was beginning to take a toll on him. The PA told him that he needed to start exercising. Griff laughed when he told me, "I can barely walk without losing breath. I don't know how I'm supposed to exercise." Adding insult to injury, they deducted two days' pay from your commissary fund for the visit to sick call.

As time went by, I became more and more accustomed to prison life. I'd established a routine and had made a lot of friends. Of course, I never got so comfortable that I forgot where I was. The unexpected shakedowns, frequent frisking, strip-searches, and occasional demeaning remarks by some of the more exuberant guards made sure of that. Nevertheless, I had a front-row seat watching the script of real-life drama unfold, written and directed by a volatile mixture of politics and religion. As each day passed, my respect and admiration grew for a group of people who I only thought I knew something about—young kids; black, white, red, and brown kids; kids who were respectful, polite, considerate, and hardworking and were problem solvers; kids with an inner constitution far more powerful than the politicians who put them there.

Names and dates of inmates continued to change in the cadre unit during my stay. As one moves on, another is quick to take his place. At times, the warden would simply yank an inmate or two out of holdover and assign them to the cadre unit for a couple of years as work was needed. More often than not, they were inmates with lengthy sentences en route to a prison facility closer to home. Having done a majority of their sentence in good conduct, the prison counselor at their previous holding facility would try and move them closer to home, where family visits weren't so burdensome. For an inmate, however, no deals are final.

One such cadre inmate was a young Hispanic named Diez, who was a little over halfway through his twelve-year, nine-month sentence. Having completed over six years in good conduct he was being transferred to a prison in South Texas, where he'd be closer to home. That was thwarted when the warden decided cadre unit needed more help. Diez was assigned to laundry fold, where the two of us got personally acquainted. Although disheartened at his sudden new and unwanted destination, he continued being the consummate worker and congenial inmate. He never slacked while working with me. I found him to be pleasant, respectful, and without complaint. He was a young, strong, good-looking kid in his twenties.

Diez was born and raised in Laredo, Mexico. He went to school there through fifth grade, then moved across the border to Laredo, Texas, with his father and started school there. They put him in a special education class, right along with mentally handicapped students, because he couldn't speak English. He knew he was smart but was made to feel dumb and unwanted. He hated it and missed his old home. On weekends during his junior high and high school years, he would return home, where his uncles and other family acquaintances would make him carry marijuana stalks on his back, crossing the river to some house where he'd leave it for whomever. He learned at a young age how to run fast and dodge the border patrol. He toughed it out at his new school and graduated, despite the way he was treated.

After high school, he got a job but continued his affiliation with relatives and older acquaintances in the drug business. To him, it was just a way of life. He married (in his words) a beautiful senorita from his home town in Laredo. They soon purchased a small house in Laredo, Texas, and spent all their time together. One night, a knock came at their door. It was an older acquaintance he'd carried stalks for as a child. He was wearing a wire. He would sacrifice Diez for his own immunity. Diez pled guilty to drug trafficking and received twelve years and nine months from the feds. With a humbling smile, he was proud to tell me he had only a little over five years left to serve.

I asked Diez what those first few days in prison were like, knowing that he'd left the love of his life and had almost thirteen years ahead of him. He said he didn't realize he was that depressed until much later, but for the first three months of incarceration, he just slept, except for eating and going to the bathroom. He also explained that he tried not to think of his beautiful senorita because it made the time seem too burdensome and long. At the time, she was still with him, although she didn't have the resources to travel the long distance to visit. He said he wouldn't blame her if she left him. He just prefers to not think about it. Call me a sucker, but I would trust Diez with anything I had.

Another victim of the holdover kidnappings was a young black man from Houston, Texas. In the unit upstairs, he pretty much kept to himself. When he wasn't at work in the kitchen, where they assigned him to wash pots and pans, he was in deep concentration on the Bible. Every evening and most weekends, he was studying and researching Scripture while the rest of us were throwing washers, playing basketball on the rec deck, or watching the TV on the large pole.

He seemed a little militant to me. Refusing to be belittled or talked down to, he was a frequent visitor to the SHU. Somehow, his demeanor and his constant search of the Scripture didn't seem to jive until I got to know him.

After a month or so, I began noticing him in the small prison library with a group of other inmates, all sitting in a circle. They would meet there several nights a week just prior to the 9:00 p.m. count. Intrigue finally got the better of me, so I peeked in one evening and asked if I could join them. He was quick to shake my hand and introduce himself as Sabre Harrison Johnson. He was holding a volunteer Bible study, and I took a seat in the circle. It had been a long time since I'd participated in a church activity, as church had long since become more of a ritualistic show to me. Nevertheless, I still had a faith and a conscience that had never let go of my heart. The prison chapel certainly wasn't my answer. Maybe this was.

Sabre would simply go around the circle asking each one what their favorite Bible story was and, with an anxious grin, ask them to share the story in their own words. When they would finish, Sabre would say, "Amen, brother, thank you." He didn't feel the need to correct or otherwise embarrass someone else's view of their story. I was more accustomed to the preachers who knew it all, who acted like it was their way or the highway! This guy acted as though he could learn as much from the students as they could from him. When the loud intercom interrupted announcing the 9:00 p.m. count, we all joined hands and closed with a prayer. It didn't seem like I was there for five minutes, much less an hour. I was more accustomed to a one-hour church service seeming like a half day.

The next day, after work in laundry fold, I was eager to introduce myself to Sabre and tell him how much I'd enjoyed the study. I did just that, and we become closest of friends. From then on, I called him Brother Johnson, and he called me Brother Guv.

The circle, as we called it, became something I looked forward to. I never thought I'd look so forward to a church service. Of course, in prison, there is no one "holier" than "thou"; we all knew we were sinners. There were a couple of obvious mentally handicapped in the circle, but they too had their turn at telling their story. Brother Johnson demonstrated the patience of Job as he dealt with them.

One evening, while Brother Johnson and I were sharing a flour tortilla and microwaved ground beef (someone had smuggled up the elevator), I asked him why he was so confrontational with some of the prison guards and staff. I even told him how he'd come across as militant before I got to really know him.

He explained to me that although he'd made mistakes that merited his prison time, he still considered himself a man and would never accept being treated as less than a man. He not only had a profound understanding of Scripture but also had the guts of a government mule. I laughed and told him I'd be anything the warden wanted me to be if it kept me out of the SHU!

The small rec deck outside of F pod was used mainly as a handball court. King of the handball court was a twenty-six-year-old kid named Cody from eastern Iowa. The feds picked Cody up at the age of nineteen for his dealings in methamphetamines. Of course, there were the usual hunting rifles and shotguns tucked away in the gun cabinet, which constituted having firearms in the commission of a crime. After serving eighteen months in a county jail, the feds came to him with an offer of significantly less time in exchange for grand jury testimony against his parents, who were also dealing in meth. Cody refused. Because he wouldn't snitch on his parents, the feds enhanced his crime on every level they could. Young Cody got a sentence of sixteen years. When I met Cody, he'd already served seven years and only had nine more to go. Despite all that, he was a remarkably bright kid and, surprisingly enough, was concerned about his future. "Gov, can you imagine me going for a job interview when I get out of here at age 35 and them asking me for a resume? I will have to say, 'Well, I've been in the federal penitentiary for the past sixteen years. I've never had a class, but I play a mean game of handball and can talk shit with the best of them!'"

By then, Arlan had shipped out to a halfway house, and I was glad of it. It was hard to sleep with him crying at the cell door every night. I had finally scored a bottom bunk. The day he left, however, I got a new cellie, a twenty-seven-year-old kid with a full-blown case of the flu. Just my luck! During lockdown times, I'd cover up best I could in the thin blanket while he was hacking and sneezing overhead.

The TV pole that was located in the center of E pod had four TVs attached about six feet above the floor. One was kept on a Hispanic channel, one on ESPN, one tuned in for the white guys, and the last kept tuned by our black brothers. In order to hear the various programs, we had to purchase a small transistor radio in commissary and tune it into the proper channel. Every so often, the director of recreation would plug in a movie that we could all watch. One night, they put the movie *Blind Side* on. I couldn't help but watch all these hardened criminals as they sat motionless and quiet during that movie. The movie was based on a true story of a wealthy white Christian couple in Mississippi that had taken in a poor black kid from the projects of the inner city. The kid went on to be an All American at Mississippi State and later played in the pros. It was a real story of hope and inspiration. The movie was the exact opposite of what I had always assumed inmates would be interested in, and in a sorted twist of irony, it was wealthy white Christian couples and their pandering politicians who had built the prisons these kids were in.

Before the movie was over, we were all interrupted by an annoying thudding sound coming from Griff's cell. One of the guys nearest his cell door finally got up to see what the racket was all about. When he opened the cell door, Griff was lying there in his own vomit. Unable to get up, he was holding a boot by the shoestring and swatting it against the door, hoping to get someone's attention. I ran to the officer's station outside the pod to summon help while some of the other guys stayed with Griff.

In a matter of minutes, the prison LTs had us all locked in our cells while they attended to Griff. Watching through the narrow windows of our cell door, we could see that the guards were reluctant to touch him in all the mess. After fetching themselves all a pair of the plastic gloves, they finally managed to get him in a wheelchair. I watched as they rolled him out of the pod, with poor Griff's head dangling, his chin bouncing off his chest. I thought to myself, *At least maybe now they'll get that kid to a hospital.* We remained on lockdown the remainder of the night.

The following morning, I was dressed and ready when the guards unlocked our cells. I never got used to being locked in a cell. We usually had ten minutes or so before our laundry boss would show up to escort us to our work station, so I fixed a cup of instant coffee, plugged in my radio, and tuned into CNN. While I was watching the news, one of the guys came over and nodded toward Griff's cell. I pulled my earphones out and walked over to peek in, and there was Griff back in his bunk. I eased into his cell and asked how he was doing. He could barely talk; he was so weak. They had kept him downstairs in infirmary most of the night but still no trip to see a doctor. He was curled in a fetal position facing the cold concrete wall, gasping for breath. It was a rather chilling place to be when you're deathly ill.

Before I left Griff's cell, a young man we called Buddha appeared in the doorway. He occupied the cell next to Griff and had also come in to check on his buddy. The two of them were pretty close, having spent time together in Fort Worth prior to their stint at FTC.

Buddha was from a small Texas town on the outskirts of Tyler, Texas. Griff had confided to me that Buddha took his first thirty days in prison pretty hard. He told me Buddha wouldn't talk and only wanted to stay in his bunk, said he wouldn't even shower for the first couple of weeks. I'm sure a lot of people facing over 120 months in a federal pen would do the same. Buddha was in for much the same as most of these young guys, drugs and guns. Of course, the guns were used only for quail hunting by Buddha's uncle and used by the feds as a prop.

By the time I met Buddha there at FTC, he'd shaken off the initial prison shock and kept himself busy. He worked out every day and went to chapel at every opportunity he had. He was the sort of guy who seemed to always appear when someone needed help or encouragement. It didn't surprise me that he would be checking in on Griff. It's a good thing too. He was the closest thing to a nurse that Griff was gonna see.

That evening after work and before the 4:00 p.m. count, I was in my cell stashing some new socks I'd smuggled out of laundry when I heard this loud boisterous laugh out in the pod. It was a voice I hadn't heard before but definitely one that merited some attention. I hurriedly stuffed my new socks inside a slit on the end of my mattress and went outside my cell door to see what the commotion was about. There was a mountain of a man dressed in the usual new arrival attire standing center stage at the entrance to the pod. He had an audience of inmates around him, obviously guys who knew him from previous federal facilities. It looked like a family reunion of sorts.

I had to go meet this guy. His laugh was contagious! The guys around him introduced me as Gov, and he introduced himself as Big Tex. He seemed to dwarf those of us standing around him. One glimpse, and I figured this kid could have picked my old Ford tractor up like a Tinkertoy. Buddha knew the kid. They were from the same general area in Texas. Tex was a black kid and a former member of the Crips, but he sure didn't act like a gangster. I couldn't help but ask him how long he'd been lifting weights. "Shit, Gov, feel dis." With that, he flexed his bicep. I swear, it felt like steel. While I was mesmerized by this seemingly gentle giant, he couldn't help but notice the growth pulling at my eyelid. The other guys were like me; they were getting used to it. "Damn, man," he said, "what the hell wrong with you eye?" I told him it had been that way for a while, but trips to sick call weren't helping it. Tex was quick to respond. "Gov, I'd tell those mothafuckas they betta fix this damn eye, else I'd be puttin' something on they ass Ajax won't take off!" With that, he broke into a boisterous laugh, and I couldn't help but laugh with him.

Using my political skills, I talked the laundry boss into putting Tex to work in laundry fold. Big Tex and I were both proud of that achievement, and we became best of buddies. He was the consummate showman, loved attention, and usually always had the floor! He could be a real politician, a Crip and street gangster, or the shy black gentle giant you'd want as your personal chauffeur.

While at work in laundry fold, we'd all share stories and, in some cases, swap lies. The storytelling would generally last as long as the work shift did. I'd tell them of fine meals and Crown Royal provided by capitol lobbyists and of trips on corporate jets with the big oilies. I told them of meeting President Clinton and nominating Al Gore at the National Convention in Los Angeles. These were stories I'd tell over and over as the guys could seem to never hear them enough. Of course, they would all want to know where I hid all the money, and could they go with me to dig it up when we all got out! I couldn't make them believe that I could get in such a mess and end up destitute. It took quite the fool to have the opportunity I'd had and manage to throw it all away.

Diez would talk of his beautiful senorita and the hopes and dreams they once shared back in their old homeland of Mexico. Not to let a good opportunity pass, Tex would butt in and ask him if he managed to get any of that good marijuana smuggled up to his cell.

Then Tony, another Hispanic who was busted for hauling cocaine in his thriving trucking business in New York, would take his turn. Tony always had the same story, and we'd all patiently listen, as if it were just as funny as the first time he told it. He claimed when the feds asked him what he was doing with fifty kilos of cocaine in the freighter, he told them it was for his personal use. He loved that line and told it to every newcomer.

Tex always had a good gangster story of brandishing automatic weapons and controlling the drug trade in the whole south side of Houston, Texas. Naturally, Big Tex had to have a bigger story than the next guy. I cut in on one of his stories and said, "Come on, Tex, you probably ran around with a bunch of white nerds when you were in junior high."

He said, "Gov, da only white dude I ever seen down in da projects was da bail bondsman. He was an old white man with a big gray beard. We all thought he was Santa Claus!"

Regardless of Big Tex's big stories, the one thing he couldn't hide was his big heart. If he thought there was a crate too heavy for the Gov to lift, he'd lift it himself.

Tex caught on that every Saturday morning, I'd be up early, dodging the guards and preparing my weekend burritos with the smuggled ingredients. He noticed I was always running short on cheese, as cheese was a precious commodity up in the cadre unit and very hard to come by. The good cheese was kept in the officers' mess hall, next door to laundry fold. It took a pretty good smuggler to get to that cheese! It wasn't like the imitation cheese kept in the inmate's cafeteria; it was the real thing. Guys who got caught trying to steal the good stuff out of the officer's diner were sent straight to the SHU!

One Friday afternoon, I left my work station a couple of hours early for another visit to sick call, trying desperately to get some relief for my eye. By the time I waited out the line at sick call and got my usual runaround, the guys in laundry had already finished their shift and were back in the unit upstairs. When I walked into the pod, I could see Big Tex sitting across the way, and I could tell he was watching me as I headed toward my cell to put my laundry bag inside. When I opened the cell door, I nearly fainted. There was a thirty-pound block of mozzarella cheese sitting on top of my locker plain as day. The unit officer wasn't ten steps behind me. How do you hide a thirty-pound block of mozzarella in an eight-by-nine cell in fifteen seconds? I could hear Tex laughing outside in the pod loud enough to wake the dead. Knowing I was probably scared half out of my wits, Tex distracted the officer long enough for me to get that block of cheese hidden. How he managed to get that big block of mozzarella out of the officer's mess hall and up the elevator escorted by the prison cops, I'll never know, but I sure had plenty of good cheese, and Tex had plenty of good laughs.

When Thanksgiving rolled around, I felt as though I'd been in prison for years. It was the first Thanksgiving in over forty years that I wouldn't be with my brothers and my boys at the deer camp or sitting around the family table for Thanksgiving dinner. Although every day was long inside the pen, holidays were the longest. We got a day off work for Thanksgiving and would receive a special meal in honor of the traditional holiday. I got up early, just as I had done every day, stood at the cell door, and waited for the guard to make his morning rounds unlocking each cell door. That morning, I started out on much the same routine as I would do on weekends. I made a cup of instant coffee, hooked my small transistor radio to the waist of my khakis, and put in my earbuds.

While having my coffee, Gage walked across the pod and wished me a happy Thanksgiving and asked how my family was doing back home. He was the same polite and respectful young man as the day I'd met him. After my coffee, I set out on my exercise routine, walking the perimeter of each of the three cadre units. I'd walk the perimeter of E pod then D pod and back down the long hallway to F pod. I'd always notice who was up early and would often wonder what they were thinking as they stared in silence toward the muted TV. I paid special attention that Thanksgiving morning.

As I walked around D pod, I saw Vance and Willie. Both were from Eastern Oklahoma and both had a history of drug abuse, showing the telltale signs of rotten teeth and tattooed arms. Vance was doing six years and Willie thirteen. They both had a humble and kind spirit that always made me feel welcome in their presence. They would have been my dad's kind of people too. Willie had no high school diploma and no social pedigree but was kindhearted as they come.

Then there was Arteuro and Tony over at the Mexican table. Tony was my coworker in laundry, and Arteuro was a veteran of the war in Iraq. Both were handsome and smart young Hispanics who showed me tons of respect, both with families too far away for visits.

Making my rounds at F pod, I noticed Brother Johnson reading his Bible and giving council to one of our mentally unstable brothers of the circle. Looking toward the rec deck, I could see Cody warming up for a game of handball. Most of the guys were all sleeping in for the holiday.

When I came back to E pod, old Fitz was outside his cell dusting off the powder, and Buddha was on the treadmill in the small fitness room. Young Petros was pacing back and forth, looking lost and miserable. His ninety-two-year-old grandmother and a younger aunt had made a seven-hour drive from West Texas to pay him a special Thanksgiving visit. One of the prison employees had turned them away because something wasn't filled out properly on their visitation form. Petros had tears in his eyes while trying to explain the mix-up to me, as if I could do something about it. There was a day that I probably could have, but not today.

Petros was half white, half Hispanic, and somewhere in his midthirties. Both he and his wife were doing time for making meth. She was locked up somewhere in Texas doing nine years, and he was doing thirteen. Petros—or Pete, as I called him—had the heart and, at times, the mind of a child. He absolutely loved playing cards with me. Whenever he'd win (which was seldom) I'd curse and throw the cards in the floor, putting on a real show for him. Of course, my fits were greatly embellished, but it just tickled him to death. I cut my walk short that morning and played cards with Pete.

After the 10:00 a.m. count that day, I got in line with the rest of the cadre unit for the Thanksgiving meal. All my fellow inmates seemed to be especially cleaned up and sharp looking, as if they were going somewhere special. For many of them, Thanksgiving dinner in the federal pen was special. The dinner was a home run! Good ham, a slice of turkey breast, green beans, mashed potatoes, and a small portion of pecan pie. Even Mr.

Chairman enjoyed the meal. The prison staff had gone out of their way to make Thanksgiving special.

After dinner, the recreation boss devised several competitive tournament brackets: washer throwing (which I hurriedly signed up for), three-on-three basketball, and even a spades tournament. After signing up for the washer-throwing tournament, I got busy looking for a spades partner. My old partner, Griff, didn't have steam enough to even play cards. When I approached Big Tex at the proposition of partnering up, he laughed that Big Tex laugh and said, "Hell no, I ain't being partners with no blind-ass motherfucker!" Then he really laughed big, as well as everyone else within hearing distance.

Though I had no formal education, representing the folks in House District 17 was a natural fit for me. The years of being a jack-of-all-trades had given me insight you can't find in a college classroom. Moreover, it was the best job I'd ever had, and I loved every minute of it! My passion was helping people who I knew and those who had no means of helping themselves. Most of the calls I got were clearly made out of desperation. I understood them because I had been in their shoes at one time or another. The ability or power it took to answer their calls of desperation didn't come from my brain, it came from the friends I had made in the legislature. I had enough friends who would stay with me on critical votes and make it, at the very least, difficult to pass any meaningful legislation without my support. So when some high-minded bureaucrat told one of my constituents there was nothing they could do to help them, I had the leverage to make them find a way to help. Nothing chapped me more than a utility company standing at the trough with their hand out while they didn't bat an eye at turning some poor sap's electricity off. That being said, I had about as much business being Democratic Party chairman as I did kissing up to those chamber board members. Chairing a political party had nothing to do with helping people and everything to do with hurting people. That's a position designed for an attack dog. I was more like the dog that got his teeth hung up in ole Roy's hubcap.

Events had been unfolding, even as I ran for my first term of office that would be the undoing of both myself and the Oklahoma Democratic Party. At the time, there were six congressional offices representing Oklahoma's interests in Washington, DC. The Third Congressional District, which included State House District 17, was considered Oklahoma's Little Dixie. It was one of the last remaining Democratic strongholds in the state. As old Doc once put it, Little Dixie democrats were Yellow Dog Democrats, meaning they would vote for an old yellow dog before they would vote Republican!

Little Dixie politics was a world all to itself, as issues there rarely reflected those in any other quadrant of the state. Political speakings were better attended and often more intense. To the crowd, it was entertainment at its best, and to the politicians, it was serious business.

One of the more heated issues during the 1990s was the proposed sale of water out of the Kiamichi River Basin to North Texas. In all reality, no one was for the proposed transfer of water, except for the Choctaw Chief and his arsenal of attorneys. Of course, the Choctaw Chief didn't have to answer to the locals. He got his votes the old-fashioned way, with lots of cash and absentee voters. Any other politician brave enough, or stupid enough, who even considered the notion of selling water was run out of office on a rail!

Every organization in Southeast Oklahoma was up in arms at the very thought of selling our water rights, so every week or two, a rally against the proposal would ensue. Naturally, every politician in Little Dixie was expected to attend and voice their opposition. A no-show was reason enough to make you suspect. To show up and give a good speech in opposition was a reelection guarantee. Since finding a politician in support of the sale was hard to do, speeches against it became quite competitive. That meant that you had to convince folk that you were more against it than your opponent was!

One Saturday evening, the McCurtain County Cattleman Association joined forces with a couple of other groups that were opposed to the sale and held a campaign speaking night on the banks of the Little River in McCurtain County.

On my way to the event, I stopped in Pushmataha County and picked up a couple of my county commissioner friends, both of whom had opposition for their upcoming elections. We made small talk on our way through the winding narrow roads from Antlers to Broken Bow, neither of us tipping our hands as to what we would say in our speech for fear the other would steal our material. Of course, I fancied myself as the king speech giver and storyteller, so I wasn't too fearful of getting upstaged.

When we arrived, the sun was beginning to settle below the pine covered Kiamichi Mountains. The event was held near a cabin tucked away in a lush green valley adjacent to the crystal clear water of Little River. Smoke from the large BBQ pit next to the rough cedar cabin was drifting above the large crowd, and people in various cliques were abuzz, eagerly awaiting the arrival of all the politicians. Appetites would be held at bay until after the speakin' was over, a trick long since learned in order to hold the crowd.

When all had arrived, the president of the Cattleman's Association stood on the porch of the small cabin and called the speakin' to order. One by one, he would introduce us politicians, each of us trying to outdo the other with our "save the water" speech.

I was particularly interested in hearing what one of my county commissioner friends had to say because I had never heard him give a speech. He was a short potbellied fellow with a western straw hat, with jeans and boots fitting for the occasion. Having been introduced, he took to the porch, walked over to one side, and stared silently off toward Little River. After a minute or two, the crowd became deathly quiet. I thought maybe he had frozen up or forgotten what he was going to say. About then, he turned and faced the crowd while he pointed toward the river. "Ladies and gentlemen," he said, "my mama used to fetch water out of that beautiful river to wash our clothes in." He went on to say, "These are the pristine waters we've baptized our kids in." Then morphing his face and demeanor from giving a heartfelt sermon to a fiery scolding, he shouted, "Now those Texans want to use it to wash the whisky out of their shot glasses and the blood off their abortion room floors!" Continuing his chastising of those dirty Texans, he worked the crowd into a frenzy and assured himself of a reelection bid.

On the drive back to his home in Antlers, the other friend and I were all but speechless. Neither of us had any idea our buddy was such an orator, especially one so full of the Holy Ghost. As we entered the city limit sign in Antlers, I broke the silence and asked our newly discovered religious orator if he had seen many black bear in the Antlers area. Without hesitation he responded, "Not nearly enough. I wish some of them would move in closer to town and eat some of these lazy ass kids roaming the streets!"

The Third Congressional District had been most notably represented by the esteemed Carl Albert. Coming from the small community of Bugtussle in Pittsburg County, Albert had gone on to become a Rhodes Scholar, attend Oxford, and become Speaker of the United States House of Representatives. He represented Little Dixie in Congress from 1947 until 1977, when he retired. One of Mr. Albert's old campaign strategists told me they literally had to find him an opponent, pay their filing fee, and generate their own race just so folks wouldn't forget he was still in office!

Speaker Albert was replaced by a young man from Bentville, Oklahoma, who had graduated from Oklahoma State University. His name was Les Atkins. He too was a Yellow Dog Democrat.

The first time I met Congressman Atkins was at a conservation awards banquet I had organized for the conservation district.

Doc, being well acquainted with Les, had invited him to be our keynote speaker. During his speech, Les unloaded a flurry of attacks on my then hero Ronald Reagan. I was a neophyte as far as politics was concerned, but I listened intently as Les pounded his fist and bemoaned the president's policy of trickle-down economics. I wondered what all that had to do with conservation, but little Les was undeterred, warning the crowd of Reagan's voodoo economics and the underhanded Republican trickery. I dared not tell anyone I had voted for Reagan, especially old Doc.

Having served as Little Dixie's yellow dog congressman for nearly fifteen years, Les decided the time was right to make a bid for Oklahoma's governor. At the same time, an unknown named Mike Mass was making a bid for State House District 17. Les's campaign theme was to "Turn the lights back on in Oklahoma." During the campaign that summer, I didn't see much of Les. I saw a lot of his primary opponent, a brash young Democrat upstart named David Walters. Les was busy working other areas of the state, figuring he had Little Dixie in the bag. The highlight of Les's campaign was these clever brochures he had printed featuring a big lightbulb on the cover. He was gonna "turn the lights back on in Oklahoma."

As told to me later by one of his campaign aides, Les and his crew were on their way to a big rally in Ada with a large cache of the brochures stashed in the rear of their station wagon. As they approached the last town within fifty miles of Ada, the aide proclaimed, "Last chance for a bathroom break. Anyone need to stop?" Les hurriedly motioned with his hand. "Ain't got time, gonna be late!" Just a few miles down the road, however, Les piped up again, "Pull over, pull over! Gotta go, gotta go!" On a long stretch of Highway 270, flanked on both sides by a good growth of Oklahoma weeds, they pulled onto the shoulder to give Les a much-needed bathroom break. Exiting the vehicle, he asked for toilet paper, which nobody had. Making the best of a bad situation, Les grabbed a handful of the new brochures and waded uncomfortably through the weeds out of sight. The driver turned to the aide and asked, "How do you think the campaigns going?"

The senior aide responded, "I don't know, but I'll bet David Walters ain't wadin' Johnson grass waist deep and wiping his ass on his own brochures!" To make a long story short, Les got his lights turned off by the new Democrat from Western Oklahoma.

After only one term as Oklahoma's governor, Walters called it quits. Both he and his family had suffered great loss in the sometimes harsh and unforgiving Oklahoma political climate. Again, little Les threw his hat in the ring, only this time as an Independent. He had either been impressed by H. Ross Perot's sudden political popularity or mad at the Democrats who had let him down in his first attempt. Either way, he was no longer a Little Dixie Democrat. Managing only to siphon enough votes from our Democratic nominee, Les handed the executive office to a former prosecutor of the Reagan Administration and a Republican stalwart, Drake Meely.

At the beginning of my fourth term in office, Les's replacement in the Third Congressional office was stepping down to take a position lobbying for the NRA. A fellow named Newt Gingrich had a new contract for America, and the Christian Coalition was going strong. Congressional Republicans offered little Les a job on the prestigious Ways and Means committee, along with restoration of his full seniority, in exchange for his changing his registration to Republican. Les obliged, and the rest is history. The long-held bitter taste of those Hoover rabbits by Oklahoma's Little Dixie Democrats had been replaced by a fear of losing their guns to the government and their souls to the devil! The little congressman I'd heard so passionately berate those wine-sipping, blue-blood Republicans was now Little Dixie's first Republican congressman since statehood.

Les's victory wasn't without a fight, however. There was a veteran state senator who took the fight personally. His name was Mr. Stokes. Senator Stokes had his own dog in the fight, a young artist and fiddle player with loads of talent. The only problem was that he would have a primary opponent—a former state senator from Ardmore who had his own following, making the pool of campaign cash somewhat limited. Les didn't have that problem. The GOP had pumped more than three million dollars into their new fair-haired boy's political war chest. Senator Stokes didn't give a damn about limited resources because he had plenty of cash. He just needed to figure out how to get it funneled into the fiddle player's campaign, and he did—by violating every federal election rule on the books!

By this time in my political career, the senator and I had a pretty good relationship; after all, we served a lot of the same constituency. He was a political icon in Oklahoma and probably the single most reason term limits had been imposed. There wasn't much middle ground for Stokes. People either loved him or hated him. Over the years, he had become somewhat vulnerable in his senate races, barely squeaking by on occasion. His last couple of races he even hitched his wagon to mine in order to get all the Democrat votes he could. He needed every last one of them! I didn't care, though. Mr. Stokes had forgotten more about politics than I would ever know. I just enjoyed his company when we rode together to OKC. I got to hear a wealth of old political stories. After all, he was plunging headlong into politics while the doctor at St. Mary's hospital was cutting my umbilical cord.

There seemed to be two sides to the veteran senator—one that was genuine, caring, and helpful and the other that was callous and calculated.

By my third term in office, his driver's licenses had been revoked as a result of a DUI. Most people viewed the DUI as just another example of the powerful senator having his own way and doing as he damn well pleased. It sure didn't seem to hinder his reelection bid the following summer. Not only was his driver's license revoked, but he was ordered to do some hours of community service. Part of that was done picking up litter at one of the state parks. He grinned when he told me how many votes he picked up while picking up trash.

The upside of his DUI for me was that it left him riding to and from the state capitol with me exclusively for the better part of a year. During those trips, he shared stories and events that were unfolding while I was busy picking blackberries with my older brother and sister.

He told of how he'd ridden the train with Harry Truman and of his acquaintance with Johnny Carson during his stint in the military. He reminisced of growing up with his siblings in the rugged hills of Southeast Oklahoma and how he'd upset a favorite McClain son in his first political race.

I drove and listened. He would chuckle when telling of his early legislation that was still on the books, like the flashpoint of Eastern Oklahoma coal. He told me of how one of his country neighbors had complained of trespassers who were stealing his pecans and how he attempted to help by passing legislation that would penalize folks for picking up pecans that weren't theirs. After passing the legislation, he discovered just how many friends and supporters he had who were picking up those pecans! He talked, and we both laughed while the stories inside him overflowed.

In the same comedic tone, he told of being indicted by the FBI for income tax evasion and how he beat them at their own game. With a menacing smile, he quipped, "It helps when you have a good friend on the jury."

He also told of how he'd represented a young marine who was facing a court-martial during the course of the Vietnam War, at no cost. The old senator wasn't about to let the federal government hang the kid out to dry, much less pass on an opportunity to be involved in such a high-profile case.

I had witnessed the flip side of the senator's personality early in my political career when I unknowingly killed one of his bills on the House floor. At that time, I didn't have sense enough to pay attention to the author's name that appeared at the top of the legislation. As chairman of the senate transportation committee, he had filed the bill in response to federal law that would withhold a portion of transportation funds from states that didn't impose a strict helmet law for motorcyclists.

I really didn't have a dog in the fight, save one neighbor who was a cycle enthusiast and had called me in opposition to the bill. Nevertheless, after the bill was introduced on the House floor, I raised my hand in opposition. Using a little country humor and appealing to freedom in the name of the stars and stripes, my debate brought on an arousing response from my House colleagues. Old John removed a small American flag from his desk and began waving it while shouting, "Here, here!" Other House members joined in. Some pounding their desks, others whistling. They loved hearing a good debate, especially one delivered with such ease against such a powerful state senator. They didn't have a clue that I was oblivious to the bill's principal author!

Debates rarely change the outcome of a vote, but this one did, and the bill failed miserably short of a majority vote.

Later that afternoon, I was summoned by the senator's secretary to his spacious senate office. Upon arriving, I could see that his office was packed as usual. Standing from behind his large conference table, he motioned me in as if I were the most important person there. It thoroughly impressed me that the senator would acknowledge me in front of what seemed to be a very distinguished group. My head still swollen from the accolades I'd received for my rousing debate, I was now ready for my sterling introduction in the senator's office.

The old senator stood, peering over his black-rimmed glasses and proceeded to give me an undressing for all within hearing distance to witness. By the time he was done, I had no doubt whose legislation I had derailed. I was stunned and thoroughly humiliated. I was on his turf, in front of his friends, and there was little I could do but take it.

My instincts were begging to curse him back; my brain, however, and the politician inside me were telling me different. So biting my tongue and swallowing my pride, I left his office both embarrassed and seething with anger.

Within a week, he came lumbering into my modest House office, hugged and charmed the daylights out of my secretary, and acted as though I was his best friend. The public scolding that had left me rattled was all in a day's work to him.

Serving as the senator's counterpart in the House was a double-edged sword. On one hand, his insight, power, and influence could help you tremendously. On the other, his half a century of political baggage was a liability. Neither the general public nor the media would allow middle ground. Getting along with him made me his crony; butting heads with him would render me ineffective. As far as I was concerned, the latter wasn't an option.

By the time I had arrived on the political scene, the senator's days of conjuring up pork dollars and worrying about his constituency had long since passed. He was perfectly content rolling with the flow, chairing his long-standing transportation committee, and pulling the strings far beyond the state's business. By then, his interests were more focused on the price of oil, the stock market, and what federal judge or prosecutor he might get appointed. As a result, an unspoken quid pro quo was developing in our relationship. I would take care of the home folk, and he would take care of the "big deals." We would ride each other's coattails.

In the midst of the ghost investigation, which came later, I went over to his capitol senate office to seek some advice. I knew that one of his old senate colleagues and a personal friend of his was on the list of accused ghosts. When I asked how his friend was holding up, the senator said he didn't know the guy. I was shocked and immediately dropped the subject. I figured the senator was either in early stages of Alzheimer or suspected me of wearing a wire. Either way, it was disconcerting to me. As I left his office, I asked his longtime senate secretary if he was all right. She pulled me in close and said, "Michael, he'll step on every head in the pond to keep his feet dry." Coming from her, I thought, that was a mouthful! She hadn't even been privy to our conversation.

Oh well, back to the campaign against Les. I had managed to avoid the campaign for most of that race, mainly because I was friends with both Democrats in the race and had better things to do than get involved in a fight between the two of them. Furthermore, whichever one won the primary, I figured would be a shoo-in come fall. I never even considered the fact that Little Dixie would vote Republican. With only a couple of weeks before the primary and against my better judgment, I let my conscience get the better of me. Knowing how Senator Stokes had vested himself in the fiddler's campaign, I stopped by his law office to lend some support. I was hoping they would send me to speak at some pie supper that neither candidate would attend. As usual, I figured all wrong. His receptionist scurried to his office to let him know I was there and ready to help out. Barking out from his office, I could hear him plainly from the waiting area. "Hell yes, we need help, we need money!" I was somewhat relieved because I knew that he knew I didn't have any money to give! Within seconds, however, he was front and center. "Money's what we need, Michael, money!"

I thought maybe he didn't know, so I told him, "Senator, I don't have any money to give."

"I got plenty of money, Michael. We just need to get it into the campaign!" He had his secretary make out a check for ten thousand dollars, payable to me, and told me to split it up among some friends, and we could all donate. Knowing full well it violated federal election laws, I took the check and did just that. I figured, he must know what he's doing. He's been a lawyer for almost fifty years! Besides, I was glad he hadn't asked me to give half a dozen campaign speeches my heart wasn't into. I had no idea how many other straw donors he had used.

Even though the senator's fiddler won the primary, he was trounced in the general election, and Little Dixie's reign had come to an end. After that election and with a seemingly untouchable Republican governor, Oklahoma's Democratic Party began crumbling like wet corn bread. Adding insult to injury, fallout from the fiddler's campaign became a weekly barrage of bad press, and Stokes was up to his ears in FEC investigations. Consequently, by the time I became Democrat party chair, the party was over.

Chairing the party wasn't without its rewards to some degree. It afforded me the opportunity to meet President Bill Clinton when he landed at Tinker Air Force Base en route to speak to families, who had lost loved ones in the Murrah Federal Building bombing. It also landed me in venues where I would meet Patrick Kennedy, Jesse Jackson, and the now infamous John Edwards. I sat within fifty feet of former President Jimmy Carter and soaked in every speech at the 2000 national convention in Los Angeles. Being Mr. Chairman also gave me opportunities to rub elbows with democratic heavy hitters statewide that I otherwise would never have met, none of whom would become lifelong friends.

Another benefit of holding the distinguished title of Mr. Chairman came in a subtle way. While my detractors were honed in on party issues, I could hone in on my role as appropriations chair. So while the right wing was busy pointing out my immorality and the left wing was crying for attention, I was sending good chunks of the state coffers back home to the poor folk. In my hometown alone, I helped fund a new fire station, a new clinic, a new senior center, and a new sports complex for the high school. I also accommodated the city with funding for a water-bottling plant, a new swimming pool, a ballpark, and new bleachers for their rodeo arena. Surrounding communities in Southeast

Oklahoma also reaped the benefits, as I rarely said no to a legitimate request. I helped with community centers, roads, rural hospital repairs, fire trucks, storm shelters, schools, museums, and I even managed to help one small town acquire a drug dog.

I was out of my league, however, trying to run with the big dogs. When shit hit the fan, it didn't seem to stick to them like it did to me. At one point, news broke that our Republican governor had received a quarter million in cash from a friend of his that was in the drug-manufacturing business. He wanted our governor to help get his product pushed wholesale via the state's prison system. When the news hit the state paper, the governor said the cash gift wasn't his. It was given to his children to be used for their college. Besides that, he reinforced his Christian values by offering to give the money back as to avoid the very appearance of evil. Now that's a Christian. I wouldn't advise that approach if you get caught robbing a bank, however! The governor also got some publicity when one of his generous political donors landed a more than generous contract to renovate the state's airplane. Being the good Democrat I was, I couldn't help but have a little fun at the governor's expense. During a parade that was organized in my district featuring both himself and my republican opponent as grand marshals, I affixed a homemade wooden airplane on a pole that attached to the back of a four-wheeler. I painted the letters "GOP" on the side of the homemade aircraft and spelled out in large letters "Governor on Parade." While the governor and my opponent led the parade in a horse-drawn buggy, one of my brothers drove the four-wheeler in circles around them. Everyone thought it was funny, except the governor. I thought he got off easy. Whenever I got bad press, it was followed up by a badge and a gun.

It seemed as though it were yesterday when I donned the thirty-dollar wig, the cheap suit, and boarded the old Lincoln with old John. Time had moved as swift as the water beneath Gaines Creek Bridge. The political landscape had changed, and so had I, but I failed to acknowledge the change in either. The ability to sign off on spreadsheets and allocations involving six-digit figures had swallowed up my sense of reality back home, and the briefcase-laden friends crowded in the foyer of my office were superficial as well. At home, I was as good as bankrupt, but I continued to operate as if there were no tomorrow. On weekends, I'd hit the slots in Bossier City, and on Monday, I'd call my banker. He was more than congenial. After all, I was Mr. Chairman. If on the auction block one could have bought me for what I was worth and sold me for what I thought I was worth, they could have made a mint!

# 20

At the start of my sixth term as representative of House District 17, the Honorable Les Atkins announced that he would not seek another term for the United States Congress. Little Dixie's Third Congressional seat was wide open for the taking. Staring down the barrel of state term limits and having as much name recognition, if not more, than any potential candidate for the prized seat, I quickly announced my intentions to run. The Third Congressional District was tailor-made for Mike Mass. I knew the folk and spoke their language. I was on my way to Congress!

In the beginning, it was all hands on deck. Fund-raisers for the outgoing Mr. Chairman and incoming Mr. Congressman sprang up rapidly. A young man with soft white hands and a newfangled laptop computer had been referred to help in my efforts to raise campaign funds. At a glance, I could tell the kid had never hit a lick in the hayfields, much less swung an ax, but he came highly recommended. I was now on a much larger playing field. The first meeting we had, he opened his little laptop and scrolled through a list of potential donors. The list was endless and the names unfamiliar. In fact, I didn't recognize any of them, save a handful. As he explained, these were folks who paid to play and were well accustomed to the game. Not that they expected any great deals, but if they call their Congressman, they sure didn't want to speak with an aide. They didn't need to know me or what I stood for. They were merely players. Although uncomfortable, I began calling, and quickly found out he was right! I began raising money from people I'd never met. My newfound fund-raising technique, combined with my popularity in Little Dixie's Third District, had me well on my way.

Despite the solid start, unforeseeable problems soon reared their ugly head. Almost midway through the campaign, the census bureau announced their latest population count, and it wasn't good. Oklahoma had lost enough numbers to force a reduction in congressional districts from six down to five. That meant reapportioning congressional boundary lines, as well as state House and senate districts, which would occur during my last legislative session and only months before the primary election. The senate proposed a plan that extended the Third District west along the Red River, encompassing areas favorable to their majority leader, who also wanted to run for the seat. The House, barely hanging on to a democratic majority, could never agree on a plan. The governor with whom I'd had so much fun in the parade submitted a plan that completely did away with Little Dixie's Third District. It combined the area into northeast Oklahoma's Second Congressional District, a seat that already had a sitting Democratic congressman. The governor won out.

I immediately began getting calls encouraging me to drop out of the race. The speaker of the US House of Representatives, Dick Gephardt, called. My good friend and former governor David Walters called. People whose names appeared on the laptop began calling. They wanted their contributions back. Absolutely no one who was anyone wanted me to force a primary race in the Second District, but I was not in a listening mood. Politically charged and ego filled, I took it personally and forged ahead, dragging a handful of loyal supporters and my family through a no-win situation.

With fund-raising all but dried up, I took to the road, a dismal reminder of my first campaign. Only this wasn't four counties, it was the entire eastern side of the state! Door knocking and event hopping was outdated and paled in comparison to the full-colored mail-outs and TV ads brought on by my opponent. I thought there might be a slim chance that the folks I'd helped over the last decade would rally in my support. After all, there wasn't a rural fire department, a county, or a small municipality that the REAP program I'd sponsored hadn't helped in some way, not to mention the special pork packages I'd sent throughout areas all over Eastern Oklahoma.

Since the sprawling Second District reached from the Kansas boarder up north to the Red River down south, I'd need the services of a driver. I recruited a former House colleague from Checotah Oklahoma named Bobby Frame. Bobby wasn't only a loyal friend, he had an outgoing personality that was genuine and real. Moreover, he could shake hands with a roomful of people before the average politician could get on the porch!

Bobby also had a quality that is rarely found in politicians, a demeanor that appeared to be completely void of an ego. He had the heart of a servant and was in no need of personal accolades. While most of us were decorating our office walls with plaques and overglorified certificates of approval, Bobby decorated his with a stringer of mounted bass he'd caught in the local farm ponds of McIntosh County.

His realness led him to be a favorite among House staffers and legislative assistants. One morning, he made an appearance in full Batman regalia, dashing in and out of House offices like a true superhero. Of course, these were antics that made House leadership cringe. They would have cringed even more had they known how much of the state's coffers Bobby was delivering to his constituency back home!

During the campaign for party chair, Senator Stokes hooked Bobby and me up with a small single-engine aircraft, allowing us to make a personal appearance at several conventions that were being held the same day across the state. It seemed as though we were cramped inside the small airplane hopping from county to county as much as we were shaking hands and campaigning delegates on the ground. That night, on the way home as we were descending over the McClain city limits, the small aircraft stalled, the lone engine sputtering at first and finally going completely silent. While the pilot was frantically pulling and pushing various levers and controls, I was all but paralyzed. Although we could see the lights on the landing strip below, we were a long way from a safe landing. Leaning forward from the small rear seat, Bobby put his hand on my shoulder and said, "Damn, Dad, wish we were a little higher up. I don't have time to make it right with the Lord this close to the ground." Lucky for us both, the pilot was skilled enough to glide in on "thin air" for a shaky but safe landing.

After serving only two terms in the House, Bobby removed himself from the political arena. He would devote full time to his family, as well as the time needed to rise above his own personal demons. Having him back in the fray of a political campaign as we traveled the narrow highways of Eastern Oklahoma was a win-win for me.

One group in particular that was a benefactor of my efforts was called Councils of State Government or COGs, as they were referred to. They were a quasi-entity of both state and federal government, and they ran the Senior Nutrition program, Rural Fire program, and an assortment of economic development initiatives. More recently, they were charged with dispersing REAP grant funds, which I had not only pushed into law but also helped the COG directors get rights to administer the program. They were all frequent visitors to my office with the high back chairs, and all were in constant need of Special Project funds.

Seeking support from this group was a no-brainer, so my chauffeur and I began our visits with the COG located in far

Northeast Oklahoma and right on the porch steps of my opponent and sitting Democratic congressman. The director there greeted me with open arms and a reassuring smile. We visited about the recent reapportionment and made small talk, and I politely asked for his support, knowing it went without saying. With his confirming handshake, I hurried from his office to make the next stop on my hectic schedule. Approaching the exit door from the building, I realized I had left my itinerary lying on a small conference table in the director's office, so I made an about-face and returned to retrieve it. As I unexpectedly entered his office, he was rehanging a large portrait of the sitting congressman neatly behind his desk. So much for my short-lived boost of confidence.

Both the legislative session and my sixth term in office were over that year. The filing deadline for those candidates who were considering state and federal offices would occur in less than a month, which meant I still had time to reconsider. The handwriting was clearly on the wall. All I need do was spit out my pride and take a cushioned job from any number of sources that would have gladly handed me a title just to get me out of the race. Pride, however, is not an easy thing to swallow, especially by a politician. Besides, I was about to meet a character that was full of inspiration and cash!

Knowing I was up against it, Mr. Stokes's law office secretary recommended I talk to an obscure associate of the senator's. They were longtime partners in a variety of business. During my twelve years in office, I had seen the guy a couple of times while he was helping out in one of the senator's campaigns but had never been formally introduced. I thought he was one of Stokes's house boys. I had no idea that he was loaded with his own cash! Within five minutes of our introduction, the guy was already laying out a winning strategy, along with a "leave it to him" fundraising scheme.

His wife had a successful business as well, and why, in all the years I had been in office, we hadn't been introduced before, I had no idea. Be that as it may, in a week's time, he had already managed to acquire a truckload of new campaign signs, along with a crew to put them up. He had a fund-raiser schedule and booked a professional recording studio to make radio ads. This guy was a one-man campaign staff! When life had you down, it really doesn't take much to pick you back up. My newfound friend had breathed life back into my deflated ego, just enough life to make me oblivious to the inevitable butt kicking I was about to take.

His fund-raising ability, along with the slick radio ads and my clever stump speeches were just enough to bring out the wrath from the well-funded congressman's campaign. I'd shoot my opponent with a BB gun, and he'd bust me in the backside with a 10-gauge shotgun! Two weeks before the election, he buried me beneath so many negative campaign ads, I was embarrassed to leave my hometown. In politics, everything is fair game, and he used it all. The only difference between him and that female prosecutor who smeared my reputation in front of a small grand jury was the size of the audience. On election night, I was humiliated in front of my own watch party. I guess you could say I had it coming. Nevertheless, within ninety short days, I went from Mr. Chairman to the laughing stock of Oklahoma politics.

The following week was eerie and distorted. For the first time in over a decade, my phone was silent. I felt like I was alone, sitting in the rubble and smoke of a bombed-out building. Thirty years earlier, my father had been in an explosion at the Army Ammunition plant near McClain. It was considered the worst tragedy in the Army Ammunition facility history. It claimed the lives of two of dad's coworkers and left him buried beneath ten feet of smoldering debris. Dad described how it felt when the explosion occurred. He said the blast was so loud and so close, he didn't hear it. He just felt a ringing sensation in his ears and felt a shock, like an electrical shock, and felt as though he were in a powerful vacuum. In an instant, he was numb and trapped in a dark, smoky place. There appeared to be a rat's nest of sorts burning just inches from his face. With a chew of Five Brothers Tobacco still lodged in his jaw, he spit the small blaze into submission. He was literally buried alive ten feet beneath the rubble. In an odd sort of way, and at least to some extent, I could now relate to the mental state of mind he must have been in. The only difference was Dad was a man of principle and character who ended up in a place of circumstances beyond his control. I was a fool's fool who ended up in the bed I had made.

After twelve years of politics, I had ostracized myself from "the Church" and, to some extent, felt as though "the Church" had ostracized me. My political groupies vanished like they did from the mansion during the ghost scandal, and although the world kept right on turning, I was lost. Over the past several years, the local papers had kept my name front and center and all positive, even during the ghost scandal. They liked my ability to keep the state funds flowing through communities in Southeast Oklahoma, but now they were silent. The only publicity I had now was an editorial by the *Muskogee Phoenix* berating my campaign signs that still littered their precious right of ways. A week or so after the beating, I was paid a visit by my new friend who'd come to the aide of my congressional campaign. The visit did pick my spirits up a bit because outside my family, no one else seemed to care whether I was dead or alive. During the brief visit, he reminded me that all was not lost and that although there were only a few months before my term expired, I was still a state representative, as well as Mr. Appropriation Chairman. He even managed to get a few chuckles out of me, something I hadn't done for quite some time. Before he left, he asked if I could muster up some state funds in a joint venture with the McClain Foundation to acquire a building he planned to convert to a manufacturing facility. He planned to call it Superior Products. I'd forgotten I still had some clout left and assured him

I'd make a few calls. After he left, however, I got involved helping my brothers prepare for a craft show and, although somewhat reinvigorated by his visit, forgot all about his request. A few days later, he called to ask if I had made any headway in obtaining the funds. Completely embarrassed, I explained that I had gotten busy soon after our visit and plain forgot, but assured him I would follow through. Thinking I needed some incentive, he told me that he'd give me 10 percent of the amount requested. Taking 10 percent of anything was the farthest thing from my mind. I was just embarrassed that I'd forgotten to make a call. After all, this guy was one of the few bright spots in my failed campaign, and taking anything for the performance of my duties as a representative would violate my oath of office.

That afternoon, I called the director of our local COG and ask if there were any funds left in my usual stash of project money, on which he kept a close watch. Most of the time, requests came directly to him anyway, and he would simply call me to let me know who we were helping next. Informing me that there was well over half a million still intact, I ask that he get with my new friend Mr. Hibbs and the McClain Foundation to see what they needed. The next day, he called me back but not with the helpful tone I had grown so accustomed to. He ask if I knew the building in question belonged to the old senator, and was I sure that was a project I wanted to get involved with. It made me mad for two reasons. First, it insulted me that he seemed to be insinuating that I would get involved in some sort of underhanded scheme, and, secondly, I figured since I was all but out of office, he would like to keep the funds to use to his own glory! I was probably right on both counts. Already a little miffed at what I thought was a lackluster performance by him and his colleagues in my congressional campaign, I lit into him. "I don't give a damn whose building it is. If it meets with constitutional guidelines and the McClain Foundation is involved, then do it!" I went on to say, "I'm not asking you to do something illegal. If it doesn't fit state guidelines, then don't do it." After hanging up, I was still furious. Here's a guy that had spent the better part of ten years sucking up to me at the state capitol, and now he wants to treat me like I was some kind of idiot. I then called Hibbs and told him to get with the COG director and the foundation and whatever capital they needed would be available. In the following weeks, the three parties worked out the details, and Hibbs, along with my help, had secured around $400,000 for his superior operation. Both the COG director and the Foundation were praised in the newspaper for their latest efforts in economic development. I was not mentioned.

My mood wasn't exactly in the best of sorts. I had no job, my finances were in a mess, and although I had fancied myself a master of politics, I'd been given a dose of its bowels. In Oklahoma, most politicians trade out for a job before leaving office. If, for example, you carry water for higher education, you go to work for Higher Ed. Carry water for the co-ops, you go to work for the co-ops, and so on. I had certainly carried water for some folk but was too dumb to do the latter.

The real kick in the rear end, however, was waking up to the fact that there was a vast difference between political supporters and friends. It's kind of like the difference between Christians for show and real Christians. Christians for show will give you their umbrella when it ain't raining, real Christians will give it to you when it is raining. People who had rode my coattails and burned my grease for the better part of a decade were nowhere to be seen. As it turned out, people I had done the least for were the most help during and after the campaign.

I had made a few friends during my time in office. One in particular was a county commissioner in Pushmataha County named Eddie McIntosh. Eddie took life and friendship serious, even back in his college days at EOSC. During a college basketball game, the home crowd had become agitated by the seemingly one-sided calls the refs were making against EOSC.

The Eastern crowd was booing and heckling the refs from the bleachers, except for Eddie. Before anyone could corral him, he was hopping across the gym floor on one foot, trying to pull a pistol out of his boot on the other one. To hell with the shouting, Eddie was going to make a point the refs would understand. No one got hurt, but ole Eddie made his point. He never got to make another basketball game there either.

While I was in office, I had called Eddie one day just to chat and to see if there was anything I could help him with, as I knew most county officials were strapped for funds. Reluctantly, he told me their rural hospital was in jeopardy of closing if they couldn't come up with $25,000, a problem resulting from an audit or some such. Eddie wasn't the kind to come to people with his hand out, and I knew that. Within the week, I arranged to send a couple hundred thousand to the Push County Hospital. I had made a friend for life.

At the beginning of my congressional campaign, when most folks thought I was a shoo-in, several county commissioners from Eastern Oklahoma had invited me to dinner at Charlie Newton's restaurant in OKC. Wanting to show their support, they took turns toasting my efforts as a good rural legislator. I couldn't help but notice Eddie glaring at one of the gentlemen across the table. Of course, he knew these commissioners a lot better than I did. When it came to the gentleman's turn to raise his glass, Eddie interrupted, calling him counterfeit, among some other choice words. Then he invited him outside for a good old-fashioned butt kickin'. Eddie knew this guy wasn't a real supporter of mine and couldn't stand watching him act the part. It ruined a good dinner party, but that's when I realized Eddie was the real deal.

After the campaign, while I was dazed by the aftershock of reality, Eddie took it on himself to help. Among his many duties as a county commissioner, he also chaired the board of our local COG. He knew I had helped that organization tremendously while I was in office. He also knew that I had personally seen to it that their director got a generous raise in salary via some special state funds. So Eddie figured I would do more good for the COG in one visit at the capitol with some old acquaintances than the director or anyone else on their staff could do in a year. He was right too! I did know my way around the capitol. Frankly, I thought it was a shame the director had to be leaned on in the first place. The raise I had got him alone would boost his retirement quite handsomely.

Nonetheless, the director came up with a contract for my services. The contract was only for six months and totaled twenty thousand dollars, which I thought was a near insult. Even then, I could pick up the phone and get the COG that amount with little effort. At least it was something, though, so I put on a grateful face. As life in the public workforce goes, however, someone in the organization begrudged my "overwhelming" contract, and I got a call from a reporter at the McClain newspaper. I just thought the news people didn't care what I was doing. The reporter began the conversation with a hypothetical question. "What would you say to someone who said you were taking funds away from the senior citizens' Meals on Wheels program to have yourself a job?" It really didn't matter how I answered the question. I already knew how the headlines would read. Adding insult to injury, the question came from the same reporter who had called me a few years earlier lobbying me to help kill legislation that would have freed county government from paying exorbitant column-inch prices to have their monthly meeting minutes printed in the newspaper (that he worked for). This weasel of a reporter wasn't concerned then about the wise use of public funds. Moreover, while I was in office, I had more than doubled the amount of funds going into senior citizens' programs, including their Meals on Wheels. In fact, I had made a special appropriation to the local COG so that they could purchase, for one of their sites, a new van equipped specifically to haul meals. All that didn't matter. What this little snooze hound wanted was a story designed to sell papers.

Whoever the jealous employee was who fed this distorted information to the paper, was like a lot of other people in the area. Most of them assumed that I was rolling in cash. The assumption came mostly from my years of living in the limelight. Little did they know I was broker than Dick's hatband! My bankers knew it, and now that I was no longer Mr. Chairman, my stock had dropped dramatically with them as well. Covering checks and rolling back loan payments came to a screeching halt. The facade was crumbling, and there was no place to hide.

While at an all-time low and wallowing in self-pity, I got another call from Hibbs. The call couldn't have come at a better time. He had a knack for making me feel like I still had some self-worth. He wanted me to drive over and meet him at the old senator's law office to discuss the possibility of working for him in a new venture called Ace Developers. I didn't let my shirttail hit my ass, and I was on my way. En route to the office, I recalled how the senator had recommended that I work for Hibbs, but that was before the campaign heated up, and I barely knew the guy. The old senator had told me that Hibbs was a real entrepreneur. I shrugged the notion off then, as I was set on Third District Congress.

Upon arriving at the law office, I strolled through the crowded lobby of folks patiently waiting their turn to see an attorney. No need to check in with the receptionist. I was far too important for that. Approaching the entrance to the senator's suite I noticed, through a cracked door, a group of people positioned around the table in his large conference room. I could see Hibbs circling the table, as if he were passing out legal documents or forms of some sort. I also noticed, from what I could see, a couple of members of the McClain Foundation, including the senator's brother, the one I had so graciously denied the opportunity to partner up with in the Randy Travis concert years earlier. Right away, I assumed they were closing on the manufacturing facility Hibbs had visited with me about weeks earlier. The senator's office door was closed, so I entered his secretary's office, where she was in her usual multitasking role, sorting through piles of paper, all the while a phone pressed between her ear and shoulder. It felt good to be back in the thick of things, so I made myself comfortable and waited for the flurry of typical law office happenings to slow.

Within minutes, I could hear voices and shuffling footsteps as people were leaving the conference room, and Hibbs beckoned me out into the hallway. He had on his usual Hawaii-cut shirt, as his midsection wouldn't accommodate a tucked-in shirttail. There were small beads of sweat on his forehead, a stack of forms tucked under his arm, and a more than pleased look on his face. He was happy to see me. It was quite obvious that Mr. Hibbs knew his way around the law office. In fact, it looked to me like he was running the place. The first words out of his mouth were, "You ready to go to work?" I couldn't have been more ready! At that, we sat at the conference table where he talked of all the projects I would be involved with that would require my political expertise and connections. Most of it would require my getting his foot in the door to places and people who would otherwise not give him the time of day. That I could do with no sweat. I was already impressed by the professional manner in which he'd helped in my campaign, but now I was even more impressed. For starters, he'd need more funds for the new Superior Products venture, which was no problem. Although I certainly didn't have the ability to move state funds like I did in the past, I could get him in to see the people that could. From there, he talked about his idea of a power plant that would require burning poultry litter that would not only generate power but also clean up a problem that had plagued Oklahoma for years. With my past involvement and acquaintances I'd made in the Department of Ag, he knew I was well equipped to get this project off the ground. I explained to him that although I would soon be officially out of office, I still wouldn't be comfortable being paid directly from state funds. He assured me that I would be compensated from Hibbs Enterprises, and I had no reason to doubt it.

This guy was partners with the senator in companies all over the state, and his wife owned a successful business, as well as a myriad of other business ventures he was involved with. His monthly income from one business alone was more money than I'd ever hope to make. This guy sure didn't need the state's money in order to live the good life.

With a handshake, we sealed the deal, and better yet, there was no contract to sign, no mileage forms, and no time sheets. I would be paid according to the success I had in hooking him up with the right people to get the job done. Even at a small percentage, I knew I would be making more than decent income. Plus, I would be back dealing with familiar faces and doing the work I did best. He also had no problem with my previous obligation with the small contract I'd signed with the COG. I couldn't wait to get started! In my mind, I had finally arrived. Before I left the conference room, he told me to go back to the secretary's office because she had something for me, and that she did! It was a check from the senator's account in the amount of $40,000. As she handed me the check, she pressed her index finger snuggly beneath the line that pronounced, "Payable for loan." The amount was suspiciously close to 10 percent of the funds I had obtained for Hibbs dog food plant. Furthermore, although I had received loans from the senator before, I hadn't asked for this one.

With a guilty but somewhat seared conscience, I took the check. My better judgment told me I had just accepted a kickback. The pressing issue of bank overdrafts and late car payments told me a thousand reasons why it wasn't. After all, it was the senator who had first recommended that I go to work for Hibbs. Maybe knowing my financial situation, he did expect a payback. Moreover, he had never so much as insinuated he wanted me to funnel money into a manufacturing facility. The fact remained, however, that it was the senator's building they had just closed the mortgage on for the manufacturing facility, and although done legally, I had been instrumental in obtaining the state funds.

The old saying "Let your conscience be your guide" didn't work for me anyway. My conscience had been telling me I was guilty as far back as I could remember. Besides that, I was in one of the most prestigious law firms in the state of Oklahoma. These folk weren't hauling hay and patching roofs for a penance either. They were successful, wealthy people who seemed obliged to take this cucumber picker into their circle.

# 21

The remainder of my first winter there at FTC dragged on at a snail's pace. The only change in my routine was the artwork I'd taken on since having some good instruction from my buddy Griff. Griff wasn't only a salt-of-the-earth kid but also a very gifted art instructor. I let the washer tossing go that winter and spent weekends sketching portraits of my grandchildren. Two nights a week, I continued in the circle of prayer and Bible study with my good brother Johnson.

Spring came and went, and so did the many faces of cadre unit. I had been away from my family in the confines of a federal pen for one year. I couldn't help but reflect on the time I had been there. I recalled how absurd and creepy the place had seemed when I arrived, how I had gagged at the smell of the prison cafeteria, how distinct and troubling the sound of the key chains were, and how odd it seemed watching TV with the aid of a transistor radio. I remembered going to and from the shower in full view of people I didn't know and how degrading it felt. I reflected on the absolute feeling of desperation when they first locked that steel cell door and the horror of being locked in with the mentally unstable. With a shudder, I recalled the strip search and the long line of inmates wearing chains, of putting my clothing and watch in the cardboard box and signing the form about my next of kin.

I thought of the more insignificant details, like drinking instant coffee from the plastic containers and the restricted access to a phone. I'm sure there were many things I'd grown accustomed to that I didn't even notice.

My eye continued to get worse, but I'd long since quit making sick call. It was a waste of time, as well as two days' pay. I had not only made friends with the young men of cadre but a lot of the prison staff as well. Of course, there will always be the gung-ho guards who like to belittle and harass a defenseless inmate, but by and large, most of them were decent folk, just trying their best to make a living. The bosses in laundry fold were class A people, as well as the bosses in safety and commissary. They not only treated me with dignity but were fair as well.

While I was affixed on nostalgia at my one-year anniversary, we got a new cadre arrival who would give me pause for even more reflection. This guy's name was Herman Delany, and he hailed from Mississippi. He was born October 20, 1951, just nine days before my birth. Although he was born in Texas, his parents were itching to move back to their old home in Mississippi. By his eighth birthday, he was a full-fledged Mississippian.

His folks were devout Baptists, and he never missed a Gospel meeting or a vacation Bible school. Just like my siblings and I, he was in church every Sunday morning, Sunday night, and Wednesday night. Delany had three younger sisters. When I asked which of his parents was the most religious, he said they both ran a pretty tight race. His dad was a deacon, and his mom made him and his sisters have a devotional every morning along with a good breakfast. He said she would make him and his sisters hold hands while she prayed, and the prayers seemed to last forever.

They lived two and a half miles from the schoolhouse and rode the school bus every day. When the bus stopped, the driver would honk the horn one time, and if they weren't out the door running, he'd go off and leave them. Sometimes the driver would honk while his mother was in the middle of one of her long prayers. Herman would crack one eye open at her and tell her the bus was honking. He said that would make her mad, so she would tell him to shut up and bow his head, then she would pray even longer, so they'd end up walking to school!

Even though Herman and I were different as night and day, the similarities of our upbringing were rather intriguing. When he was a senior in high school, he was six two and weighed 185. My height and weight were exactly the same when I was a senior. He was a star on their high school football team, and I was captain of mine. We both narrowly missed Vietnam because our lottery numbers never came up. I attended a class B high school, and he attended a class A. His dad pushed and pushed him to excel in sports. My dad could care less about sports. He pushed my brothers and me with a crosscut saw. His music was Jimmy Hendrix; mine was Johnny Cash and Merle Haggard. When I graduated high school, I had short hair and believed the establishment was always right. When he graduated, he had long hair and hated the establishment! I left home on a Greyhound bus; he left on a Honda 350. I left home to stay with my dad's sister in Texas; he left home to stay with his mom's sister in Florida.

Old Herman never settled down from the time he left home. He joined the hippie scene, did drugs, made drugs, and never married. He never held a job more than a couple of years and was never responsible for anyone other than himself. He moved from city to city and even lived in Alaska for a year.

I did the exact opposite. I left home, found a job, got married, raised four children, and stuck to the grind. I guess you could say that after high school, he turned left, and I turned right. Nevertheless, we both ended up in the federal transfer center!

The nearly a year's worth of prison life and bunking with old man Powell was taking a toll on Fitz. I'm sure he'd had better sleep on the streets of El Paso than he was getting in Powell's cell. At times, he'd take laughing spells for no apparent reason.

He'd been stuck in Powell's cell for nearly a year but wasn't as fortunate as I was. Moving to another cell was out of the question because no one wanted to bunk with either of them. Fitz failed miserably in the personal hygiene department. If it weren't for the medicated powder, you couldn't sit next to him. Some of the guys called him minute man because he was always in and out of the shower in less than a minute.

I was one of the few cadre inmates who would even talk to old Fitz. He sauntered over to my table out in the pod one evening, all the while laughing hysterically, a hideous, crazy kind of laugh. He wouldn't sit next to me, or anyone else for that matter. He'd just stand there long enough to say what he had to say and then amble off to himself. When he got to my table, he stopped laughing, like he'd turned it off with a switch. "Well, my man," he said, "I was offered a bottom bunk yesterday, but I turned it down. I've decided I'm going to stay in there with old Powell and make him smell my shit until he leaves! He can spray me with all the powder he wants. Screw him!" Then he went on to say, "Mr. Mass, there I was, a sixty-year-old man living out of a garbage can. Couldn't qualify for a cup of coffee. I tried to get help, but people laughed in my face, so I tried to rob a bank, and what do they do? They give me free room and board, three meals a day, and now they're gonna spend $6,000 fixing my mouth with oral surgery. Now you tell me what's wrong with this country!" With that, he ambled on off to himself.

FTC did have dental services and, from what the guys told me, a pretty good dentist. I never took them up on their dental service. I just wanted my eye fixed before I went blind. It struck me as odd that they would furnish a dentist when other health services were so lacking.

Of course, a lot of things about BOP struck me as odd. The structure of the massive facility itself had to have cost no telling what. When the federal government builds something, they don't take shortcuts or look for bargains. Back when I served in the House, there were a lot of schools in my district begging for funds to build classrooms. I'm sure the cost of this prison facility alone could have built a dozen schools in Southeast Oklahoma. Moreover, the boys on the landscape crew had been busy for the past couple of weeks with jackhammers, removing sidewalks outside the facility. The warden was having them replaced with heated sidewalks! The boys on landscape thought it was funny, considering the mild winters we have in Oklahoma.

Not long after Delany arrived, Griff took another turn for the worse. He'd decided to try and make it through the line for lunch call but stalled out before he could reach the elevator. Several of the guys helped him back to his cell. He looked pale and ashen.

That evening, as Delany and I were exiting the mess hall, Delany asked one of the lieutenants who was posted at the exit if we could bring a tray up for Griff. The lieutenant was a female we all called Leather Face behind her back. She wasn't one of our favorites. She was quick to send us on our way, saying Griff could come get his own tray when he got over his "tummy ache!" When we got back upstairs, ole Delany whipped up a plastic bowl full of ramen noodles and brought them to Griff's cell. Griff thought he was hungry, but he couldn't eat.

The following day was pretty much a routine day there at FTC. We all made our work stations and went about our business, each in our own way, dealing with time the best we knew how. By lunchtime, word was getting around that young Griff had finally gotten his visit to an outside hospital. According to his cellie, Griff had a bad episode during the night, so he hit the cell's panic button. He told us a couple of the guards, along with one of the LTs, removed Griff from the cell, and that was the last he'd seen of him.

That afternoon just prior to the 4:00 p.m. count, a voice came over the intercom calling a town hall meeting in E pod. Town hall meetings were a common occurrence in the cadre unit. They were usually called when the warden felt a need to chastise or correct the unit as a whole or if certain new restrictions or guidelines were being implemented.

This town hall would be different. The warden wasn't there. Instead it was the prison chaplain flanked on either side by FTC lieutenants. Young Griff wouldn't be coming back to cadre. He was dead. The meeting was very brief and very somber. Prison officials would give no details, and if questions were to be asked by cadre inmates, they would be asked right then, although a pretty clear message was sent that questions wouldn't be all that welcomed. After all, what were we going to ask? Why did BOP let him die? I don't think so!

With that, we were ushered to our cells and locked down for the 4:00 p.m. count. During count, both my cellie and I lay on our bunks in silence. All I could think of was Griff, the kid of meager means with the quiet subtle humor, polite and respectful, my spade partner and art teacher. I thought of his mother back in Fort Worth and how she'd take the news. No one deserved such an indignant death, especially young Griff.

After count, the pod was abuzz with whispers of Griff's passing. A couple of the cadre inmates talked a little too loud and were swiftly shipped to a different facility. BOP made it clear there would be no discussion of Griff's death.

To pacify an otherwise tenuous situation, the prison chaplain announced a memorial to be held in Griff's honor. The special memorial would be held in the visitation room in order to accommodate cadre inmates who wanted to attend. It was a pretty feeble attempt at showing that BOP really cared, as far as I was concerned.

The day of the memorial, we were all escorted by guards to the visitation room where Lieutenant Leather Face was posted front and center. To her credit, she made no attempt to fake her feelings. She was there to keep order, not mourn. The prison chaplain mustered up some good words to say about Griff, but that's what prison chaplains are paid to do. A few of the guys sang a gospel song, and the memorial service was over.

After Griff's death, my attitude went down the drain and, along with it, my patience. The hands on the big clock that hung over the Co's office seemed to have all but quit turning. The noises of dominoes slapping against the hard-surface tables and my new cell mate's snoring were only amplified. For a good while, all I could dwell on were negative thoughts, like BOP installing heated sidewalks while letting my friend Griff die a slow and miserable death.

The negative thoughts weren't just limited to the Bureau of Prisons. I thought of the federal prosecutors, whose job came from political favor, and the plaques adorning their office walls that came off the back of kids like Griff. I thought about the old senator, found incompetent to stand trial while he bragged publicly about his portfolio. Then I thought of this place, filled with the less fortunate and the mentally impaired. I thought of politicians whose bellies were filled with shrimp and fine wine while they handed out tax relief for the big oil that fed them. I thought of the doctors, and yes, even the governor, who pushed drugs for the pharmaceuticals and were rewarded with goody bags, season football tickets, and cash. Then I'd think of the less fortunate drug pushers whose reward was a cell. I thought of my own former self-righteous indignation toward those whose shoes I hadn't worn.

Not long after Griff's death, we got a new unit manager at cadre, a transfer from El Reno who loved showing himself. First day as our new chief, he came strolling through the unit whistling "The Merry Month of May." Beginning with the first cell in E pod, he went from cell to cell, throwing everyone's personals out in the pod floor. Stripping the bunks, he'd use his feet to drag the bedding out into the unit. The eerie whistling didn't stop until he'd ransacked every cell. Before exiting E pod, he stopped and, in a real show of authority, said, "Have a nice day."

After the incident, I went out on the rec deck with Gage, Big Tex, and a couple of the other guys. I was grumbling about the repugnant new unit manager and prison life in general. Big Tex broke out in one of his big laughs and said, "Guv, you ain't in da White House no mo, you be in da big house." All of them had a good laugh at my expense! I had my own laugh the following afternoon. Risking a trip to the SHU, I smuggled new sheets and blankets out of laundry fold. I stashed them beneath E pod laundry in one of the huge laundry carts and held my breath while being escorted up the elevator. I felt like a real convict after furnishing the guys in E pod with new linens!

My dismal attitude, combined with the annoying festered eye, was beginning to get the better of me. As far back as I could remember, I was always able to find the humor in a bad situation, but I had lost even that. My loathing for the government and moreover, wallowing in self-pity wasn't helping time move any faster either.

That night, after Bible study in the circle, I stayed for a much-needed talk with my good brother Johnson. I was sixty years old and had never sought counseling from anyone, mainly because I always thought I was the one who should be doing the counseling! Nevertheless, there I was in all my glory, begging a young black inmate for a much-needed glimmer of hope.

I shared with Brother Johnson every loathing thought I'd ever had for myself, as well as others. I told him the long and painful story of self-betrayal, as well as betrayal of friends that landed me in prison. I told him how I'd managed to lose every dime I'd ever worked for, including my retirement and my home on the banks of Gaines Creek. I told him of the friends I'd helped who now wouldn't give me the time of day. I vented my disdain for the feds and how they'd much rather get to a headline than the truth. He sat quietly and patiently while I spilled my churning guts.

When I finished, he put his hand on my shoulder, and with an understanding smile, he asked, "Is that all, Brotha Govna?"

I felt a little foolish. This kid was doing far more time than I was, and I was quite sure had lost just as much, but he certainly didn't act like it.

"Brotha Govna, it's mighty hard giving up everything you ever owned, but it's even harder to give up your pride." Somehow, Brother Johnson managed to skip all the counseling and get straight to the point as he continued, "You see, Brother Govna, you went from Mr. Chairman to inmate 04581-063, from somebody to nobody, and that right there is where the good Lord wants you to be. He can't work with Mr. Chairman, but he can work with Mike Mass. You see, Brother Govna, the potter can't work with the sandstone until it's been broken down to clay."

By then the loud intercom announced lockdown for count. "Everyone, get to your cell." It was time for the 9:00 p.m. count. That night, I slept better than I had in months. I didn't even hear the rattling snore of my cellie. When the guard unlocked the cell that morning, I was dressed and ready for work, and my attitude was finally off high center!

The job in laundry fold had become a rut. Notwithstanding the painful knees and feet from standing on concrete rolling up clothes, our crew had been split up from the constant moving of inmates in and out of cadre. Tex had moved to work down in R&D (receiving and discharge.) Rick had finally reached his outdate and had gone to the halfway house. Both Diaz and Tony would soon be shipped to another facility. I needed a move myself.

During lunch break that day, I approached my laundry boss about the prospects of a new job, anything but pots and pans. As it turned out, one of the boys in safety had been sent to the SHU just the day before, which left a job opening right next door to laundry. Both the laundry supervisor and the safety supervisor worked out an agreement that moved me out of laundry fold into safety.

The new job in safety brought some much-needed relief for my knees and ankles. The safety department was responsible for delivering the various cleaning agents and chemicals to the holdover units. We also filled orders for guys that did the sanitizing in R&D, as well as the mess hall. Although there was still plenty work to be done, the job allowed me a lot of sitting-down time. Moreover, it was a much-needed change of scenery as well as company.

Inmate health services picked up dramatically in the wake of Griff's death. I suppose it could have been a coincidence, but within days of Griff's memorial, a rash of cadre inmates were being sent for outside health services, including myself.

It had been just over a year since I'd first signed up for sick call seeking some relief for my eye, and I had long since given up on any notion of seeing a doctor. I knew something was afoot when I noticed my name on the call-out sheet hanging on the poster board outside the pod. I had finally rated a visit to see a real doctor! Down on second floor medical, the doc recommended that I be sent out to have the growth inside my eyelid removed. Because of security reasons, of course, I wouldn't be told when.

A few days after the visit, I'd just got back to my cage in safety after the noon chow line when a guard came in and asked if I was 04581-063. He escorted me to the elevator and on to the second floor, down the long corridor to R&D. I was strip-searched and handed a change of clothing. For the trip out, I'd wear the same issues I was given the first day I had arrived: the T-shirt, elastic-waist kakis, and canvas shoes.

After changing clothes, we headed down another long corridor past several large holding cells that I hadn't seen before. They reminded me of the holding pens back home at the livestock yards, where cattle were crammed awaiting their final destination. Once we passed the large holding cells, we came to a sally port used for loading and unloading inmates from a bus. There was a white prison vehicle waiting there in the sally port.

I was put in the back seat, with a cage separating myself from the front seat, and locked in. The guard then started the white vehicle, and we were on our way. He drove us out of the large sally port and on through the same guard shack that I'd come through over a year earlier. I couldn't help but look through the rear glass as we left the monstrous prison compound.

It was the first time I'd been on the outside of a building in a long time. I didn't miss a tree or a blade of grass as we sailed along I-44 north toward Baptist hospital in Oklahoma City. As we passed other vehicles or they passed us, people seemed to stare at the prisoner behind the cage. It felt surreal.

We pulled into a small parking lot at the rear entrance of a small clinic not far from the Baptist hospital. As we exited the car, a receptionist motioned us to the rear entrance. The doctor and his female assistant were somewhat standoffish. I'm sure they didn't know if I was a pedophile or an ax murderer, as the guard kept little distance between himself and me. They had me sit in a chair while the doctor examined my eye. There was none of the polite small talk that usually occurs between doctor and patient. I was a convict.

The doctor gave me a shot under my eyelid and immediately made an incision and started digging at the growth with a large pair of tweezers. I dug my fingernails into the arm of the chair while he dug and pulled. It was over in less than ten minutes. He stitched my eyelid, put a large white patch over my eye, and sent us on our way. We were back at FTC by 2:30 p.m. About the time we arrived back at the prison, the shot he gave to numb my eye was just beginning to take effect!

When I got back to E pod, all the guys couldn't help but notice the large white patch. They knew I'd made a trip out into the world. They all wanted to hear about it.

Naturally, several of the guys were anxious to help me with whatever I needed. Gage fixed me a cup of coffee, and young Cody had already retrieved my laundry from the laundry cart, folded it, and tucked it away in my cell locker. Big Tex wanted to know what the nurses looked like. I told him there were two nurses, both of them young, and quite attractive. I told him they held my hand and rubbed their fingers through my hair while the doctor put me gently to sleep. I told him the beautiful nurses slipped me their phone number before I left. The bigger I lied, the more we all laughed! It was, however, a relief having the eye ordeal over with.

Poor old Herman Delany also got caught up in the rush of health services. His cellmate had been approved for a visit on the outside for a colonoscopy, but the guard on nightshift lost his paperwork. He knew what cell the inmate was in but didn't know which one was to be prepared, so he took them both to the SHU, where they were ordered, as per the prison doc, to drink a half gallon of liquid designed to clear out the bowels. Although the guard didn't know which of the two was having the procedure, he was playing it safe and wasn't about to take a chance on getting the wrong inmate prepared. Herman and his cellie ended up being locked in the same small cell sharing the toilet all night. Although Herman looked like hell the next day, we couldn't help but get a laugh at his nauseating ordeal. Adding insult to injury, when they unlocked the cell door the next morning to take his cellie out for his treatment, they sent Herman on down to his work station cleaning pots and pans. Herman said, "I tried to tell the guard there wasn't anything wrong with me, but he told me to keep my piehole shut."

The next morning, the guards had no sooner made their rounds unlocking the cell doors than Philly came scurrying through the pod, visibly shaken. Philly was Brother Johnson's cellmate and one of the more mentally impaired who Brother Johnson had fostered during our prayer circle. He had come over from F pod to tell me they had taken Brother Johnson during the night and was sending him to another facility. Of course, we had no idea where. We knew he had a few years left of his sentence.

About then, another of our evening prayer circle attendees came over to join us, a young black kid name Shaw. Shaw was bipolar. If he ever got off his medication, we could tell it right quick. He'd be praying one minute and cursing the guards the next! Poor kid spent a lot of time in the SHU and still had twenty years ahead of him in the federal pen.

Shaw knew of Brother Johnson's departure too. They had opened his cell earlier than usual because he was on a special cleaning duty down in the mess hall. Although they hadn't unlocked the door leading out of the unit, he could see the guards escorting Brother Johnson to the elevator through the reinforced glass window. He said Brother Johnson hollered through the door, "Tell Govna they shipping me out, and you two stay outta trouble!"

I hadn't even got the chance to thank Brother Johnson for our visit a couple nights earlier that had left me feeling much better about myself. It was really no surprise to me that they would ship Brother Johnson out of cadre. He was a leader of sorts, and prison officials don't necessarily like inmate leaders. He wasn't a leader in the sense of trouble making, nor did he ever presume to be a leader. That role just came to him naturally. He wasn't afraid of the SHU or any other punishment BOP had. He believed he represented the temple of God. Therefore, he would accept no treatment that made him feel less than a man. I admired him for his courage and the ability to stand up for himself when he knew he was in the right. He had filed every grievance available on prison staff when none of the rest of us had the guts to. Moreover, he didn't just file them for the heck of it; he filed them when they merited filing. Johnson had developed a tradition of praying our fellow cadre inmates out as they completed their sentences and were on their way to a halfway house or another prison destination. We didn't get an opportunity to pray him out.

Despite the unexpected departure of our inspirational brother, time seemed to pick up the pace, at least for me. My eye was on the mend, and my new job in safety was a change I needed as well. I was back tossing washers out on the rec deck, and my spirits were much improved. Naturally, our prayer circle and Bible study wasn't the same. Different ones tried filling Brother Johnson's shoes, but the attempts were feeble at best. Brother Johnson was a scholar of the Bible but didn't come across as a know-it-all. He just had a natural, and I believe, God-given talent to teach and to lead. Philly and Shaw were lost without him, and I'm quite sure that time slowed for them when he left.

Another pleasant surprise came when my safety boss allowed me to help out in commissary. My friend Oso, the gangster from south OKC, had worked in commissary for a couple of years. Every so often, they'd let me go help him fill orders for our fellow cadre inmates when they were shorthanded. Oso was like Gage and I when it came to the Oklahoma Sooner football team. We were all die-hard fans. The closer college football season got, the closer the three of us got.

I also found out while working in commissary that Oso was afraid of bugs. Although the muzzle end of a 9-millimeter Glock pistol didn't bother him, the sight of a cricket would nearly make him faint! Even gangsters have their weaknesses. I told Oso that if I ever decided to go gangster in south OKC, I was going to carry a big bug in my holster! Oso didn't see the humor in my comment; he didn't even like talking about bugs. There were two boss men in safety that rotated shifts. One was black, and one was white. The two of them were like the bosses I'd had in laundry and the boss in safety, all stand-up guys. If my good brother Johnson could have been fortunate enough to work for any one of these men, he would never have had to file a grievance.

Switching my work time between safety and commissary was a real boost to the otherwise monotonous routine and helped make my time go even faster during work hours. It also allowed me to spend work time with fellow cadre inmates who I'd only seen slapping dominoes up in the pod.

Commissary days were Monday and Tuesday. On Monday, everyone whose last name began with *A–L* went shopping. On

Tuesday, the *M–Zs*. Inside the commissary, there were four aisles about eight feet long. On either side of the aisles were shelves filled with items for personal hygiene and grocery items—rice, ramen noodles, crackers, sardines, tuna, peanut butter, soft drinks, coffee, chips, and small bags of hard candy. The hygiene aisle hosted toothpaste and brushes, shampoo, antibiotic ointment, do-rags, soap, etc.

Inmates would take their turn in line as the boss man scanned their various items and deducted it from their commissary fund. Working there allowed me to see which inmate used a certain brand of instant coffee and so forth. This came in handy when I was running low and needed to do a little bumming. It also allowed me to distinguish inmates who had little outside help and relied only on the meager pay from their cadre job. They usually ordered ramen noodles or saltines.

I noticed that Billy, with whom I worked in safety, watched his p's and q's while ordering his commissary items. Billy had no support from family, except for his aging grandmother, who'd bring his two young daughters for a yearly visit. Living on a limited social security budget, she had no means of helping support his commissary fund. Billy didn't complain, but it helped me understand why he seemed so anxious and volunteered for every available extra detail.

One of his extras was a part-time job in companion watch, where he was paid extra for monitoring inmates who were primarily suicidal. FTC had no shortage of those type of inmates. They were kept in a stripped down cell about twice the size of mine. There was no bunk, no locker, and it was all concrete. In the middle of the cell is a stationary concrete slab rising about twelve inches from the floor, used for a bed. In one corner of the cell was a stainless steel commode and drinking fountain combined. The front of the cell is thick unbreakable Plexiglas so the inmate can be seen and monitored around the clock. The inside is kept at a cool 65 degrees. The inmate inside is given only a smock, no shoes and no clothing.

The companion watch documents every word and action of the suicidal inmate. A good number of these inmates routinely urinate or defecate in the floor or smear feces on the large unbreakable glass. They're kept there until they figure out how to at least act sane. Those are the inmates who weren't wealthy enough to be declared incompetent.

One such inmate being monitored by Billy was a young black kid they'd found in one of the holdover units hanging from his top bunk by a sheet. Unfortunately for the kid, they found him in time to save his life and promptly put him in suicide watch. He'd been in the federal pen for six years and had thirty years to go.

Another kid who Billy kept watch over was a young white boy. Billy laughed and said the kid was crazy as a loon. He said the kid lay in the floor naked trying to get the plastic wrap off a bologna sandwich and would push it back toward Billy trying to get some help unwrapping it.

The boss man in safety also had a cadre inmate assigned specifically to keep inventory. Safety's warehouse alone had enough supplies to stock Lowes home furnishings—scrubbers, buffers, chemicals, fire extinguishers, cleaning and buffing pads, gloves, etc. The inmate assigned to this duty was a twenty-three-year-old black kid we called JR. He was also from Missouri and sharp as a tack, both mentally and physically. JR could add, divide and multiply quicker in his head than boss man could on his computer. He was also one of the most considerate and respectful young men I'd ever been around. While everyone else in cadre called me Gov, JR insisted on calling me Mr. Mass. I knew JR was at the beginning of a sixty-month stay and never bothered asking what he was in for. I did know, however, that a kid of his intellect and personality would have been far more useful outside this facility of wire and steel. By then, I was growing a little weary of learning all the personal stories. I assumed JR was like most of the other young men: hit with a baseball bat when he could have been handled with a switch.

Like a lot of the others, JR had been raised by his grandmother, who managed to have a card or letter for him at every mail call. At break times in safety, Billy, JR and I would play a quick game of gin rummy and swap stories of our days out in the free world. Like the guys in laundry fold, they were fascinated by my sometimes embellished political escapades.

Billy kept himself focused on the next good laugh or the next good meal. Talking of future plans was the farthest thing from his mind. Prospects of a productive life was a dismal proposition at best. JR, on the other hand, loved talking to me of his future plans. He wanted to go to college and make something of himself. I simply encouraged him all I could. I knew his long road ahead wouldn't be easy, but who was I to extinguish his hopes.

After a couple of months on the job in safety, boss man took the three of us for a special detail in one of the holdover units. As of yet, I'd only caught glimpses of holdover through the narrow glass window at the entrance door when we delivered laundry or cleaning supplies. I found out that every so often, prison management would manage to shift inmates in an effort to empty one of the large units for a good cleaning. The three of us would be stripping and waxing the entire unit. When we entered the unit, I couldn't help but stand in awe at the massive space filled with rows upon rows of eight-by-ten cells, like a double-decker ship, rows of cells on top of rows of cells. I fully comprehended why the large holding pens down in R&D were necessary. A facility designed to hold and transfer literally herds of human beings.

Holdover inmates weren't quite as lucky as cadre inmates. Their mattresses made ours look like Serta or Tempur-Pedic! Billy called me over to one of the cells to show me where he'd inscribed his initials when passing through this facility a few years earlier. You couldn't even see the sky from their recreation deck; it was covered, with one TV mounted high on the wall. Billy said most fights in holdover occurred because of arguments over what channel would be watched on the shared TV. He said, "Gov, be glad you're not stuck in one of these units. They suck." I believed him. I was just there to scrub the floor, and even that sucked.

# 22

By the time I was officially out of office, Hibbs had the details firmly intact as far as my role in Ace Developers. It worked out great for me. By the time my legislative pay ended, I was on the payroll of Hibbs Enterprises. The $40,000 check I'd gotten a couple months before was pretty much gone. I had paid a few bills, bought some antiques, spent a few bucks trying to turn a metal building into a restaurant, and gambled a lot.

The weekend trips to Bossier City had slowed, but stops by the local Choctaw Indian Casino were on the increase. The tribes were beginning to use slots that were not only comparable to the sophisticated class 3 machines in Vegas and Bossier City but better and faster. Although Oklahoma hadn't given the green light for either class 2 or class 3 gaming, it was more lucrative for the tribes to do it anyway and pay a fine now and then. Most of the tribe's slots were installed by a company with deep roots in the slot business. They got their percentage right off the top. The good thing for the slot manufacturers and programmers was that state bureaucrats didn't understand all that class 2 and class 3 jargon anyhow. They could program the machines to do basically whatever they wanted them to do. Gone were the days of the one-arm bandit where odds were a factor. These machines were nothing short of one big computer program that could be turned on and off with the flick of a mouse. You could cram all the hundred-dollar bills you wanted into one, but you weren't going to feed it into submission. If you were lucky enough to be in front of one when the computers server was on, you could turn a twenty-dollar bill into a thousand quick bucks.

I got lucky enough on many occasions. I just didn't know when to quit or how. Either way, as long as I had a paycheck coming, they were going to get their share.

I had stopped by the local Choctaw Casino one night and, within an hour, had gone through several hundred dollars. Down to my last few bucks, my better senses told me to cash the ticket in so I could at least get enough gasoline to get back home. When I slid the ticket through the small cage opening, the gal on the other side slid my thirty dollars back, with a hand-scribbled note under the cash. I didn't know her from Adam, but evidently she knew me, or else thought she did. I took my money and discreetly peeked at the note. It was nothing more than the ID number of one of the five hundred-plus slot machines in the building.

It intrigued me enough to spend the better part of an hour hunting for it. I was about to give up when on my way out the back entrance, I spied the number atop a high limit slot machine. The minimum bet was five bucks, so at the most, I could press the button four times and keep ten for gas. I'd already gone through five hundred dollars. What was twenty more? The very first lick the screen turned red and, with the free spin, landed on double, double, triple bars for $800. I went back to cash the ticket and was eager to tip this generous clerk I didn't know, but by then, she was nowhere in sight. I guess her shift had ended. Heck, she could very well have been the one who cashed my eight-hundred-dollar ticket, and I didn't recognize her. I sure wasn't going to ask. After twelve years of being in political office, I often ran into folk I didn't recognize who seemed to know me. It was an embarrassing but common occurrence for me.

Before I would delve into the various Ace Development Company projects that Hibbs had outlined, he wanted me to spend time at the state capitol introducing him to various politicians. I not only got it, I loved it! This was right down my alley. So when the 2003 legislative session began, I was back at the state capitol but playing a new role. I was now viewing the process through the eyes of a lobbyist. It was like still being in the legislature, only without the hassle of committee work, deadlines, a ton of phone calls, and all the other headaches that came with being a legislator, and it paid better! I understood then why most lobbyists were former legislators. What a perfect fit! I couldn't believe I was getting paid for this. It was like a dream come true.

Prior to beginning our capital rounds, Hibbs drove me a few blocks down Lincoln Boulevard past the capitol complex to an office where he ran one of his many business ventures. He introduced me to his secretary/receptionist and a business partner there and explained I would be getting paid through that office. It just kept getting better. This guy was surely a genius and, just like the senator had told me, a real entrepreneur! Adding to it all, he was the "gentlemen's gentleman." We rarely entered an office where he didn't have a box of chocolates for the receptionist, whether he knew her or not. I think that stemmed from being the smart, overweight kid in a small Southeast Oklahoma school he attended when he was young. While most of the boys excelled in basketball, rodeos, and deer hunting, he preferred hanging out with the girls and participating in student council activities. Early on, he'd figured out that the only way he was likely to get in on a game of tag football was if he brought the football, then let them keep it when recess was over! The girls were much easier and cheaper to get along with, and so were the teachers. He gushed when telling how he and a famous country music star were best buddies in high school.

Hibbs's background of evolving into a suitable social life served him well in a building packed with politicians, legislative assistants, and secretaries. Bearing gifts for the women and buying cocktails and dinner for the men came quite naturally, and he had more than plenty of takers. When you're picking up the tab, you're welcome at anybody's table. That session of the 2003 legislature, Hibbs and me became quite the popular duo. Since I was no longer a threat in political circles, I seemed to be even more loved, if that were possible. Of course, it helped having a sidekick with an open checkbook and one that was more than willing to participate. We would get him in an office, and before we would leave, he had either made a contribution to the politician or the political action committee of their preference. By session's end, Hibbs had personally sponsored successful fund-raisers for the incoming Democratic governor, a new second district congressman and had contributed to every major Democratic PAC in both the House and the Senate. He had also contributed to the campaign coffers of all the major players in the House and senate. We would have no problem getting state matching funds for the newly formed Ace Developers, and I soon found out that it was much easier getting state funds appropriated from the outside. Although Hibbs didn't have the capitol as well greased as did the oil companies, utilities, and pharmaceuticals, he had it greased enough.

In between buying dinners and rubbing elbows with the political big shots, I was working in earnest on the list of projects my new boss had outlined. Foremost was the power plant project. I thought the idea had some merit since burning chicken litter would serve a twofold purpose. Oklahoma poultry producers had been under the gun for quite some time because of water quality issues directly related to chicken litter. Getting rid of the litter and making power all at the same time would definitely be a plus. I had made several visits with folks at the Department of Agriculture, all of whom thought the idea had merit. I had also met with directors of Grand River Dam Authority in hopes of finding a buyer for the power. Since the idea would have required participation on the state level, enabling legislation would also be necessary.

While I was busy in the power plant project, Hibbs was supposedly pushing forward with the manufacturing facility. So far, it was nothing more than the building he had managed to purchase and a lot full of used grain bins, augers, and conveyer lines he'd purchased from a bankrupt facility in Muskogee. It would be a lengthy and painstaking process, at best, to get the plant in working order, and since I was responsible for helping acquire state funds for the project, I was naturally concerned to see it completed. Trying not to be too pushy, I prodded Hibbs as best I could to get the facility completed, but he seemed more interested in finding bigger and better deals to pursue.

While I was up to my neck in working out details for the power plant and Superior parts were strewn all over hell's half acre, Hibbs came up with another idea for Ace Developers—building dorms for a small college in northeast Oklahoma. According to Hibbs, we could make good money as developers of the deal. I thought to myself, *This guy already has more going than we can say grace over, but it's his dime.* So off I went! I was now in the college dormitory building business. Of course, I already knew every college president in the state, so it did make a little sense, but at the same time, this project wasn't my cup of tea. I didn't know a thing about the construction business, and from past experience, I knew dealing with a college president was a dubious proposition at best. Not very long into the dorm project, however, Hibbs came up with yet another brilliant scheme, and this one did pique my interest. We were now going to develop a casino for some Indian tribe. All we needed to do was find us an Indian who had bona fide Indian trust land, get his tribe to buy into the idea, and presto, we'd develop a casino. I was beginning to think this guy was either a complete idiot or the smartest guy I'd ever met. Either way, he was paying, so I began to give less of a damn about the merits of his thought process. In less than a year,

I had run a failed congressional race, helped kick-start a manufacturing plant, become a lobbyist, a power plant expert, a dormitory developer, and now I was going to help develop a casino!

I figured the casino idea, which was just the latest of many, would also be a flash in the pan before he was on to another harebrained idea, but it wasn't. Tribal gaming had become Oklahoma's new black gold, and casinos were cropping up all over the diverse Oklahoma landscape. The problem was, the only white men who could get their fingers in this lucrative pie were the slot manufacturers out west. I didn't see it as that abnormal that Hibbs would try and get a piece of the action, so off we went. We were now wining and dining Oklahoma Indian chiefs or their proxies.

Chasing down Indians who had land that was still considered eligible for gaming was all-consuming, and Hibbs dropped every project we had going, including the manufacturing plant. I was still trying to figure out how Ace Developers was going to develop something as expensive and far-reaching as a casino, but I sure didn't want to appear dumb, so I didn't ask. Besides, I was getting paid just as I'd been promised and not a day late, and all my job had become was getting Hibbs through an open door. Hibbs's checkbook didn't seem to have a bottom. He spent more on steaks and liquor than I did on cow feed for sixty head of cattle.

Hibbs was a real talker. I don't know if anyone ever understood a word he said, but it sure sounded smart. After weeks of running down false leads, we finally found the perfect prospect in an old Indian fellow who had land in federal trust that was ideally located near Interstate 40. He was willing to dance, but we still had to get the tribe's approval in order to get a casino sanctioned. With some good old-fashioned Hibbs hospitality and a couple of council members I knew, we had a meeting with the chief, his full tribal council, and their attorney. Hibbs gave one whale of a presentation. I didn't understand a word he said or a chart he displayed, and from the looks of everyone else in the meeting, I don't think they did either. The chief seemed preoccupied with a pen that didn't want to retract and was busy taking it apart and putting it back together while Hibbs was talking. The rest of the bunch, except for their attorney, were all fighting sleep. After Hibbs forty-minute presentation, all we needed was approval from the council. I knew we were in trouble when they all starting talking it over in their native tongue. They had a good fifteen-minute discussion, with the chief getting in the final word, and then silence fell while they all stared at Hibbs, as if they thought he also spoke their native language. I leaned over to one of the council members who I knew and asked him what the chief had said. He leaned back toward me and said, "Chief said, 'Nah.'"

Despite being paid on time, I was beginning to get a little embarrassed by all the failures, especially when I was the one responsible for getting Hibbs the audience. Failure didn't seem to register on Hibbs, however, as he was intent on getting in on the gaming action. Moreover, I could sense he was getting a little perturbed by my subtle loss of zeal. Be that as it may, we had spent the better part of an entire legislative session wining and dining legislators and Indian chiefs with very little results.

In the waning days of that legislative session, the nearly five-year federal probe into the fiddler's campaign was finally coming to a head. All the focus had been on the senator, who was now in and out of the hospital, suffering from fluid at the base of his spinal cord. At times, he seemed to be plumb out of it, but who knew? I remembered how he had denied knowing his senate colleague and friend of thirty years who was knee-deep in the ghost investigation. Medical issues or not, absolutely no one could put a finger on the functions of his mind. Regardless, it was time to pay the fiddler.

I wasn't very concerned about repercussions as far as my role in that campaign. The list of straw donors was a mile long, and there had been no mention of any of us in media reports. Besides,

I had already been confronted by the feds, and they assured me that I was not a target of their investigation. The senator was heavily fined and forced to resign his senate seat of fifty years. His loyal secretary was also fined and put on probation. The entire three-year drama and untold thousands of dollars spent by the lengthy federal investigation could have all been avoided if, three years earlier, the senator would have simply acknowledged the FEC violation and paid half the fine he ended up paying.

The senator's resignation triggered a string of events that would ultimately be my undoing. A hometown boy, the son of Hartshorne's longtime mayor, had successfully run for my old state House seat. He now wanted to leave the House midterm and run for Stokes's vacant senate seat, which opened up my previous seat in the House. That is where Hibbs's next brilliant idea came into play. He wanted me to run for my old House seat, which was the last thing that I wanted to do. With term limits firmly intact, the best I could do was serve one and a half terms, which would be three years. I also knew that starting all over as a freshman legislator, I would be powerless.

Saying no, however, was never an easy thing for me to do, especially to someone who had been as helpful to me as Hibbs had. I also felt that I had gotten Hibbs to a place where he could do his own politicking without my help. I also figured it was a nice way of his telling me that he no longer needed my services. He offered to do all the fund-raising, and to my surprise, he also offered to keep me on his payroll. What more could I ask for? Fund-raising was three-fourths of the campaign, and I knew he would raise more than I needed. Besides, it did my heart good to know his insistence wasn't based entirely on getting rid of my services. So I obliged. I knew I would be a shoo-in. I knew everyone in the old district. I'd built a new fire station and senior center in every community and helped get jobs for a lot of them.

That summer, I campaigned, Hibbs raised the money, and as I had expected, I sailed back in office with a good tailwind.

The venture back into the limelight wasn't without its personal costs, however. With the rapid growth of social media, there was a McClain-based website called Insider. It was basically a site where all the naysayers could air their complaints. Most of them had to do with Stokes, the undeveloped manufacturing plant, and insinuations of unsavory politicians. I had personally never owned a computer, but the website had become so popular that the local news media was beginning to print its venom. I had also noticed a different spin by my republican opponent during the campaign. Not so much the standard abortion and gay rights accusations but more on a personal level, as he chided my basic morals between right and wrong. I also couldn't help but notice his campaign signs cropping up in a few business fronts and lawns that at one time had displayed my own. What made them more noticeable was the fact that they were displayed on property owned by my church brethren, some of whom had spent a lot of time with their hand out in my old appropriation office. There was a movement afoot and definitely not to my benefit! I guess you could say my ears were burning. It would also be fair to say I had earned the cold shoulder from some of my church brethren. After the mansion years, and promenading around the state as Mr. Chairman, my reputation preceded me. Stories of the mansion grew bigger with each telling, and I was a stalwart at all the casinos. My gambling had grown to an addiction, but I hid that pretty well from the people closest to me. I stopped by the local Choctaw casino one night and within thirty minutes had hit three jackpots totaling over $4,000. An acquaintance noticed the wads of cash I had and approached me for a little help, as he wasn't quite so lucky that night. Rather than ask for some cash, he offered to write me a check, so I gave him $200, and he wrote me a $200 check. When I left the casino that night, all I had in my wallet was an IRS form for the jackpots and the $200 check. The check even bounced.

I had absolutely no illusions about going back into office. I knew there was a faction of folks in my own party who would despise my return, even though they wouldn't show it outwardly. They already had enough of what they perceived as my reign in the House. I knew I would be powerless, and I knew the House speaker would be pressured not to place me in any position of power, and I was okay with that. I'd had enough of myself too! I was going back for one reason—to boost my retirement. When my constituents called for help, I'd give them the standard political runaround. That was all I could do.

With less than six months before I would be sworn into office, there was some personal housekeeping to be attended. The gambling, along with my miserable luck at ranching, had forced me into bankruptcy. I was too lucky at the slots. Over the period of just a couple years, I had hit numerous jackpots, ranging in amounts from $2,400 to $10,000. The problem was carrying the cash around for a few days, then feeding it back to the machines. Before I knew it, I had accrued as much income from gambling as I had from working for Ace Developers, and I hadn't paid taxes on it either. I paired down my ranching operation by selling my remaining cattle for pennies on the dollar and sold off land I'd paid $500 an acre for, for $300 an acre. I was upside down on everything, from the cars I drove to the house I lived in. To top things off that fall, I got slapped with a $25,000 fine from the FEC for my one-day role in the fiddler's campaign.

Having settled the old FmHA young farmers' loan with a considerable write-down, I refinanced my house and forty acres with a local bank. The rest of my financial ruins were boxed up and taken to a bankruptcy attorney who would file the necessary paperwork free gratis, which were mostly deferred banknotes and the $40,000 loan/kickback from the senator. The young attorney asked if I were being pressured to pay the $40,000 that was marked as loan. I told him the story of how the loan came to be, and because of the senator's health and preoccupation with the

FEC scandal, I hadn't even had the opportunity to thank him for it, much less discuss a payment schedule. He advised me not to include it in the bankruptcy proceedings since there was no agreement yet reached as far as repayment. That was fine with me. As far as the Internal Revenue Service was concerned, however, there were no provisions in their books for bankruptcy and no forgiveness.

By the time the 2004 legislative session rolled around, I had gotten my personal finances in order as best I could, save the IRS. That dilemma was proving near impossible, as we were constantly shifted from one IRS agent to another. It was quite obvious that I had lost more money at the casinos than I had won, but those losses didn't seem to count. It's pretty hard to keep records of cash flowing through the slots.

Within the first couple weeks of my first session as the "once again" representative for HD 17, the FEC released the names of the straw donors in the fiddler's campaign that happened nearly four years earlier. The press jumped on it as if it were yesterday, and yours truly was back in the headlines. The House Republicans, who were only one seat short of taking control of the majority, pounced on the opportunity like a shark on a wounded seal. Calling for nothing short of my resignation, they were preparing a resolution for censorship. With the media fanning the flames, it became a feeding frenzy. The House speaker summoned me to his office, where he and his leadership team were frantically trying to salvage their slim majority. The speaker explained that he could hold off the Republican resolution of censorship for one day, but after the weekend recess, there was no stopping it. With a majority of only one Democrat, he also wasn't sure he would garner the votes to defeat it. He recommended that I take personal privilege on the House floor and beg for forgiveness. Well, I could beg all I wanted, but I hadn't felt forgiven since I was twelve years old and I sure knew this wasn't a place of forgiveness.

In all my previous twelve years serving in the legislature, I hadn't seen or heard as much drama or clamoring for a cleansing. Drake Meely had written every governor in the United States promoting the drug Dilantin for his wealthy pal while accepting $250,000, and even that hadn't drawn this much ire. I had seen two legislators get in a fistfight over which one would get to schedule his pastor as preacher of the week. We had all read audit reports of hundreds of thousands of dollars going into welfare to work contracts that produced little more than a fat salary for political patronage. Even that hadn't brought out this much disdain. Oh well, success in politics is a lot like success in gambling. Being in the right place at the right time pays big dividends. Wrong place, wrong time, however, sucks.

To make a long story short, I took to the well and gave the best apology I could. Being contrite goes a long way at disarming your enemies but, in my case, not long enough. Soon after my remarks, a Republican from Western Oklahoma took to the mic and reminded his fellow House members that although my apology was an honorable gesture, it didn't erase the reproach I'd brought on such an august body. He also pressed the issue of censorship and, with a few more damaging remarks, had his troops rallied once again for my head on a platter. The resolution would be brought for a vote on the following Monday.

That very weekend, the Republican who had so passionately pleaded for restoration of dignity and honor to such an esteemed body was charged with sexual battery. According to a police affidavit filed with the charges, the Republican legislator sat down with a group of women at an Oklahoma City motel lounge and began making lewd comments. One woman alleged that he told her to change into boxer shorts and a T-shirt and join him in the hot tub. The woman then claimed that he followed her into the motel bar and grabbed her buttocks. The woman ran to an elevator to leave, but he pried the doors open. According to the police affidavit, she contacted hotel staff for assistance in escaping the intoxicated Republican legislator. News of his unfortunate incident broke over the weekend, and when I returned to the capitol on Monday, not one word was mentioned of my censorship. The following day, he was charged with one count of sexual battery. My, how the worm turns. Both sides of the fickle House isle seemed to quietly call it even.

No sooner had that storm passed than Hibbs was back at the capitol with chocolate in hand and a credit card, begging for hungry legislators. He seemed to have exhausted his run at the casino business and was back on the power plant notion. Having dodged more bullets than I had deserved, I was in no mood to be involved with legislation helping Ace Developers while on its payroll. Having my legislative salary back was sufficient enough, so I removed myself from Hibbs's payroll, as I felt more than confident I could resume my role for Ace Developers after my remaining three-year stint in the House. I was quite sure a conflict of interest would be in the making.

Hibbs seemed to be oblivious to the fact that I was no longer capable of wielding the power I'd had before leaving the legislature a year earlier. Although I could exhort and otherwise cajole my fellow legislators, I could make nothing meaningful happen on my own. The days of simply inserting cash amounts in the appropriations process were over. Undeterred, Hibbs was as happy as a pig in the sun, so long as he could round up political company for lunch and dinner. Aside from his various companies, his wife's business, and a myriad of Ace projects, he had also managed to form a nonpropfit foundation, the likes of which could accept state funds for suitable projects, especially his projects!

He had formed the foundation during the previous session while I was lobbying my old buddies for state funds. The local COG was too slow for his liking. He preferred working with people he knew. The foundation was another brainchild of his that was both impressive and expedient. Officers of the foundation included the vice president of a prominent McClain bank, a former employee of the Agriculture Stabilization and Conservation Service, and a federal probation officer, among others.

I was more concerned with progress on the manufacturing plant. It had become the major topic of the mean-spirited Insider and was swiftly becoming the whipping boy for the local newspaper. Moreover, McClain city hall had fallen victim to an FBI investigation concerning leave buyback schemes involving certain city officials. The newspaper, along with an overly exuberant editor, was making mention of the city hall scandal in the same breath as the lagging progress on the manufacturing plant. With that $40,000 loan haunting my conscience and the senator out of sorts, I was beginning to sweat bullets. Hibbs shrugged my concern off with a laugh, assuring me that the plant was well on its way, with employees already at the helm who would have it up and running within the month. All I could do was hope he was right. Simply paying back the so-called loan was out of the question. I had long since gambled that away.

Midway through the legislative session, Hibbs had become relatively and suspiciously quiet. He had finally figured out that I didn't possess the clout that I once did and was spending more time leaning on my friends who did. That was fine by me, but it still didn't settle my anxieties over the yet to be opened manufacturing plant. Having left the capitol for the weekend, I decided to pay a personal visit to the plant, wanting to see for myself what progress was being made. As I pulled into the plant's entrance, my fears were somewhat put to rest. From the outside, I could see the large grain bins firmly in place, several conveyors crisscrossing about, and a completed loading dock. I noticed Hibbs's expensive SUV parked near the office entrance, as well as several other vehicles. Plant employees, I presumed. What a relief!

My relief was short-lived as I entered the front office door. There, sprawled about the main office were a half dozen newly manufactured slot machines with wires and computers tangled in between. The handful of people there were so busy attending the computers and various slot control devices, they didn't notice my entrance. Standing amid all the wires was Hibbs, Hawaiian shirt and all. He did notice me and turned red as a beet, obviously embarrassed. It was an awkward moment to say the least, but I wasn't his daddy and sure wasn't in any position to chew him out. After the initial shock of my sudden appearance wore off, Hibbs began to explain his latest venture and assured me the Superior Products facility was only a temporary location for the machines. He introduced me to one of the fellows operating a computer that had wires running to one of the machines. Hibbs had flown him in from England to program the slots. This was one project Hibbs had left me out of. I assumed he had reached an agreement with a tribe and wanted this deal all to himself. I was beginning to have serious concerns about this guy.

Hibbs went on to explain that although it would be nearly impossible to develop a new casino, getting his own machines in them was the next best thing. He also said he'd been meaning to call me for some time, but he'd been so busy he'd procrastinated. He also assured me that he would need my help in getting the slots placed in various tribal gaming facilities.

At that moment, I was far more concerned with seeing Superior Products running on those empty conveyors. The local paper was relentless in their editorials chiding both Hibbs and the McClain foundation for the plant's lack of progress. It was only a matter of time before I would be a recipient of the same disdain. Once again, Hibbs promised to get the facility completed.

As life in small towns go, word of the newfangled slot machines soon leaked. Just days after I had unexpectedly discovered them, the local police paid the plant a visit. Satisfied that the slots weren't in use, they merely warned Hibbs that he should waste no time in moving them to a proper location. The damage had been done regardless. Word of the slot machines that were being programmed and stored in the infamous manufacturing plant spread like wildfire. It certainly reenergized and refueled both the Insider and the newspaper.

The visit I made at the plant gave me great pause for concern. Although I had repeatedly questioned Hibbs in regard to proper use of state funds, I was now ready to question someone with a little more authority. Seeing those slots scattered around the manufacturing plant had left me seething and wondering. Not that I had suddenly turned savior of state funds, but I sure didn't need any more attention on that miserable building I'd helped him acquire.

The following Monday, I rounded up a dozen legislators, including some of my buddies whom I'd lobbied to put money into the newly formed nonprofit foundation. I explained to them that I had concerns over the state funds that had gone to the foundation created by my genius partner. I stopped short of telling them I thought he was crooked but made my point well enough that we all got an audience with the state auditor. Once in the auditor's office, I laid all the cards on the table in regard to the nonprofit foundation and explained that our concern was that of using state funds within the confines of state guidelines. I explained to the auditor that although there were prominent and qualified people on the foundation's board, it was in its infant stages and merited watching over. The auditor appeared to know all about the foundation and confirmed its authenticity. He also assured us that the money could be audited and that he had no reason to believe any improprieties were taking place. Silently, I let out a huge sigh of relief! Of course, I didn't mention slot machines, and there was really no need to. Hibbs had assured me that operating capital for his slot operation was strictly out of his Hibbs Enterprise account. All I needed to hear was some assurance that my "suspect" partner wasn't creating more problems on top of the $40,000 loan that was still making me sweat. The visit with the auditor was confirmation enough.

Just the day after my buddies and I had our sit down with the state auditor, Hibbs showed up at the capitol right on time for lunch. My old mansion roommate and a couple of other close legislator friends all boarded the big SUV, with Hibbs as our chauffer and our lunch ticket. During lunch, Hibbs explained his latest venture into the gaming business and offered us all opportunity to participate. He would need our tribal acquaintances in order to get his new machines placed in various casinos. This job would be completely out of the realm of state government, legal, and very lucrative. All we needed to do was work out the details of payment, whether he paid a flat rate for every machine we got placed, or a percentage of the take. Either way, it sounded like a sweet deal. My buddies were just as intrigued as I was.

Before any details could be worked out, there were other pressing issues at hand. The tribes were currently trying to push a bill through the legislature that would legalize class 2 gaming. Although they were already using class 2 machines, this would free them from the antagonizing fines they were paying and other red tape issues with the tribal gaming commission. People involved in drafting the legislation were mostly slot machine vendors with one purpose in mind, making sure that *their* slots were the only ones to be legalized. The numbers and complicated codes that were being drafted into the legislation were ambiguous and near impossible for any lay person or legislator to understand. My buddies and I did understand this much: Hibbs's machines weren't gonna be included without some help. We took our issue to the governor's chief of staff and explained that it made no sense to support legalizing class 2 machines that would only benefit out-of-state, deep-pocketed slot manufactures. We informed him of Hibbs's venture into slot manufacturing and requested that language in the bill accurately reflect codes and numbers that would include Hibbs's machines. The governor's offices agreed and were amicable to the idea, but the out-of-state slot vendors who were primarily drafting the language balked.

This was big money to them, and they were not in a mood to share. After a good long battle and the threat of not garnering enough votes to pass the controversial gaming bill, they finally caved in. Hibbs's machines would be involved, and my buddies and I would support the bill.

By the close of session that spring, Hibbs had opened a brand-new facility in McClain called Native Games. It was a large impressive building and literally full of slots. It was an enterprise all in itself, with at least a dozen employees busy building machine bases, and assembling complicated wiring harnesses. The hotshot programmer from England had his own office, complete with high-tech security and locked doors. For a gambling addict like me, standing among all that was like a crackhead in a warehouse full of dope. I was now getting a bird's-eye view of the business from the inside out.

The beginning of that summer, I tended my oversized garden just as I had for over two decades. The garden was my sanctuary, and though it demanded vigilance and hard work, it was the only place I could truly relax outside of the one week I spent at deer camp with my sons. The previous twelve years I had served in the legislature, I had used it to host a large gathering of my constituency, as well as political powers from all over Oklahoma. The gathering was called the Corn Fest. With help from my family and some close friends, we'd prepare a dozen large briskets in my homemade smoker, several hundred ears of the fresh sweet corn, and slice a full bushel of ripe tomatoes. The third Saturday of every June, cars would stream down my quarter mile stretch of gravel driveway in anticipation of the homegrown feast. Some came simply to sink their teeth into the long golden ears of fresh sweet corn and consume all the hickory-smoked barbeque their stomach could hold. Others came to rub elbows with the powers to be. Tables, all the chairs we could round up, and hay bales were scattered beneath the large oak and pine trees in my yard to accommodate the crowd. It was one of the finest outdoor feasts in all of Oklahoma.

This summer would be different. After that pummeling I got in the congressional race, I was in no mood to be the generous host of years gone past. If only the people who had sheared off all those ears of corn would have voted, I'd have come closer to winning than I did. It was quite the rude awakening after a dozen years of glad handing and backslapping to find myself that alone after losing that race. I had come to the realization that I had better spend my last two years in office taking care of myself. There would be lots of canning and freezing to do this summer.

Aside from the garden that summer, I was neck deep into the slot machine business. I'd let my secretary handle all the constituent calls, just like most politicians did. Gone were the days of my spending countless hours on the phone trying to find someone a job or get their kids out of jail.

Hibbs was busier than ever courting the Indians, and I was right along with him. We attended a big gaming convention in Tulsa where all the hopeful slot manufactures gathered to show off their wares. It was quite intriguing to see the machines manipulated to hit an assortment of good jackpots. I had always had the notion that slot machines were based on odds. I was fascinated to see how easily they could go from hot to cold with the click of a mouse.

Things were beginning to look up. The unannounced visit at the manufacturing plant by the local police had finally shaken Hibbs up enough to get things rolling there, and the local press was preoccupied with the city hall scandal. We had also managed to get Hibbs's machines into a handful of the small tribal gaming facilities. The major tribes were harder nuts to crack. They seemed set on using the slot manufactures from out of state.

Prospects of a good income from placing slot machines just added fuel to my already chronic gambling habit, not to mention the constant visits to casinos while peddling our goods. You would have had to hold a gun on me to keep me from putting money in a machine, even when my purpose of being there wasn't to gamble. I had a friend who was managing a casino for a tribe in northern Oklahoma, who years earlier had worked in my campaigns. I paid him a visit knowing that if there was any way, he'd let me place Hibbs machines there. After our visit, I passed by some high-limit slots, pulled a $20 out of my wallet, and, on the second press of the button, I hit a $2,400 jackpot. On the way home that night, I stopped at several more casinos. After all, you can't drive more than thirty miles in Oklahoma without driving past one. By the time I got home, I had lost not only the $2,400 jackpot but everything else that was in my wallet. In the gambling addiction, your money evaporates, but the IRS forms don't.

Before the summer was over, my buddies and I met Hibbs at a good Italian restaurant, where he gave each of us our small percentage for the machines we had placed. It wasn't much, but it was a start. We were responsible for our own taxes, just as I had been when I got income from Ace. I paid all my taxes to the slots. After the luncheon with my buddies, we were off to Guthrie, Oklahoma, for a dinner meeting with other gaming consultants he'd hired. One of them was an old high school friend of mine who was now working for the tribal gaming commission. The other was a chubby, no-nonsense kind of gal, whose day job was representing legal matters for a small tribe in Central Oklahoma. Hibbs was spreading his tentacles as far into the gaming business as his checkbook would allow, and that was pretty far.

Hibbs had a thing for Guthrie and was acquainted with a lot of folks there. He had worked with the historical city for several years trying to establish a trolley system that would run parallel with its city streets from one historical venue to another. He owned a caboose and an old steam engine, along with some other antique railcars, and had them stored there. I'm pretty sure I'm probably the one that helped him buy the railcars he owned years earlier, before I even knew the guy existed. I recalled how old

Senator Stokes had come lumbering over to the House floor during a late-night session as we were trying to wrap up a general appropriation bill. He wanted me to earmark $300,000 for the Guthrie historical society. At the time, I found it odd that Stokes would be interested in helping the city of Guthrie since it wasn't even remotely close to his senate district. I didn't question him, though. He rarely asked me to earmark funds for anything, so I just did it. I did alert the good representative from Guthrie that we were sending state funds to his area, so he could take credit.

Hibbs was also enamored with the old theater in Guthrie that was used as a performing arts theater. He would often charter a bus and take groups from home to watch the performances. He had also used Guthrie as the location for holding political fundraisers, most notably, for the newly elected Democratic governor and the new Second District US congressman.

At times during lockdown, I'd catch myself pacing back and forth from the narrow window looking outside to the cell door window facing the empty pod. It was only three paces from one window to the other, but I made a lot of trips. I had nearly fourteen months behind me, as my second summer on the inside was winding down. I couldn't help but think of all the young guys locked inside this very facility who had already spent more time in a county jail, and that was before even learning of their final sentence. From the view outside my window, well beyond the outside wire, I could see the scorched dry grass and withered leaves left from the searing summer heat. Inside the prison fence, all was lush and green. Although I didn't see much to be proud of from where I stood, I could see the huge American flag waving proudly high above the coils of razor wire. Some things seem to just make us proud, whether they make sense or not. Regardless, I could tell by the view outside that prison time was getting short for me. In less than six months, I would be viewing this place from a rearview mirror. The flood of inmates never slowed in the giant holdover units. They kept coming and going like cattle through the stockyards. Cadre unit was a constant change as well, and I was now on my seventh cellie. Newcomers, from my perspective, were almost predictable, as they came in with the latest fad in publicity and politics.

Two of the latest arrivals, both in their mid-forties, had gotten caught up in a conspiracy of selling OxyContin, a prescription narcotic. They both looked like deer caught in the headlights as they exited the large elevator and entered their strange, new home. One would be my last cellmate.

The one ending up as my cellie was dirt-poor and, like most of the others, had a court-appointed attorney. He got hooked on Oxy the legal way, as prescribed by his doctor after a car accident left him with a ruptured disk. To support his addiction, he delivered Oxy to others, who like himself had become addicted to the powerful drug. Most of them were family and people he knew. His supplier had been busted and, saving himself from a lengthy prison stay, snitched on his couriers. Lucky for my new cellie, he wasn't an outdoor sportsman. There were no hunting rifles in his mobile home, or he'd be doing a lot more time than the two years he ended up with.

Another of the new arrivals in the early fall was a young black man named Walker. He had been busted on a marijuana charge three years earlier and received five years' probation. Since then, he had cleaned up his act, gotten married, and had an eighteen-month old child, with another one on the way. He supported his young family as a handyman, helping his older brother on remodeling jobs. With three and a half years of probation behind him without incident, he had taken his wife out of town to see her mother and failed to report for his monthly drug test. His parole officer cut him no slack and sent him to see the judge. The judge gave him six months in the federal pen.

When he told me who the "tough on crime" judge was, I was embarrassed to tell him I knew the guy. He was minority floor leader when I first got elected to the House. A congressional delegation of party affiliates had got him appointed to a federal judgeship. I can almost assure you that guy never had to paint a house!

In early October, one of the new cadre inmates was a victim of the warden's kidnapping from holdover. He was a king-sized fellow of Hispanic descent we called Premo. Caught in the usual safe street initiative that leveraged guns as a means of long convictions, Premo was doing a sixteen-year sentence. His family originated in old Mexico and later established themselves in South Texas, where as a child, Premo helped his father raise and train quarter horses.

Not long after high school graduation, Premo left home to stay with relatives in Colorado to help them start a ranching operation of their own. Wavering from his strict upbringing, Premo fell in with some guys who hooked him up in the marijuana trade. Being more of a rancher and less than a drug dealer, Premo was easily caught by the feds. Of course, his uncle there in Colorado had plenty of hunting rifles that were used to enhance his crime. Premo refused to snitch out his new so-called friends, thus bearing full weight of the penalty himself.

He completed his first five years in a medium facility in Big Springs, Texas. When his points finally dropped, qualifying him for a lower security facility closer to his home in Colorado, his prison councilor recommended a redesignation. Premo would finally be going to a camp facility in Florence, Colorado, where he could get some much-needed visits from family. As in most cases, he would be routed through the OKC federal transfer center, waiting there in holdover until the next prison bus or plane could ship him on to Florence. Unfortunately, the warden needed to fill an empty bunk in the cadre unit, and Premo was the unlucky pick. His redesignation closer to home would have to wait another two years.

Premo went to work in utilities, where Griff used to work, and I would see him often as the utility crew would come to safety for supplies. We became fast friends when I found out commissary didn't keep his favorite brand of instant coffee in stock. I got the boss man to include Premo's brand in our next commissary shipment. After that, Premo thought I was no less than the Godfather himself. It still made me feel good inside to help someone, and it made Premo feel good to know someone.

After mess call every evening, I would alternate playing cards between Pete and Premo and still manage to get a game or two of washers in with some of the other guys. Premo's eyes would light up when he'd tell me stories of the famous quarter horses he and his father had raised and, like the rest, would hold his enormous belly while laughing at my political tales.

By the time college football was in full swing, I was down to counting the days, and so were Big Tex and Gage. On Saturday afternoon in E pod, you'd find Gage and me squarely in front of the TV pole, with our transistors tuned in to watch Sooner football. In D pod, Oso and a couple other Okie inmates would be doing the same. Gage and I had a little extra pep in our step knowing we were both soon to be released. We had a little extra pep in our jaws too as we taunted our fellow cadre inmates with the crimson-and-cream toboggans Oso had crocheted for us. Oso wasn't only a gangster who was frightened of bugs but could crochet with the best of them!

In the days leading up to the Big 12 Conference championship, Gage and I were in full throttle, razzing our fellow inmates of our unbeatable Sooners. It was OU versus Mizzou, both unbeaten and both vying for the Big 12 crown. Naturally, JR, Billy, and other Missourians were doing the same for their team, and since OU had beaten Texas in the Cotton Bowl, all the cadre's Texas fans were pulling for Mizzou.

The evening prior to kickoff, Gage and I were on one side of the pod and most everyone else in E pod on the other. The TVs on both sides of the pole tuned in to the big game. Big Tex shouted above all the noise, "Look at Gov! Blind mothafucka actin' like he can see the TV!" Even Gage had to laugh.

Mizzou ran the opening kickoff back for a touchdown, and the entire pod went nuts. They couldn't give Gage and me enough hell. OU answered the Mizzou touchdown on their ensuing drive, so Gage and I did our own little end zone dance.

Fortunately, the unit CO was a football fan himself and paid little attention to the ruckus surrounding the TV pole. Ordinarily, that kind of pandemonium would have landed some inmates in the SHU. Mizzou went on to claim both the victory and the Big 12 title that afternoon. Billy, JR, and the others got the last laugh and rode Gage and me pretty hard. For a brief three hours, everyone's time went fast!

The celebration for young JR was short-lived. The following Monday, the safety boss interrupted JR's daily inventory count for a private consultation. He had the grim task of informing JR that his grandmother had passed away. For all practical purposes, JR's grandmother had been his mother most of his life. JR took the news pretty hard, and he slid to the concrete floor with his face buried in his hands. He sobbed uncontrollably for the better part of an hour. Billy and I tried, but our consoling did little to ease his grief. The boss in safety went well beyond his duty as a prison guard and supervisor. He stayed by JR's side most of the day. Knowing that getting an inmate out of prison to attend a funeral was next to impossible, boss man pulled every string he could. Try as he may, however, there would be no funeral pass for young JR. You're lucky if you get out of the federal pen for your own funeral, much less your grandmother's.

The closer my out date came, the slower time seemed to go. I had done most of my time on adrenaline. It reminded me of my early high school days when I suited up for my first varsity football practice. Back then, the seniors had a special initiation in store for the freshmen who'd be coming to the high school as sophomores. The initiation was degrading and very painful, as told by those who'd been through it. Initiations took place on the mile, a stretch of dirt road that began near the practice field and looped around a wooded area leading back to the school. Most of it was well out of view from any school officials. Before any football drills would occur, the entire team had to run the mile as a warm-up. Somewhere, during the course, sophomores would meet their doom.

Although the initiation had never killed anyone, it sure didn't sound like anything I wanted to go through with. Not only that but my imagination had let fear grow to an unimaginable proportion.

As we exited the field house and gathered near the dirt road, the coach blew his whistle. It was time to run the mile! I lit out in a full sprint and didn't look back. All I could hear were the footsteps of those frightening seniors. I was far from an athlete, but I rounded the mile well ahead of the pack and in record time.

The coach was astonished to see me hotfooting it back so quickly. There wasn't another kid within sight behind me either. I impressed the coach so much, he signed me up for the high school track team running the 440. I never came close to winning a track meet, but then, I wasn't running on adrenaline either. I had done most of my prison time the same way I ran that mile—on adrenaline! Now that full reality had set in, every hour seemed more like a day.

A few days before Big Tex was getting released, some of the guys insisted that I go to a special Bible study that was going to occur on a Wednesday night an hour before lockdown. I hadn't been to that chapel in over a year and swore that I wasn't going back. Delany was grinning big when he said, "Gov, I guarantee you, if you go, you won't miss another Wednesday night until you leave here." The grin got me, so on Wednesday evening at 7:45 p.m., I followed the group to the large elevator, where we'd be escorted to the chapel below.

I had never seen so many of my fellow cadre inmates interested in a Bible study. Big Tex even crowded into the elevator. In fact, the on duty guard had to make two elevator trips.

As we entered the chapel single file, old Delany rushed over to a small bookshelf and grabbed an armload of hymnals to pass out. It was obvious that he'd had prior church training. He placed two of them on folding chairs positioned on the front row, saving prime seats for both himself and me.

After we were all seated, a middle-aged couple walked in, a husband and wife team who were volunteering their time to share the Word with us lowly inmates. One glance was all I needed. I completely understood old Delany's grin.

The husband was a scrawny little fellow. He was carrying a guitar case that appeared to be as big as he was. His wife, however, was nothing short of a retired runway model gone evangelist. She was wearing gray slacks and a white form-fitting button-up shirt. The top button of the shirt was unfastened and for good reason. She couldn't have pulled it together if she tried. Delany was cutting his eyes over, trying to see my reaction, and his grin was only getting wider. I'm quite sure the expression on my face was everything he'd expected. I was stunned! Just the weekend before, my daughter had been turned away from visitation because her four-year-old was wearing a sleeveless T-shirt. She had to find a Walmart in Oklahoma City and buy my grandbaby another shirt before they would let her in to visit.

Nevertheless, I had a front-row seat at quite a show. Tex leaned up from the row behind and whispered, "I bet that ole crooked eye can see now!"

The woman's little husband strummed a few chords on his guitar and sat quietly on a stool while she preached with all the fervor of a TV evangelist. She strutted back and forth holding the Word of God in one hand and our undivided attention in the other.

I could never forget her lesson plan. After about a dozen "one last scriptures," she drove home her final point. "Your thoughts make you who you are," she said. "Keep your thoughts on the Word, and you can live completely free of sin."

Oh well, the Wednesday-night chapel visit made about as much sense as anything else that I'd ever had a front-row seat to in politics, where politicians jump through hoops like little circus dogs, entertaining the crowd and pandering to the latest political fad, with the media both acting and reacting to whatever sells. They were like preachers, all of them, with their own points of view and directions to heaven.

As bad as I hate to admit it, I never really understood the big deals in life. My brain just never developed to that level of sophistication. The big important deals always seemed to just sail over my head, like seventh-grade algebra did. I'd just gone with it and acted like I understood it and went along in order to get along. My answers to the "big questions" were always far too simple and still are. Older brother was like that as well. We were coming back from a gambling trip to Bossier City, Louisiana, one night and had to rake pennies and nickels out of the floorboard of the car in order to pay a seventy-five-cent toll fee on the Indian Nation Turnpike. While we were looking for loose coins, I asked him if he thought we might have a gambling problem. He said, "It's only a problem when you're losing!"

Back in my old high school football days, we had a coach who was like that as well, always having simple answers to sophisticated questions. His name was Haskell Jennings.

Although Hartshorne was a relatively small school, we played against opponents who had athletes who went on to stardom. In 1969, we played Eufaula for the 10-B conference championship. Our team was made up of mostly poor country kids and a handful of Native American boys from the neighboring Jones Academy boarding school. We may have had one pretty good athlete, and it certainly wasn't me. Eufaula had all three of the famous Selmon brothers: Lucious, Lee Roy, and Dewey. All three went on to have successful college careers, and a couple of them would become top-notch NFL players. Nevertheless, we beat them for the 10-B crown.

A lot of teams came to Hartshorne boasting future greats, only to get a sound whipping from Coach Jennings. The Henrietta

Hens came with a rocket-armed quarterback named Troy Aikman. A few years later, Eufaula came to town with another future All American J. C. Watts.

Despite the talent that Coach Jennings faced, he somehow managed to pull off victory after victory, so much that he was later inducted into Oklahoma's High School Football Coaches Hall of Fame. Anticipating a profound secret formula, a reporter asked how he managed to consistently win with only a handful of mostly average athletes. Coach Jennings said, "Gosh, I just figured if I'd teach them the basics of how to block and tackle, they'd do pretty good." Coach Jennings would never have made a good politician!

By the time the first session of my final two-year term in the Oklahoma House of Representatives rolled around, my wagon was firmly hitched to Hibbs, along with all his harebrained ideas. In all reality, it had become pretty well hitched the day I took that $40,000 check/loan/kickback from the senator's secretary.

As I had grown accustomed to, nothing went smooth for very long while working for him. Just as I was beginning to feel comfortable about the progress on the manufacturing plant and our new venture into the gaming business, Hibbs took yet another turn. The slot machine business just wasn't fast enough to suit him. Working with tribal governments was a different ball game than working with any other form of government. They might order a truckload of machines one day and want you to move them out the next. Hibbs thought he was doing a good job wining and dining the tribal hot shots, but in the casino business, there was always someone who could buy a bigger bottle of wine. Although he wouldn't admit it, he couldn't play ball with the really big boys.

His latest scheme absolutely trumped every bad idea he'd ever come up with. He now wanted to apply for water rights out of Lake Eufaula, one of the largest manmade lakes in the country, and sell water to towns along Interstate 40 all the way to

OKC. People in Oklahoma were already stirred up about water rights. We'd been in battles with North Texas and the tribes over water rights ever since I'd been in office. To top it all off, we'd been in the worst drought Oklahoma had seen since the Dirty Thirties. Eufaula lake levels were already well below normal, and the folks who had expensive boat docks now sitting on dry land sure weren't going to sit still at the prospects of sucking it down even lower, especially to send it off to OKC.

Hibbs, however, was oblivious to anything remotely related to common sense. He had friends on the Water Resources Board in OKC, so common sense had nothing to do with it. I couldn't talk him out of it. I knew that the idea would stir up a political hornet's nest, bringing both Hibbs and myself right back into the media's crosshairs, and would be impossible to do even under the best circumstances, but you can't talk to a guy who thinks he's smarter than everyone else.

I also found out that Hibbs had gotten himself at odds with old Senator Stokes, the very guy who had taken Hibbs under his wing and partnered with him in some very lucrative business deals. According to Hibbs, Stokes was mad at him for not including him in the casino business. That made a little sense to me, but what didn't make sense was the fact that Stokes's long-time secretary was also on the outs with him. They both had been his closest confidants for a very long time, but they weren't now.

I hadn't even talked to old Stokes in a year. I knew he'd had a lot of health issues, and I also knew he was livid over losing his senate seat. He'd expected all those straw donors to take the fall for him. He wasn't accustomed to taking his own medicine. Whatever the case, I knew nothing good would come out of the three of them being at odds, so I steered clear of that mess.

That first session of my last term was miserable and a pretty good sign that my chickens were coming home to roost. Not only had the Republicans taken control of the House, but all my old buddies were gone as well. Sitting on that House floor completely powerless was akin to being in a casino flat broke. Besides that, these Republicans were taking no prisoners. They had my old guru and budget analyst, who had helped me ship money to the poor folk all those years, escorted out of the building like he was a criminal. They left no stone unturned in that capitol building. House staffers who had worked there for years were either demoted or fired. The takeover was like being under martial law. I already had a bad guilt complex, but these Republicans were all but carrying handcuffs with them. Making things even worse was the fact that every time I looked up, there was Hibbs in his big Hawaiian shirt, stirring up the murky waters of Lake Eufaula.

Just as I had presumed, it wasn't long before Hibbs's latest conquest had the good folk around Eufaula Lake up in arms. I was smart enough to stay well away from this doom-ridden project, but it didn't stop the protests and god-awful press. The riff between Stokes, Hibbs, and Stokes's longtime secretary had also turned into a war. It got so bad that Stokes fired his secretary. Now how smart was that? She had helped sweep his dirt under the rug for years, and now he was cutting her loose? Not only cutting her loose but leaving her crippled by the hefty fine and federal probation he'd gotten her into. I didn't know much about it all, but I knew one thing, shit was about to hit the fan!

In the midst of all the chaos, I get a call from the old senator, who I hadn't heard from for the better part of a year. Without warning, my secretary buzzed his call into my office, and when I picked up the phone, he immediately started rambling on about that crooked Hibbs. All the stuff I'd heard about their fight was now being confirmed. The last time old Stokes mentioned Hibbs to me was when he recommended that I go to work for the brilliant entrepreneur. Now he was calling him a crook and wanting me to steer clear of him. A little late for that, I thought. Stokes wasn't one to chitchat or ask your opinion in the matter, especially when he was on the war path. He rambled on about the misdeeds of Hibbs and his old secretary and hung up. That was the last conversation I ever had with the old senator.

Back in McClain, the city hall scandal was wrapping up with the city manager going to trial for all kinds of alleged maleficence. Both the young editor and crusader for the local newspaper and the infamous Insider were taking half the credit for cleaning up city hall and were now vowing to cleanse the shady business behind the manufacturing plant. The local newspaper and the feds were on a full-blown honeymoon!

Meanwhile, feeling their oats from gaining control of the Oklahoma House of Representatives, Republicans in the city were on a cleansing mission of their own. Foremost in their sights was one of the last remaining statewide democratic office holders, the state auditor. His nemesis was the Republican whom he'd defeated in the general election who had now become the state chairman of the Republican Party. These guys weren't like Democrats, who seemed to be satisfied with smearing their political rivals in the newspaper; they wanted convictions! At issue in the auditor's office was none other than the ties he had with Hibbs, Stokes, and an alleged cozy relationship with their private businesses.

While all these events were unfolding, I was becoming paralyzed with fear. I could sense serious trouble, and all I wanted to do was bury myself in a casino somewhere.

The fight among Stokes, Hibbs, and Stokes's secretary had now turned vicious. None of them seemed to care or acknowledge the cloud of suspicion we were all now under. Their only goal was getting their own pound of flesh. In fact, they were as brazen as to sic investigators on each other. I soon realized that I was merely collateral damage to the whole lot of them.

Toward the end of that unsettling session, all the state associations were busy putting on their end-of-session parties. The takeover didn't seem to affect any of them or the lobbyists. They just crawled out of one bed and into another. Although mingling about in one of the sine die parties wasn't at all appealing to me, I decided to force myself to at least attend the firefighters' association's shindig. There was the typical large crowd there, but it was quite obvious that new faces were now getting all the attention. I spotted one of the old House secretary's sitting at a table full of people, with an empty chair next to her. She had been a loyal secretary to one of my best buddies in the House for years, so I made a beeline to sit next to her. There weren't that many friendly faces in the crowd anyway. Although I considered her a friend, she was one of the biggest gossipers in all the state capitol. I knew that if there were any secret movement afoot, she couldn't help but tell it. I no sooner sat down than she leaned over and whispered, "I hear the feds are looking at you and the boys," meaning my buddies who would be in the slot-promoting business with me. My heart sank plumb to the bottom of my Tony Lama boots. I don't remember leaving that reception or the state capitol at the close of that session. I needed time in my garden.

I was always one who was very adept at smearing myself without the help of anyone else. Nonetheless, I had plenty of help, whether I needed it or not. I guess you could say that in politics, that goes with the territory.

Back in my Chamber of Commerce days, I met a guy who ran a small electrical business. A real good ole boy. He was relatively new to the area, having been raised in Northeast Oklahoma. I met him on the heels of the Randy Travis concert, after which a lot of folk thought I was a real event organizer. We became buddies of sorts, so based on the fact that he ran a small business and was outgoing, I recruited him to serve on the chamber board. Naturally I needed friendly board members, especially in light of the fact that the chamber manager, whom I'd replaced, still worked there and had a knack for stirring up trouble at my expense.

Not long after getting my new buddy appointed, we were sharing stories from our past and making small talk. He went all the way back to his childhood. The story he seemed most proud of came about when a new kid moved in next door. He was fourteen years old at the time and said the new kid was a year or two younger, redheaded and chubby.

Welcoming the new kid to the neighborhood, he hid behind the hedges in back of his parents' house and fired a round of rat shot from a .22-caliber rifle into the boy's side as the chubby youngster was coming out to play.

Poor kid didn't know where or from whom the shot came, but he ended up in the hospital getting rat shot removed from his waist and hip. I then asked, "Why did you shoot the poor kid?"

He laughed a hideous laugh and said, "I didn't like the little bastard's looks."

That story told me a lot about my new "best friend" and like a fool, I'd been promoting him as a chamber board member. Later on, I wasn't one bit surprised to learn he'd become my chamber nemesis's ally and confidant.

When I resigned from the chamber as executive director, I was more than glad to rid myself from the likes of that guy, as well as a few other chamber types! Fate, however, wouldn't let it be that simple.

I went on to work with my brothers and later elected to the Oklahoma House. After serving only one term, the fiddler, whose house district adjoined mine, resigned from his House seat to run for congress. My former trigger-happy friend ran for and won the empty seat. I cringed.

Trying my best to be cordial to my new colleague, I knew to keep my distance. Like the odor of dog dung tracked inside, that too proved impossible to avoid. He soon made himself welcome as a frequent mansion guest and, keeping true to form, brought his unwelcome antics with him. One evening, with the mansion filled with guests, he positioned himself on the front lawn, shooting potatoes from a homemade device on to the School of Science and Math that was located across the street.

The next morning, there was a note attached to our front door from officials of the prestigious school. It wasn't a pleasant note either. My mansion roommate and I were thoroughly embarrassed.

More than a decade later, the sharpshooter was golfing buddies with the federal investigator assigned to my case. I could feel the rat shot!

By now, Stokes and Hibbs had let their personal fight spill over into a civil lawsuit, hurling their insults and accusations publicly. They both had enough money to burn a wet mule, but evidently that wasn't enough for either of them. They would each be damned if the other got one cent more of their private business than the other and didn't care who got caught in the middle. Hibbs, who had finally emerged from Stokes's shadow, full of ambition and greed, and Stokes reeling with anger at losing his senate seat and taking the hickey from the fiddler's campaign.

Having got all the mileage they could squeeze out of the McClain city hall scandal, the local area-wide newspaper honed in on Stokes, Hibbs, the manufacturing plant, and me. The young editor, who was as full of ambition as he was of himself, was printing headlines and editorials on a tabloid level, warning his good readers to not be shocked by what might be uncovered. The rumor that I heard was true, and the FBI was having a field day between depositions filed in the civil suit and the barrage of publicity about the manufacturing plant. The newspaper boys were ringing my phone off the wall, but I wouldn't answer. One thing I did know, no good would come from talking to them.

With the session over and the headlines swirling, I planted myself square in the middle of my garden, hoping I'd wake up the next morning and realize it was all a bad dream. It's hard to sleep with your eyes open. That $40,000 check from Stokes-via-Hibbs may as well have been a million. It would not have been haunting me any worse.

When I was in fifth grade, I stole a handful of test tubes from the grade school science class. I smuggled them out of school in a worn-out book satchel one of my friends had given me. I don't know what I thought I was going to do with them. They just looked so cool to me. By the time I got off the school bus that afternoon, I was a nervous wreck. I just knew that at any moment, the grade school principal would come looking for me. Carrying that old book satchel around was like holding a bag full of dynamite. It was easy to slip those tubes in that satchel, but it was a nightmare toting them. I buried those test tubes that very evening a good long way from the house, hoping I could get rid of that gnawing, haunting feeling in my gut. It had helped me no better than hiding in my garden was now. I couldn't even bury that $40,000 check, as if it would have helped anyway. I was never good at hiding my guilt.

The garden wasn't helping, nor was withdrawing on my forty-plus acres on Gaines Creek bottoms. I couldn't focus on anything. The headlines, the rumors, and my conscience were beginning to eat me alive. Having been home and out of touch for a few days, Hibbs's big maroon SUV came pulling into my driveway. In the passenger's seat was Stokes's estranged secretary. They both had an odd grin on their face, as if this untangling mess was merely some kind of game. In an odd sort of way, it was a little comforting that they drove up. One of them had come up with an amount, and the other had handed me the check that was now eating my guts. Maybe they had the answer that was gonna make it all go away. They sure didn't appear to be sweating like I was. Hibbs invited me inside the SUV. The three of us were going for a drive. Driving the back county roads, both Hibbs and his companion spent the better part of an hour trying to convince me what a rotten SOB Stokes was and how it was all his fault that the feds were now sorting through everyone's dirty laundry. They weren't telling me anything I didn't already know. I felt like the whole lot of us were rotten SOBs. I also knew that this mess was as much Hibbs's fault as it was anybody's. He'd made a bungled mess of everything I had seen him touch for the past year.

Why the secretary was so involved, I didn't have a clue, but she seemed just as wound up as Hibbs. Other than bad-mouthing Stokes, they both seemed overly concerned with my well-being. Although neither of them had not so much as mentioned the $40,000 loan since the day I received it, they couldn't seem to shut up about it now. The secretary was the very one who had put a real emphasis on the word *loan* that was written at the bottom of that check. She wasn't singing the loan song now. According to her, it was a bona fide kickback from Stokes. Hibbs would glance up at his rearview mirror as if to take note of my reaction while I was sitting in the back seat taking it all in.

Having made our country drive and confidential visit, we pulled back into my drive. Before I crawled out of the back seat, Hibbs assured me this would all blow over soon, especially if his old partner would keep his mouth shut. (Like everything else he got involved with, he was also an expert on how the FBI operated.) Hibbs then recommended that I get over all the rumors and headlines and go on with business as usual. After all, he still had a few slot machines in a casino or two up north and would need me to accompany him there in a few days.

After they left, a thousand thoughts crossed my mind, and not a single one was good. The best I could hope for was that maybe Hibbs was right, this would all blow over. One thing, however, was for certain. There was no longer any question about the $40,000. The unbelievable part was that I had never, as of yet, talked to the old senator about it. Moreover, if he was interested in building a manufacturing plant, why didn't he ask me to get the money for it? He sure didn't have a problem asking for the $300,000 for Hibbs's trolley project in Guthrie several years earlier. It was too late to talk to him now. He was engaged full throttle in his battle with Hibbs.

In the weeks following the precarious meeting with Hibbs and the secretary, the rumors and headlines only intensified. The feds were interviewing everyone I had ever had any dealings with, but neither the feds, nor those folks, were talking to me about any of it. After several failed attempts at reaching me by phone, the young ambitious newspaper editor ran a story with the headline reading, "Where's Mike Mass?"

In the midst of it all, Hibbs was ready for another drive, and again, Stokes's former secretary went along. This time, we were en route to a casino in Northeast Oklahoma, and the conversation was a little more pointed. Hibbs not only wanted me to testify as a friendly witness in his civil suit against Stokes but also suggested that I contact the feds and tell them how Stokes had given me a kickback for getting state funds to buy his old building that had been previously used as headquarters for the fiddler's campaign. He went on to assure me that the feds weren't the least bit interested in me but wanted Stokes real bad. I was speechless! How dumb did this jerk think I was?

When we reached the casino, we were greeted by a fourth party—the chubby tribal attorney who Hibbs had recently hired on as another in his long list of consultants. The four of us went to a secluded diner where conspiring against Stokes would continue. I was somewhat shocked to learn that she seemed to know as much about the unraveling mess as I did. It was quite obvious that both she and the secretary were a lot tighter with Hibbs than I was. The woman had a whale of a personality. She talked to me as if we had been lifelong friends and, speaking from an attorney's point of view, or so she claims, suggested I follow Hibbs's lead. This was all nuts to me, and I'm quite sure by my expression, they could all tell I wasn't buying their goods. Hibbs ideas on how to solve legal problems were as goofy as were most of his entrepreneurial ventures.

The drive back home was uncomfortable, to say the least. Hibbs knew he wasn't being successful in enlisting my support in his scheme, and I was beginning to wonder what else besides the $40,000 loan I had gotten myself into. I also knew there wasn't anything that was simply going to blow over.

Bright and early the next morning, I hightailed it to Tulsa. There was an attorney there I had known quite well from my days as party chairman. He was on the party's executive board and had represented me before the DNC when disgruntled party members were challenging the results of my election. I spilled my guts to the trial lawyer, beginning with the $40,000 check up until the trip I had taken the night before. He asked if I had shared this information with anyone else, and of course, I hadn't. "Then don't," he said, "To anyone." He went on to tell me that he'd be glad to represent me at no cost. He was just that kind of person, and I figured he would help. We had become relatively close during my party chair days. Before I left, he warned me again to keep my mouth shut and if I were paid a visit by the federal investigators to call him immediately. I felt better after leaving his office than I had since the day I cashed that haunting check. He was on the case, and boy was I relieved. When I got home that evening, I changed into my overhauls, put a cigar in my mouth, and worked peacefully in my garden until sundown. That night, I slept better than I had in months.

The next morning was literally like the dawning of a new day. I had finally relieved my conscience by telling someone about the guilt I had carried for nearly a year. Moreover, it was someone who would help sort out the tangled web I was in. By the time I had poured a second cup of coffee, the phone rang. It was my friend and now my attorney. I was glad to take the call and pleasantly surprised he'd been working on my case so soon—that is, until I answered. Just after the hello, he informed me that working for me would be a conflict of interest, wished me the best, and hung up. I didn't have to guess what the conflict was. I knew. The old senator.

By midsummer, I was nothing more than a bundle of nerves. The FBI investigation of the old credentials I forged for old Sam paled in comparison to this one. I only had to sweat that one for a couple of weeks before the agents in their black suits and crew cuts came knocking. This one, however, was torturous. I knew they were questioning everyone I had ever dealt with, both at the state capitol and at home. I couldn't figure out why they hadn't come to see me yet. I knew they'd already pulled my bank records. It surely wasn't that difficult to find that $40,000 check, compare it to the amount of money sent to the manufacturing plant, and add things up. The up-and-coming young editor with the sensational editorials and the federal police seemed to be feeding off each other. They both had good practice under their belt during the course of the lengthy fiddler's campaign investigation and the city hall scandal, and they now appeared to be on the trail of the largest organized crime spree since Al Capone.

Almost going unnoticed, with the limited press coverage, was a local county official who had embezzled just over thirty thousand from the county coffers. She had fallen victim to the local casino, and her bad habit had led to her demise. The investigation was wrapped up pretty quick by the local DA. She was ordered to pay the money back and put on probation. I noticed, because her circumstances and mine were eerily similar, even the amount of money involved. I felt for her as well as myself. Being considered a much larger catch, however, my plight wouldn't be solved as quickly or as harmlessly!

At the center of all the madness was the ugly civil suit between Stokes and Hibbs, which was now on the court docket and being played out in full view. Entering into its second day in court, a county sheriff's deputy rolled up my driveway. I thought to myself, *Well, here it is, the day of judgment. But why the county?* When the deputy got out of his truck, he didn't have handcuffs. He had a subpoena. Since I wouldn't voluntarily join Hibbs's quest to battle Stokes, he would drag me into it. The move to subpoena me turned out to be brilliant on his part and costly on mine. Before I could take the stand, Stokes settled with Hibbs. Within a week, however, the old senator filed a lien on my house and forty-seven acres on Gaines Creek bottom. The subpoena to have me as a witness for Hibbs convinced Stokes that I was just as much his enemy. The lien he placed on my home made a pretty good case that the $40,000 check was indeed a loan, at least good enough for him.

After the settlement, the feds ramped up their investigation, leaving no doubt they were out for blood. They raided Stokes's law office and Hibbs's home. They also raided his Native Games gaming facility, private offices, and even the business that was operated by Hibbs's wife. The sudden move rattled Hibbs to his core. I was already rattled and had been for quite some time.

The next day, Hibbs called, wanting to meet me as soon as possible. I really didn't want to be anywhere around him but had little choice. It had become quite evident that there was far more to this tangled mess than the $40,000 check, and I needed to know where the next shoe would fall. We met in an offbeat parking lot, and I climbed in his big SUV for another countryside drive. He began spilling his guts to a laundry list of brazen and calculated illegal activity dating back to the first day I'd met him while running for the US congressional seat. With every breath, he used the term *we*, as if I had helped him mastermind every detail. Right away, I assumed he was wired. I was well accustomed to him talking like an idiot, but he was off the chain now. When he finished regurgitating all the sorted details, he laid out his plan to cure it all. The plan not only involved feeding Stokes to the wolves but my buddies in the legislature as well. In his words, "I'm not going to the federal pen," and "I don't care what it takes." He went on to say that if I had taken his advice about going to the feds earlier to do Stokes in, this would have all been over. He said "we" were gonna have to puke on everybody, and even puke a little on ourselves. To sweeten the deal, he had already paid a $5,000 retainer and secured me a lawyer as well. I felt as if I were caught in another episode of the *Twilight Zone*.

I never really knew whether Hibbs was wired that day or not, but he'd made one thing perfectly clear. I was screwed! I didn't know the lawyer Hibbs had hired for me, but I knew I needed one. I planned to use him, only not in the way he had suggested. I went that afternoon, and sure enough, the attorney was expecting my visit. Before the lawyer could even pick up a pen, I asked that he get the US attorney for the Eastern District of Oklahoma on the phone. I was ready to tell him of a $40,000 check I'd taken over a year earlier and was ready to take my medicine. Not only that, I wanted to tell him of my disturbing country rides with Hibbs, whether he already knew or not. The lawyer, taken aback by my request, recommended that I first tell him my story and let him do the navigating. I said, "No, thanks, get me the US attorney on the phone now!" He got him on the phone in a matter of minutes, with me sitting in plain sight across his desk. He explained to the chief federal law officer that I was his client and was ready to talk.

The attorney's response was without hesitation. "We're not ready to talk to Mr. Mass," he said, "but he is definitely a target and one we consider the kingpin."

The look on that lawyer's face alone was enough to scare the wits out of me. I'm sure this was somewhat out of his league since he mainly dealt with divorce and child custody cases. We were both in over our heads, and my life, as I had known it, was over. To the lawyer's credit, he did confess that this case was a little much for him and recommended I find someone else. Since Hibbs had paid this guy's retainer, I wasn't counting on much help anyway. It was only then that I fully understood the magnitude of trouble I was in. The $40,000 check that had haunted my conscience for so long was only a blip of the radar screen. I was now considered the mastermind and kingpin of some serious organized crime.

While I had been politicking the multitude of Hibbs's projects and recklessly gambling my money away, Hibbs had been helping himself at the state's buffet of appropriated funds. The host of upstanding citizens and friends whom he'd bought and paid for were squealing like pigs. People in law enforcement make their living off folks who "kiss and tell." Everyone who had handled or mishandled one cent of money going to one of Hibbs's many projects were pointing fingers, and Hibbs would soon be pointing his.

The feds were operating a lot like some of my redneck deer-hunting buddies, who would sit in a tree for hours on end waiting for that trophy buck to come by. They weren't a bit interested in the meat, but they wanted something they could hang on their wall.

The relationship with Hibbs, as well as my relationship with Stokes, was now officially over. They were both lawyered up with the best council money could buy. I was quite alone, a lot like the fictional character "Tar-Baby" I had read about as a child. No one wanted to be around Tar-Baby for fear of getting a little tar on themselves.

By the time my final session in the legislature rolled around in February of the following year, I was completely worthless. If someone would have opened a jailhouse door, I would have gladly walked in and let them throw away the key. I just wanted some relief.

Being back at the capitol did, however, help jolt me somewhat back to my senses. That was a place where there was never a shortage of lawyers, and I needed one pretty bad. I'm sure most of them knew it too, from the way they were seeming to avoid my company. One lawyer in particular had gone from lawyer to House Speaker to US attorney under the Clinton administration and, after that, a lobbyist. In fact, he was a lobbyist who had more than frequented my old appropriation office. He was the ideal candidate from whom to ask a favor, so I asked my secretary summon him to my powerless and secluded fifth-floor office. I could plainly see the patronizing look on his face as he came in holding his little black briefcase in both hands, clearly a posture that said, "I'm in a hurry." He was never in a hurry back when I held the purse strings.

Hurry or not, I had him sit down and listen to my long and sad story in every detail and all but begged for his help. Friends didn't come cheap those days. He would need a retainer in the amount of $10,000. I was so worn out, both mentally and physically that I didn't argue, figuring I could raise the money through family and the few friends I had left. We shook hands and made the deal. I wasn't asking him to be a trial lawyer. All I wanted was a plea agreement, to simply confess to my role in this god-awful mess and take my punishment. Of course, I couldn't help but ask what he thought the punishment might be. With his background as a former US attorney, I assumed he would have a ballpark idea.

"I think we can get you a Martha Stewart–type deal, but it will take some time," he said. He told me to try and forget it all as best I could, that he'd promptly contact the Eastern District prosecuting office and begin some dialogue. Once again, I felt a little relieved.

Funny how events had come full circle. I would spend my final session in the legislature much as I had my first, withdrawn and secluded, only for a different reason. The hardest part of it was realizing I could no longer hide the fact that I had broken my oath of office by accepting a kickback, and telling my children would be the hardest thing I would ever have to do. I had several breakdowns that session—two or three in my hotel room and one in my office. Uncontrollable bouts of shaking and crying. Evidently, the purging of guilt. It had been nearly four years since I took that check, and I was feeling not only remorse but the pressure as well.

After the visit with my latest in a string of attorneys, I went home for the weekend recess and told my family what I had done. Their forgiveness was swift and real, as I knew it would be. It didn't lesson the shame I felt, but it was definitely a load off my shoulders. Now it was time to wait, both on my attorney and the public humiliation I knew was coming.

During my heart-wrenching confessional rounds, I had stopped by my older sister's house. We had always been close, as we both cherished our days back in the blackberry patch and often joked about our Sundays spent listening to Brother Ronald's long sermons. Both she and her husband were what I considered devout Christians. They never missed a church service or an opportunity to help someone. It was nearly as hard telling them as it was my children.

As the three of us embraced and cried together, my sister told me they knew that I had been in trouble for quite some time. An acquaintance of theirs who attended the church over in McClain told her that their Sunday schoolteacher and deacon had said a special prayer for me during one of their classes. The deacon also happened to be one of the FBI investigators. I'm sure he was worried about my soul. I was also now sure how rumors got started.

Nearly three months had passed before my lawyer finally came back with results of his one-sided negotiations with the feds. He pulled from his briefcase a document nearly the size of an Oklahoma City phone book. It was my plea agreement. As he handed it over, he explained that it was the best he could do and recommended I read it over the weekend. I didn't need the weekend. I already knew it didn't take that much paper to explain what I had done. Glancing through the first couple of pages was enough for me. It contained words like *conspiracy* and *money laundering*, just to name a couple. Right away, I was angry at my pandering lawyer. He hadn't negotiated one thing, certainly not ten thousand dollars' worth. It appeared to me that the feds wrote this document word for word, with absolutely no regard for the truth, much less any intervention. The so-called plea agreement was so outrageous, I didn't give it another thought. I handed it back and asked him to get me a face-to-face meeting with the feds.

By then I had cried myself out. I didn't have any tears left. Being remorseful and accepting the scourge for what I had done was one thing, but taking a hit for crimes I had never even thought of was something else. I hadn't merely been thrown under the bus, I was being used to lessen jail time for the real kingpin! The problem was, once you've danced with the devil, you become the devil's dance!

While waiting for my lawyer to arrange the face-to-face meeting, which strung out another two months, the deacon's name cropped up again. He had paid a visit to my younger brother, who is a Gospel minister. During his "brother-to-brother" visit, he urged my brother to convince me that I needed to come in for my own good. I'd been trying to come in for nearly two years. This deacon was a real piece of work, I thought. This guy wasn't worried about my soul; he was worried about corroborating Hibbs's lies and satisfying the insatiable appetite of the local press who had built him and his counterparts up as Saviors of Southeast Oklahoma. He knew full well that I was no kingpin, or they would have raided my home and office just like they did Stokes and Hibbs.

# 25

The people I met in the FTC and the stories they shared, never ceased to amaze me. Being on the inside was like taking a huge filter off the typical documentaries you see on television that only highlight a minority of trouble making convicts.

I will never forget the first shower I took in that prison. Of course, I was still somewhat in shock, and certainly wasn't comprehending the fact that I was now in a place that was a "catch all" for every human virus and disease known to mankind. Afflictions and ailments were carried here from border to border and beyond. Be that as it may, I entered the shower in my bare feet. By the next morning, the spaces between my toes were red as a beet and appeared as though they'd been drenched in acid. Fortunately, one of the guys out in the pod had noticed me coming barefoot, out of the shower. The next day he came over to my cell with a pair of shower shoes and a tube of cream for curing jungle rot. He didn't know me, and I certainly didn't know him, so I figured he surely had an angle. To my surprise, there was no "angle". He simply took pity on this new arrival and had the wherewithal to help. He barely hung around long enough to accept a mere 'thank you.'

Within the next couple of weeks, I became well acquainted with the guy. His name was Terrell and, although he looked much older, he was only forty-three years old. The receding hairline and the gray in his hair came about from stress, not age. His home, in his former life, was in a suburb of Hollywood, California where he had run a successful limousine service for nearly a decade.

Having more of a reserved personality, the occupation of limo driver suited him to a 'T'. Except for a belligerent passenger once in a blue moon, the job allowed him to be his own boss and operate at a pace of his own choosing. He didn't earn a lot of money, but enough to provide a decent living for his wife and three young children. By the time he turned age 36, he had managed to pay off the limo and move his family into a modest, but nice, brick home in a good neighborhood. For Terrell, however, as for the most of us, the storms of life seem to hit when we least expect them.

One morning he got a call from a distant relative, whom he hadn't heard from since graduating high school. Like most relatives that seem to appear at the most awkward times, this long lost cousin needed some help. He was down on his luck and needed a place to stay while looking for a job. Terrell wasn't the kind to turn someone away, especially family.

Even though Terrell hadn't seen the guy in years, he had heard through the family grapevine that he wasn't exactly the "working type." He was more of a bum, who went from one family member to another, getting for free whatever he could before moving on.

Figuring, at the very worst, the uninvited relative would only put them out for a week or two, Terrell convinced his wife to put on her best face. While she scurried about trying to arrange a spare room on short notice, Terrell drove several miles across town where he picked his cousin up.

As Terrell suspected, his cousin was traveling pretty light, with only the clothes on his back, and a small canvas duffle bag. Terrell could tell right away the cousin didn't look like someone interested in going to work, but gave him a cordial greeting and acted as though he was happy to see him.

When they arrived back at Terrell's home, the cousin was quick to pull a one-hundred-dollar bill from his pocket, offering it to Terrell's wife as a token of appreciation. As any gracious hostess would do, she insisted he keep the money and reassured him that they would be glad to help him out for a few days. Terrell couldn't believe he had any money at all, much less a one-hundred-dollar bill.

While Terrell was making his limo rounds the following day, old 'cuz' was helping himself to the residence phone. Unbeknownst to Terrell, cousin wasn't looking for a job, he was dealing 'crack cocaine' via Terrell's home phone!

It didn't take Terrell but a couple of days to realize his cousin was up to no good, but Terrell's personality wasn't one of prying or asking questions. Besides, by the fourth day, cousin was ready to leave. He just needed Terrell to take him on a few 'house calls' to say 'hi' to some old friends, then he would be quietly on his way.

Terrell said, "Man, I figured he was doin' somethin' no good at those places, but like a damn fool, I just kept on being his chauffeur and, "Sho-nuff, bout' the third stop, police cars came upon us from every direction." They hauled me off in handcuffs, right along with Cuz and a couple other people that were in that house." He went on to say, "That little duffle bag he had was plum full of cash, dope and even had a gun in it." "I never saw any of it, but that's what that little lawyer they gave me said."

After Terrell got caught up in the 'drug bust', the federal prosecutors took over. They pulled his telephone records, which verified calls being made to a known drug dealer. They also impounded the limo he had worked so hard to pay off. When the dust finally settled, the court appointed lawyer managed to get him a 'plea bargain' of only fifteen years in the federal pen.

At the time I met Terrell, he had already served six years of his sentence. The first eighteen months of his stretch were done in an overcrowded county jail. He still had nine years left to serve.

The various federal facilities he had been doing time in were all too far away to make frequent visitation from his wife and three children possible. He had seen them only twice in the past six years.

I could only listen in disbelief while he shared his story. Well, maybe not total disbelief. After all, he was black, driving a limousine and hauling another black dude, with a bag full of dope, around. He never stood a chance!

Terrell managed to keep just enough money on his books, from doing 'extra duty work' to make weekly calls to his wife and kids. When I asked him how he managed to keep his sanity, he said, "Man, I just take it one day at a time."

Another favorite of mine there in the cadre unit was a thirty-two-year-old black kid named 'Washington.' We first met in the prison library prayer circle. He was about midway through a sentence of seventeen years. I didn't ask him what he was in for, but I could tell he had no support from home. On commissary days, he usually bought saltines, ramen noodles and a small bag of butterscotch candy. He was a heck of an athlete out on the small basketball court, but always played in his prison issue work boots. He didn't have enough money on his books to purchase tennis shoes from the commissary order list.

On Sunday mornings, while I was tuned in to my favorite bluegrass gospel music, I would see him pacing circles around the small rec deck with his own radio and earbuds. He would stop every so often and raise his hands high above his head, as if he were giving praise to the Almighty. I soon found out that he was listening to his own favorite gospel music. I'm sure it wasn't bluegrass, but it must have been very inspirational to him.

Washington was just one of many young, black men I became acquainted with there at the FTC. Very few were complainers. Unlike a lot of us white folk who were "born on third base" while taking credit for hitting a triple, these young men went on as if they weren't surprised at all to be living in a federal penitentiary.

Back in the old cucumber picking days, dad leased some land that joined my Grandpa's farm. It was only a half mile from our old home place, and was a handy place to graze our small herd of milk cows and a Hereford bull we called 'Zeto.' The lease was Rock Island railroad property, where remnants from past coal mining days were still scattered about. At the entrance to the property was an old abandoned tavern, once frequented by the mine workers. It made for a good place to store hay in the winter for Zeto and the milk cows. Except for an antique pot-bellied stove and the rusted stovepipe, the old building was bare.

Every summer, older brother and I would cram all the square hay bales it could hold into that old shack, save a small area around the old stove. Afterwards, we would latch the door and bid good riddance to the old tavern, along with the half dozen wasp nests we had to dodge, while stacking the hay. We wouldn't be unlatching that old door until well into the following winter.

One particular year, however, we had an unexpected early winter cold blast. It got cold enough that my Dad decided to get into that stash of hay and feed a few weeks earlier than usual. As we drove up the Indian Highway toward the lease, we could see white smoke billowing from the roof of the old tavern. Dad went into panic mode! We thought the whole place was going up in smoke, hay and all.

Nearing the entrance to the lease property, however, we could see that the smoke was only coming from the rusted stove pipe protruding the roof. It looked almost spooky, as I'm sure smoke hadn't come out of that old pipe for decades.

Dad quickly made his way to the tavern's front door. He didn't know who, or why, someone decided to build a fire in that old stove, but he knew it was dangerous as hell, considering the place was chock full of hay.

When he yanked the door open, there sitting on a bale of hay, was old Charlie Sisco. Poor old Charlie was a vagrant of sorts and looked like the classic 'Hobo.' His old face was round and his nose cherry red from both the cold weather, and the effects of alcohol. The ragged clothes he had on looked as if they had been slept in for months.

He had taken up residence in our makeshift hay barn and was burning our hay in that old pot-bellied stove, one block at a time, to keep himself warm. From the looks of all the empty whiskey and beer bottles, he had been living there for quite some time.

Nevertheless, old Charlie was only a couple more drinks, or a good wind gust away, from burning the whole place to the ground. Dad extinguished the fire and left no doubt in Mr. Sisco's mind that he would have to find himself a different place to live.

If old Charlie lived in this day and time, he would be a prime candidate for the federal penitentiary charged with "breaking and entering, concealing stolen property, (in a pot—bellied stove) and substance abuse and……too poor to hire a lawyer.

# 26

My last session in the Oklahoma House of Representatives had come and gone, and my garden was in full swing, when finally came word that the meeting I'd requested was scheduled. I'd need to bring my wife along as part of the deal. We met my lawyer at the entrance of the building that housed the US Eastern District FBI. We cleared security, and took a seat, waiting for our name to be called. After a brief wait, the chief prosecutor approached and led us into a large conference room with a long table surrounded by the all-too-familiar high back chairs. These chairs, however, were black and all occupied by an assortment of federal police. We took our place at the table as the prosecutor laid out a dozen different packets in front of us, each containing felony indictments ranging from conspiracy, bribery, and money laundering to bankruptcy fraud. There was even one indictment of income tax evasion. Two of the counts would involve my wife. As was explained by the feds, with no questions made by my attorney, conviction on the least of the indictments on my part would carry a federal sentence of eighteen years to life. If I took the plea, as formerly written, my wife would not be charged, and I would receive a maximum of five years that included a downward spiral pending my cooperation in the ongoing investigation. So much for the Martha Stewart type of deal.

Contemplating eighteen years to life in itself was like a nightmare, but serving my innocent wife up as a sacrifice on the altar of justice was out of the question. The feds had me. I would swallow the lengthy plea, warts and all. It would be called one count of mail fraud.

My brothers, who had stood firmly in my corner during so many campaigns, were now accompanying me to my formal arraignment. I couldn't help but wonder if even they hadn't felt betrayed, but they were the kind of brothers who stayed put, both in good times and bad. Younger brother, the minister, was a great campaign speech giver. I think my opponents would rather have faced me on the campaign stump than him. The other two knew nothing of political correctness, but that didn't stop them from helping. Their specialty was taking down the opponents' signs, which would often make me cringe.

The three of them had adjoining shops on a large lot in the hometown that at one time was a booming lumberyard. Two of them had a wood shop, and the other had a metal fabrication business. We'd often meet there, the four of us, discussing campaign strategy and getting a good laugh at someone's expense.

One day while the four of us were standing in the drive separating the two shops, an old fellow drove up and asked to look at an old antique Ford the metal fabricator was selling. We all stood there as he looked the car over inside and out, with my brother pointing out all the explicit details. The old gentlemen asked how my campaign was going. He said he knew of my opponent but had heard that the Mass boys were hard workers, as well as pretty good people, so I could expect to get his vote. Before taking his leave, he wanted to take a peek in the trunk of the old vehicle. The trunk lid seemed to be jammed, so my brother had to do a little extra prying to get it unlatched. When he finally did, the lid sprang open, and campaign signs, relieving themselves of the compression, boiled out of the trunk like a covey of flushed quail!

They weren't my signs either. I was embarrassed, but later on, we'd have many a good laugh about that episode.

None of us were laughing now as we climbed the intimidating granite stairs of the federal courthouse. Inside the courthouse, the prosecutors and the media were all there, awaiting their day in the sun. My legs were like jelly, and I had not one ounce of dignity to muster. I stood before the judge as my lawyer entered my plea of guilt. Having confirmed all my sinister deeds, as described by Hibbs and his new federal pals, she asked if I understood that I was admitting to the charges and whether or not I had been coerced. It was my final chance to set the record straight; a real fleeting thought. It was like dangling from a wire a hundred feet above the pavement and having someone say, "If it's too hard to hang on, just turn loose." I'll hang on, thank you.

The ceremony was rather brief. In a matter of moments, I went from upstanding citizen to convicted felon. Although I was somewhat aware of the voices and movements around me, the following hours were like drifting through a haze. It brought back memories of a hunting trip on Rattlesnake Mountain years earlier, when a sudden cold front ushered in a dense blanket of clouds and fog. For a while, I was lost. I knew where I was. I just didn't know where I was going. The mug shot, the finger printing and processing by the young US Marshals, and the reporters and photographers scattered about the hallways—all of it was up close and personal, yet seemed so very distant. Before I left the courthouse, the parameters of my probation were set, pending a day for formal sentencing. This included where I was allowed to travel, who I could and couldn't talk to, and the stripping of my Second Amendment right to possess or carry a firearm. Sentencing would not occur until the feds had run down every lead, as provided by Hibbs, and squeezed every last drop of blood out of me that they could get, which wouldn't be that much. I didn't have very much left to give them.

The public flogging was now at hand. By the time my brothers and I got home that evening, my mug shot was being broadcast statewide on the six o'clock news. It would take the young editor back home a little longer. He would save his thrashing for the big Sunday paper. Aside from his bold headlines, he did a half-page editorial where he called me "evil, vile and heinous." He went further to say that I had climbed the backs of my own grandchildren to gain favor in a public office where I could pillage, plunder, and steal. I could say nothing. My lips had been sealed by both the feds and my attorney.

Other than tarnishing an otherwise flawless name handed down from generations of hard work and sacrifice, I was also branded as being cooperative with the feds. The connection left me being viewed as a snitch, a snitch in bed with Hibbs. I didn't have anyone to snitch on other than myself, but who knew? Hibbs was keeping to his word. He was puking on every politician he'd ever known, including my friends, and the feds were expecting me to confirm his every word. I may have taken a kickback, gambled, and drank whiskey, but I wasn't going to be a snitching puppet! Hibbs's word alone at face value wasn't worth much when put to the test by a real defense lawyer. He was facing nearly four hundred felony counts ranging from conspiracy to campaign fraud to the child pornography found on a computer in one of the private offices he owned. The feds needed confirmation of his tales by a reliable crook like me. The feds didn't care how crooked he was; they just wanted some politicians heads to mount upon their walls!

Not knowing when but knowing for certain I was bound for the federal pen, I set out to get things in order for my wife, who by then was battling diabetes, degeneration of the spine, and a host of other illnesses that would prevent her from working. Foremost, I was making sure we both had a place to live when it was all said and done. By then, I was several payments behind on our house and forty-seven acres. Family and friends chipped in to catch up on the late bank payments, and the bank agreed to hold off calling in the note until I could sell off highway frontage enough to clear the note. We had a buyer for the frontage in less than a month. We would use the money to clear our taxes and pay off the bank, leaving the house and garden spot free and clear.

Meanwhile, the old senator and his brother were keeping as close a watch on my affairs as the feds were. With the help of a bank employee, the senator's brother was monitoring progress on the sale of my land. This was the same brother who had demonstrated his vindictive prowess twenty years earlier over the Randy Travis event. Just days before closing on the sale, the high and mighty McClain bank sold him the note on our property. A week earlier, the old senator had filed a lien on the same property, calling in the $40,000 loan that had plagued my conscience for so long. It was proof enough that, at least for him, the $40,000 was indeed a loan. I couldn't believe the Stokes brothers were pulling such a brazen stunt in full view of the public and in the midst of such a wide-scale FBI probe. Although I didn't like it, I understood it. In the same predicament, my brothers might have done the same. Moreover, I couldn't believe the bank had such audacity. The strings the senator could pull seemed endless. The Stokes were taking no chances, should I dance for the feds like their former partner Hibbs was.

It was only a matter of weeks afterward that the feds indicted the senator's brother for "witness tampering." The bankers in charge should have been indicted, but evidently they wore golden slippers. This was political hardball at its best, and I was playing out of my league.

The wheels of justice moved rapidly for Stokes's brother. With the jurors behind closed doors a little too long for comfort, he plead guilty to one count of witness intimidation. While awaiting his sentence, he succumbed to a fatal heart attack. The note to my property, however, remained in his estate.

By then I was completely numbed by the years of political battles and the more recent political scandals. Somehow, losing my home and property didn't seem that shocking. Obtaining council for civil litigation in this matter was out of the question. I was broke and had been to the well of family, and what friends I had left more than I wanted to already. I was down to a court-appointed lawyer, such as it was.

With Hibbs at the helm, the FBI probe was getting wider and deeper. They were now handing down federal grand jury indictments that included Stokes, the state auditor and his wife, and my old mansion roommate. Satisfied that I would be doing no more than five years in the pen, I was anxious to talk. Thus far, my story hadn't been told. The sooner I told it, the sooner the madness would end. The feds were anxious to talk to me too!

In my first official interview, the prosecutor and investigators hurled questions so fast I could barely keep up. They were like a pack of half-grown hungry hound pups knocking the dog food out of your hand before you could pour it in their bowl. I thought to myself, *These guys are idiots*! Most of the questions were so farfetched they didn't deserve an answer. I had been acquainted with Hibbs long enough that I could hear his contriving behind every one of them. Other questions were based on the level of two-bit greedy gossip, like, "Did you ever hear Stokes call so and so a bitch?" and "What women were your buddies sleeping with?" These were all aimed specifically at Democrats, mostly dating back to the mansion days. They were to the point of butting in on one another. The lead prosecutor was an implant from somewhere up north. He wasn't as privy to the local gossip as his two investigators were. They were both locals, including the deacon. The lead man could barely get a question in edgewise. He finally put a stop to the circus, obviously out of frustration, and suggested they all let "Mr. Mass" tell his story.

I was impressed. First time I'd been referred to as Mr. Mass in months, and up until then, any story I had told was either negotiated or filtered through these guys. Boy, was I ever ready to tell my story!

I began with the first time Hibbs and I were formally introduced and how he'd been so helpful in my failed congressional campaign. I explained the relationship I'd had with the senator over the years and how I had stayed with him in his OKC apartment while he was in bad health. I told them how his mind appeared to be slipping at times. I went on to explain that after the congressional race, Hibbs had asked me for help in obtaining state funds for his manufacturing plant and how his initial request had slipped my mind. I described in detail his second request, which left me embarrassed that I'd forgotten. I told how he offered me a 10 percent kickback as incentive to follow up. I told them how I'd initially refused any notion of a percentage and of my contacting the local COG, all done legally and in line with constitutional authority. I told them how I chastised the director for balking and that I'd also told him if it lined up with constitutional guidelines to get it done. I explained that Stokes himself had at no time asked me to help in obtaining funds. I was careful not to leave out the smallest detail.

I described the day I went to the law office and told them how the $40,000 check had been handed to me, marked as a loan. I admitted that it may as well have been a kickback and felt for sure that it was when I took it. It felt good to finally unload the guilt I'd carried for so long.

I began to notice a couple of them glancing at their watches, the way grown-ups did back when Brother Ronald's sermon would get a little too long. I didn't care if they weren't interested, I was telling my story if it hair-lipped the governor!

From there, I told of every harebrained project I'd worked on under the auspices of Ace Development. I told about the day I discovered slot machines in the unfinished manufacturing plant, the visit to the state auditor's office, the agreement we reached for placing the slots, the various fund-raisers at Guthrie, etc.

Realizing from their body language that my time for talking was about up, I skipped forward to the most important part of the story—the part where Hibbs had spent weeks trying to coerce me into framing the old senator and finally even my House colleagues and friends.

By the time I finished, it was painfully clear they were buying none of it. I may as well have been talking to a fence post. Both the feds and the media already had their story. They just needed to prove it. After all, a good story was far more glamorous than the truth. I had no reason to lie; my fate had already been sealed. Moreover, the public scourge couldn't have been worse if I had murdered the pope.

After the interview that left both me and the trigger-happy investigators disappointed, I was told to keep my mouth shut and was free to go. They'd call me when they needed me. I was happy to go. I didn't like them, and it was clear they didn't like me. Besides, I had a lot to do while making preparations for a long prison stay.

Not many people are in the market to hire a fifty-seven-year-old ex-politician and convicted felon awaiting his sentence, but I had somehow managed to get a job running a power washer. The former Mr. Chairman, who had not so long ago wore the Tony Lama boots, khaki pants, and starched white shirt, was now in a pair of overalls and knee-high rubber boots, washing grease from the diesel bays in the local truck stop. I didn't feel a bit sorry for myself; I deserved what I was getting, but the embarrassment I'd caused my family was unforgivable, not to them but to myself.

A couple of months had passed without me hearing a word from the feds or my court-appointed lawyer. The outside thermometer was reading 103 degrees, and I was in a sludge pit, blowing grease sky high with the nozzle of the high-pressured steam washer. The pay-by-the-minute Walmart phone began buzzing in my pocket. By the time I crawled out of the pit and shut the machine down, I'd missed the call. It was my lawyer, who I called back immediately. He told me to meet him at the McClain Federal building in one hour. The two local FBI agents wanted to visit, so I went, grease, sweat, and all.

I promptly met my attorney at the courthouse, where we were asked to take a seat in one of the small interrogation rooms and wait. It wasn't long before my teeth were chattering. Coming from the sweltering heat, drenched in sweat, to an overcooled interrogation room was quite chilling. The two investigators finally arrived—the "deacon," who acted like my best of Christian friends, and his sidekick, who acted like my worst of enemies.

The one I'd labeled as sidekick had been a longtime local resident. In all my years of public service, I had never met the guy, nor had any reason to, up until this meet. Although he lived in my house district, ten miles from my home, I'm quite sure the guy was never a supporter of mine. He was a neighbor to one of the old-timers who attended the same church I had while growing up. I always had the old neighbor pegged as a busybody, as he always had his nose in someone else's business. I had run into the old busybody a couple of weeks earlier in the local grocery store. He was quick to let me know that he was neighbors with the FBI agent who had been working my case. He then had the audacity to tell me if I'd just tell the truth, his fine neighbor of the badge would do me no harm at all. I wanted to tell him as well as others what I really thought but instead continued being politically correct.

Soon after they entered the bone-chilling interrogation room, the "Deacon's sidekick" pulled a spreadsheet out of his briefcase and laid it in front of me on the small table. It was a spreadsheet straight from the state capitol appropriation office. I had seen thousands of them. Highlighted on the sheet were several columns of numbers that varied in amounts from ten thousand to thirty thousand dollars. They wanted to know where the money went and what I had done with it. Upon closer examination, I realized the spreadsheet before me was money appropriated the year following my bid for congress. They had been so busy in their large-scale takedown of political corruption that they'd missed the fact that I wasn't even in office that year, and I didn't bother trying to tell them. They weren't a bit interested in what I'd had to say before, so why try now?

As they scrolled through the highlighted amounts one at a time, they demanded to know where the money went. The money had obviously been appropriated to the nonprofit foundations Hibbs had formed, but according to them, it was nowhere to be found. As they pointed out each number, I simply told the truth. I didn't have any idea. The "bad cop" was outraged, and he informed me that they could renege on the plea agreement and send me straight to trial where I'd face eternity in prison. When he finished, he stormed out of the room. The "deacon" placed a reassuring hand on my shoulder and said, "I know you didn't take it. You gave it to your old mansion roommate, didn't you?" It was a classic good cop/bad cop. I just shook my head in disbelief. I didn't know what my legislative buddies did for Hibbs and didn't care. It was none of my business. Hibbs was more than willing to implicate them simply because they were politicians, and he knew the feds were hungry for the heads of any prominent Democrat. The "bad cop" stormed back in as quickly as he had left. "Are you willing to take a polygraph?" he said. Without hesitation, I said yes. My lawyer was kicking me under the small table. "We need a minute to discuss this in private," he told the exuberant investigator.

"Take all the time you need," they said and left us alone in the small room.

When they left, the lawyer advised me not to take the polygraph. He said if it proved positive, they'd disregard it. If I failed, I could be in worse trouble. I didn't care. I wanted to take it. My lawyer called them back in the room and told them that against his advisement, I would take the polygraph. The "bad cop" told me to be back at 10:00 a.m. the next morning. They'd have their polygraph specialist there. I was glad to get out of that cold room. Before I could get home that afternoon, my lawyer called and told me the polygraph had to be postponed, due to the machine being tied up elsewhere. I may not have been a college graduate, but I knew people, and I knew that those guys weren't looking for the truth. I wouldn't hear from the feds until the day I would be sentenced.

By then, the magnitude of Hibbs's entrepreneurial skills and the wake of destruction they'd left behind had come to a pretty sharp focus. The fund-raisers we held in Guthrie for both the democratic governor elect and the newly elected second district congressman were a sham. Hibbs had raised over sixty thousand dollars for each of them, using mostly straw donors, all the while chiding his old partner Stokes for the mess he'd made of the fiddler's campaign. The foundation he'd created was also a sham, at least according to the outstanding board members. Who would have thought he could use the caliber of people on that foundation board as mere puppets, but he did. Evidently, there were also large sums of cash missing from the various enterprises he'd taken on using state funds. He had even managed to get his wife money for her operation using state funds. Lord only knows what funds were used to build the slot machines. He'd also used straw donors in the state auditor's campaign, as well as using cash to circumvent FEC regulations. The string of blatant state and federal infractions were endless.

I don't think Hibbs ever viewed himself as a criminal mastermind, nor do I think he ever intended to be one. Lord knows he didn't need the money. His years as Stokes's underling in the oil and gas business, and later other private initiatives, had made him flush with prosperity.

In my view, for what it's worth, I think he was thrust out of the chute on a real bull when he should have been riding a calf. For years, he had watched the old senator operate from the shadows. The old senator, however, was cunning and wise. Up until his mind started slipping, he was a master at operating on the fringes of the law. A lot of his dealings may not have been ethical, but he knew how to keep them in the realms of legal. Not only did the old senator know the law, he'd written most of it.

With Stokes's health both mentally and physically deteriorating, I think Hibbs wanted to take on the role as the new Stokes, trying to immerse himself into politics and deal making literally overnight. It took old Stokes fifty years. Hibbs was going to do it in three. Problem was, Stokes hadn't as yet completely slipped, and the two of them collided. Young Hibbs had climbed aboard a bull he couldn't ride.

When the feds got involved, Hibbs got a lesson in Politics 101. Every store-bought friend he'd made was quick to point their finger at him. Hibbs thought all those friends he'd bought were true-blue. He didn't know that when the ship started sinking, they were the first to bail. The blundering mess of state funds could have, and should have, been called into question by a number of safeguards. The McClain Foundation, the nonprofit foundation, the COG—any of them, at any point, could have put the brakes on, but they didn't; and the straw donors? All faithful employees of his private business, and quick to point him out.

Feeling as though the world had turned on him, he felt justified to do some turning of his own. He offered me the chance to do the same. When I didn't, he viewed me as fair game along with anyone else that stood between him and the federal pen.

By the time the feds had figured out that I wasn't lying (and if they thought I was, you can bet your hat they'd have given me the polygraph), it was too late. They were stuck with Hibbs as their sole witness to a conspiracy put together by the political bosses.

The auditor and his wife were convicted mainly of campaign violations, having considered themselves good friends of Hibbs while he had fed them to the wolves.

Stokes was found "incompetent" to stand trial, all the while begging to differ. The local paper quoted him as saying, "If you think I'm incompetent, ask my banker."

My former colleague and old mansion roommate had also been indicted on charges ranging from conspiracy to fraud. He was acquitted of all charges. I was a witness for his defense. After his trial, the federal judge chided the US attorney's office for what he called a "political witch hunt." He went on to say it was the worst case of "federal police bullying" he had seen since his time serving on the bench.

There were others on the list, as provided by Hibbs, but the feds had run out of steam, and I was certainly no help.

My sentencing was finally at hand. After years of probing, interrogating, and filing affidavits, I was the only crooked legislator they had. It had been nearly six years since I took that $40,000 check. I was long past ready for my cleansing.

At sentencing, my entire family packed into the courtroom, standing with me to the bitter end. I stood before the judge next to my court-appointed attorney. To our right stood the "deacon" and his boss. They argued the fact that I had been no help, and so far, as they were concerned, the full five years was break enough for me. The "deacon" stared at the floor while his boss did the talking.

When the feds finished driving in their dagger, it was my lawyer's turn. He explained to the judge that although my answers to their questions weren't what they wanted, they were truthful. He explained that I had owned up to my part and had been at the feds' disposal for nearly three years, never failing to answer their every beck and call. He respectfully requested the write-down that had been negotiated during my plea.

With that, the judge had his say. He basically reiterated what the feds had said, that I hadn't been helpful and that he had seen little remorse. The judge's remarks weren't any surprise to me. He hadn't seen any remorse. My remorse had long since been displayed in privacy and within the confines of family and very few dear friends. Displaying remorse in front of anyone else would merely have been a show.

The judge then turned to me and asked if I had anything to say. I had just three words. “No, Your Honor.” Satisfied I’d receive the full sixty months, I was just ready to get it over with. I’d already been through nearly ten years of hell. What was five more? I’d lost my retirement to the state, my home to the Stokes, and my basic rights as a citizen to the federal government. I still owed the IRS and now awaited my fate in a federal penitentiary.

The judge opened his mouth to declare sixty months, but twenty-four came out instead. The court had shown mercy. I was now property of the FBOP, the Federal Bureau of Prisons. I would self-report as soon as bed space was available.

# 27

Prison time eventually passed for both Gage and Big Tex. Gage had completed the ten years carved out of his life, and Tex the six. Gage left just as quiet and unassuming as he was the day I first met him. Tex left with the same flare as he came in with. I could hear his boisterous laugh as he boarded the large elevator for the last time. I certainly have no way of knowing what those young men were like on the outside, but on the inside, they were a joy to be around.

My own prison time was drawing shorter by the day, and my formula for passing time was staying busy. On Sunday afternoons, I passed time at the Texas Hold'em table out in the pod. Of course, gambling, being illegal in prison, had to be done on the down low. The inmate running the game was in charge of keeping secret books on who owed who the various commissary items that were used as tender. Risking a trip to the SHU, I was a stalwart at the friendly poker game. Premo and Tony were regulars as well. My propensity for operating on the fringes had always been a weakness and, where gambling was concerned, a real thorn in my side.

Back during my unsuccessful bid for congress, legislation was introduced that would outlaw cockfighting in the state. Opponents of cockfighting bemoaned the cruelty to the birds, and cited the derbies as sites of illegal gambling as well. Being on the side of the cockfights, I was invited by their capitol lobbyist to attend a cockfight down near the Red River. He wanted to get the group acquainted with me and hopefully raise a little money for my congressional campaign.

Although I'd never been to a cockfight, much less owned a rooster, I agreed to make the Red River trip in hopes of raising campaign funds. When we pulled into the facility's parking area, I was amazed at the number of vehicles. There were makeshift booths scattered about the area selling T-shirts, caged roosters in the back of pickups, and country kids darting in and out of the rows of vehicles as if they were at the county fair.

As we walked into the massive enclosed arena, it was elbow to elbow. One woman was sitting at a bench with a bloody apron, sewing up a wounded rooster like it was a pair of torn jeans, and a fellow in one corner was hawking the latest in knives and gaffs.

The arena itself had a platform enclosed in wire, where the owners would position their birds for the next fight. The fighting cage was surrounded by bleachers full of people, all cheering on their favorite rooster, some with fistfuls of cash. This being my first cockfight, I was somewhat in awe of it all.

My lobbyist friend ushered me right up to the arena cage for a bird's-eye view. People were cheering, and feathers were flying. In less than a minute, that particular match was over. One bird was the victor, the other headed for the woman in the bloody apron. The crowd was still cheering and anxious for the next bout. When the owners exited the cage with their birds, my lobbyist friend entered. I figured he'd point me out, politely ask for their support, and let them get on with their sport. Instead, he not only introduced me but invited me into the ring to give a speech.

I was pretty adept at off-the-cuff speeches, but I didn't know anything about the sport of cockfighting. Making matters worse was five hundred people staring at the politician who was about to interrupt their otherwise favorite pastime. As I entered the ring, I could hear the murmurings of disdain. It would be a real test of my political savvy. With mic in hand, I said, "Folks, I don't know one damn thing about cockfighting. In fact, this is the first cockfight I ever saw. I'm a ridge runner from the hills of Southeast Oklahoma, where I follow the best coonhounds in the state. The only thing I know about your sport is this: people want to outlaw it because they say it's cruel to the birds. Well, from what I've seen here, it ain't near as cruel as kicking a coon out of a tree in amongst six grown hounds. So if you'll send me to congress, I'll make a deal with you. You help keep those bleeding heart liberals outta my coon hunting, and I'll help keep them out of your cockfighting!"

The speech was short but drew a whale of applause and a showering of cash, I didn't know the details of their side bets, but I was pretty sure that taking political contributions this way was a no-no! Standing there half petrified, my lobbyist friend, who was on his hands and knees picking up cash, said, "You gonna just stand there or help pick this stuff up?"

Here I was, a decade later, risking a trip to the hole over a bag of Cheetos and a box of ramen noodles. Nevertheless, the Sunday afternoon poker games helped make time go by and were entertaining as well. I could remember a time when there weren't enough hours in the day. In here, there were too many hours in a day. Time in prison is a dreadfully slow and maddening process.

For the most part, I had avoided keeping up with any news of the outside, except, of course, keeping up with my family through letters and visits. My last few weeks there at FTC, I began catching glimpses of CNN and occasionally skimming over the big *Oklahoma Daily* that one of my buddies received during the daily mail call. The sudden change in interest, I believe, was an unconscious effort at acclimating myself to the outside world. Most notably in the news, was the BP oil spill in the gulf and the Rod Blagojevich political scandal. On a more local level was news concerning an old friend and foe who had, years earlier, blindsided a chubby kid with a round of rat shot. The public revealing of his character certainly didn't come as news to me.

After my demise, he went on from the House of Representatives to win a statewide office and seemed to have the world by the tail. As of late, however, things weren't going so well. While campaigning for his third term in the statewide office, he'd attended a big rodeo final at the OKC fairground, after which he went to a party in one of the local hotel suites. While at the party, he got drunk and stole a guitar that belonged to a world champion bull rider. Later that night, hotel security busted him, and he wound up in the Oklahoma County drunk tank. Needless to say, he lost his statewide seat over the well-publicized ordeal. Getting drunk may not have hurt him, but the public had little tolerance for a thief.

Another tidbit of local news caught my eye as well—the rising tide of tribal gambling revenues in the midst of a flailing economy. The report cited Oklahoma's tribal take on gambling had exceeded three billion in just one year. Oklahoma's entire state budget wasn't much more than that. The report also listed Oklahoma as having more tribal casinos than any other state in the nation. I couldn't help but think to myself, *A lot of social security checks going down the slot drain, and I had a hand in it all.*

I had seen a lot during my stay at FTC, more faces than I could ever hope to remember, people from every walk of life and every ethnicity, faces and personalities that reminded me of people I'd known throughout the course of my life, almost as if they had been reincarnated and came back to travel the BOP.

I witnessed some fights as well, most resulting from flared tempers that amounted to a punch or two, followed by a trip to the SHU. One fight was a little more serious. A guy we called Pit Bull, who was lacking somewhat upstairs, got into it with a young man from Los Angeles. The skirmish started in D pod over differing channels on the TV pole. After a good fistfight, Pit Bull resorted to a small sharp pencil, which he used as a knife.

He inflicted several puncture wounds to the back and neck of the young Californian. The kid from LA wound up biting a good portion of Pit Bull's thumb off before prison officers finally broke it up. Both guys were soon shipped to different locations.

I saw my share of prison guards, some of which seemed to thrive at the prodding and belittling of the more harmless inmates. One of the more exuberant little fellows evidently didn't like my looks any better than my old friend did his chubby neighbor. Early on during my incarceration, he did a strip-search of my cell and found a pill in my locker that didn't seem to belong there. It was an antibiotic one of my buddies gave me for my eye. The little guard gave me one heck of an interrogation, but I was no more inclined to be his puppet than I was to the feds who'd put me there. He called in backup—two lieutenants, the prison councilor, and the nurse I'd been to see about my eye. Of course, the prison nurse confirmed he had never given me an antibiotic. At the time, I didn't know you could go to jail inside a jail. The interrogation lingered on for the better part of an hour. I was sentenced to twenty hours of extra duty. The little guard didn't so much as touch my cellie's locker, which always stored an abundance of spent snuff. Several months later, the same little guy threatened to body slam me for stepping over the wrong line while going for a random urine test. We all called him Barney Fife behind his back.

Then there were the guards and supervisors who were some of the best people I'd ever been around. They treated inmates with the same dignity they would any other human being. Those were the kind who realized it was only by the grace of God that they themselves weren't on the other side of the very door they were locking.

I also saw my share of thugs—inmates, young and old alike, who sported their prison tattoos as if they were a badge of honor. Those were the kind who would learn a sinister trade on the inside that they couldn't learn to do on the outside. To them, the revolving door of prison was merely a way of life. By and large, however, most of the kids that I served with in the cadre unit belonged in any number of places other than a prison. A good job would have solved most of their problems. Mental health counseling and proper medication would have sufficed for others.

It's pretty hard to live in such close quarters with a group of folk for months on end without seeing what they're made of. The same was true while rubbing elbows with politicians crammed inside the state capitol building. It often crossed my mind how well the boys in cadre could have run the people's business from inside the state capitol, if the two groups could be swapped. They certainly had a better grasp on real-life issues. I know for a fact that they would have fared better there than the politicians would have in here. Inside these walls, real-life drama was playing out. Inside the capitol, show business was playing out—endless hours in caucus, planning the next strategy to trip the opposing party, Democrats against Republicans and Republicans against Democrats, one side trying to trump the other with the next good show, a Bible in one hand, a gun in the other. Meanwhile, the poor and disenfranchised fend for themselves.

Despite the fact that we Democrats controlled Oklahoma politics for decades, we failed miserably in adequately funding our public schools or paying a decent wage to those who teach our children. Now that Republicans are in control, we blame them for crowded classrooms and failing grades.

While we Democrats bellied up to the tribal buffet of Las Vegas style gambling, the far right kicked and screamed of the perils of gambling. Now that they're in control, Oklahoma gambling only flourishes, sporting a casino in every county and, in some counties, more. Moreover, the rate of personal bankruptcy filings go up at much the same rates as casinos do. According to Oklahoma's own estimates, as much as 10 percent of its population has become compulsive at the slot reels, and over a hundred thousand residents could be diagnosed as pathological gamblers.

With nearly four thousand churches preaching the Gospel, Oklahoma leads the nation in cramming single mothers into prison. Their silent cries for help fall on deaf ears. Along with other Bible belt states, Oklahoma also leads in showing the country how to incarcerate the highest percentage of our overall population, ranking fourth in the nation. Little wonder our leaders spend triple the money to lock a kid up rather than teach or rehabilitate them. Nevertheless, the show must go on, and as bad as I hate to admit it, I too had a starring role.

Within a few days of my out date, Philly and Shaw came over to my cell. Like a couple of young Jehovah's Witness without their bicycles, they were adamant that I spend one last Bible study with them in the prison library. They had been somewhat reinvigorated by a new pastor who had been recently assigned to our work unit.

The new reverend was from Kansas City, Missouri, who, aside from his preaching, ran an apartment complex. According to him, the feds accused him of trading Section 8 housing for sex. By his own admission, he was having sex with several young girls but still denied trading Section 8 housing for it. Regardless, his new home, for at least the next couple of years, would be FTC.

I wasn't at all interested in listening to the new rev rattle his gums, but spending one last session in the circle was the least I could do for Philly and Shaw. I knew how the both of them had missed Brother Johnson and our special prayer circle in the prison library.

During one of the sessions before Brother Johnson had left, the subject of death and life beyond the grave came up during one of our prayer circles. Naturally, all eyes were on Brother Johnson for the answer. It wasn't Brother Johnson's style to assert his beliefs or opinions on such matters. He did, however, have an uncanny ability to lead us to our own conclusions.

He had us open our Bibles to 2 Corinthians, singled out a scripture, and had Shaw read it. We all patiently waited as he stumbled over the words. "For we know dat if our earthly house of dis tab-er-nac-le were dis-solved, we have a building of God, a house not made wit hands, e-ter-nal in da heavens."

When he finished, Brother Johnson turned to me, and said, "All right, Brotha Govna, tell 'em bout your garden." I didn't know what that had to do with death, but I did know something about a garden. I began by telling how as a boy, I'd follow my grandfather down the long straight rows of sweetcorn, potatoes, okra, and watermelons. I got several amens when I described how sweet and crisp Grandpa's watermelons were. I told of how it gave me such pleasure to watch my own grandchildren as they followed me along my own garden rows. Then I described in detail how my garden looked that early spring morning the day I left home.

Brother Johnson smiled as he turned his Bible to the book of John and read aloud a red-letter passage. "Verily, verily, I say unto you, except a kernel of wheat fall into the ground and die, it abideth alone. But if it die, it bringeth forth much fruit."

Turning to me again, he asked, "All right, Brotha Govna, what do you do with that little seed before you can get that big stalk of corn with those good roastin' ears?"

"Bury 'em in the ground," I said.

"Then what happens?" he asked.

I described how the outer shell of the seed rotted away as the new green shoot sprouted above the ground.

"And how long that same process been' takin' place, Brotha Govna?"

"Ever since I was old enough to watch Grandpa," I said.

The guys in the circle were deathly quiet and hanging on every word of the conversation between Brother Johnson and me. Brother Johnson's smile only got wider as he explained that God had put in motion a natural order of death and life so that even folks who couldn't read could understand his great mysteries. Enough had been said. As mentally impaired as they were, young

Philly and Shaw even got the picture. As we left the library that evening for the nine o'clock count, Shaw grabbed my arm and said "Govna, I got big life ahead of me." I could plainly see that he was lost in some happy thoughts.

Making sure that I kept to my promise, Philly and Shaw came over to E pod and gave me their personal escort to the library prayer circle with the new rev. That night, the reverend from Kansas City couldn't get a word in edgewise. Philly and Shaw kept interrupting him, demanding that I tell the story about my garden. Of course, my gardening adventures didn't make quite the same sense without Brother Johnson's presence, but it sure seemed to satisfy Shaw and Philly. I'm sure the new reverend was as glad as I was that the visit in the prayer circle would be my last. The only thing more frustrating than a politician not being able to talk is a preacher's tongue being held at bay.

The day I thought would never come finally arrived. I would be escorted down the same large elevator that transported me to cadre unit the day I arrived there. The night before, I was given a full cadre send-off. The boys in E pod spread one of the tables with a giant jailhouse nacho. Several of the guys from the D and F pods came over as well. Premo brought a special treat he'd spent hours making—a burrito made of crushed corn ships, kneaded into dough and filled with cheese, and small slivers of jalapeno peppers. It was a send-off fit for a real governor.

The next morning, young Pete followed me to the elevator. He insisted on carrying my laundry bag as if he were my personal bus boy. I wished he could have left with me. The ride down the huge elevator was nowhere near as daunting as the ride up all those months earlier. I had been well acclimated to prison life.

From the elevator, I was escorted to receiving and discharge. I'd trade my khakis for a polo shirt and a pair of denim jeans that were a size too small. From there, I was escorted by the commissary boss through the same corridors of concrete and steel that I entered through nearly two years before. As he shoved the large glass door open to the outside, I was overcome by a flood of emotions and fresh air. Through the tears, I could vaguely see my family, as they were waiting in almost the exact spot they had let me out on that hot summer day on June 25, 2009.

Every so often, curiosity gets the best of people as they convey to me a rather obvious observation that could easily be construed as a question. "Boy, I'll bet it felt good to get out of that place." In all honesty, I still don't know what it felt like and perhaps never will.

From the parking lot outside the transfer center, I had thirty minutes to report to the halfway house located just off I-40 in OKC. I was still property of the Bureau of Prisons. The halfway house was an old motel converted to accommodate roughly 150 ex-cons jumping another hurdle on their way to the outside world. The experience is supposedly designed to reacclimate inmates to civilian life. It was run by a handful of overwhelmed counselors who accomplish little more than a babysitting service for BOP. The concept sounds good but is about as practical as any other layer of government bureaucracy. Every hour on the hour, a loud bell would ring, alerting the residents of count time. In between being counted, we'd be assigned little chores, like cleaning doorknobs or sweeping the sidewalks. There were people in the facility who'd been in prison for as much as thirty years. They'd get no more rehabilitation to the outside world than I would get. The process only served to further confuse them and demean what little pride they had mustered in prison on their own.

After my required stay in the halfway house, my sons picked me up, and we drove straight to an office in southern Oklahoma where a federal parole officer would lay out the terms of my two additional years of probation. We'd begin with an ankle monitor that would alert him in the event that I should wander too far from the house. It did allow me, however, to get a job in my brother's café, where I could earn a few bucks to pay on the fine that went along with my sentence. Eventually, the two years' probation expired as well. I had paid at least a portion of my debt to society, but once a felon, always a felon. I can no longer own, carry, or be in the vicinity of a squirrel gun. I can't run for office, although I wouldn't if you paid me to, and have been deemed unfit to vote. You can, however, find my credentials to preach in book 3, page 475 in the courthouse of Pittsburg County, Oklahoma.

CPSIA information can be obtained
at www.ICGtesting.com
Printed in the USA
LVOW04s1115150816
500440LV00027B/806/P

9 781683 522195